AAT

Management Accounting: Decision and Control

Level 4

Professional Diploma in Accounting

Course Book

For assessments from September 2017

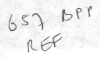

657 BPP
REF

Second edition 2017

ISBN 9781 5097 1210 6
ISBN (for internal use only) 9781 5097 1229 8

British Library Cataloguing-in-Publication Data
A catalogue record for this book is available from the British Library

Published by

BPP Learning Media Ltd
BPP House, Aldine Place
142–144 Uxbridge Road
London W12 8AA

www.bpp.com/learningmedia

Printed in the United Kingdom

Your learning materials, published by BPP Learning Media Ltd, are printed on paper obtained from traceable sustainable sources.

Contents

Introduction To The Course

Syllabus Overview

Purpose

This unit teaches students management accounting principles and concepts. Students will understand the nature and importance of different concepts such as cost behaviour, cost analysis, standard costing and contribution theory. They will know when each technique should be used to aid the planning and decision making of an organisation and the subsequent analysis for control purposes.

Students will learn the key performance indicators that should be used to aid the performance monitoring of an organisation and the techniques for assessing changes to an organisation. The student will build a toolbox of techniques, understand the nature of these techniques and know when each technique should be used.

Alongside *Management Accounting: Budgeting, Management Accounting: Decision & Control* prepares students to be valuable members of a management accounting finance team. It is a mandatory unit that builds on the fundamental concepts and techniques introduced in foundation level *Elements of Costing* and advanced level *Management Accounting: Costing*.

Learning outcomes
On successful completion of this paper, learners should be able to:
1. Analyse a range of costing techniques to support the management accounting function of an organisation
2. Calculate and use standard costing to improve performance
3. Demonstrate a range of statistical techniques to analyse business information
4. Use appropriate financial and non-financial performance techniques to aid decision making
5. Evaluate a range of cost management techniques to enhance value and aid decision making

Assessment structure

The *Management Accounting: Decision and Control* assessment is a 2½ hour computer based test, which comprises of 10 tasks. Learners must demonstrate competence across these tasks by scoring at least 70%.

This unit is about monitoring and managing financial performance. Learners will have the skills and knowledge to be able to analyse information on income and expenditure. They will then be able to use this to make reasoned judgements to support the decision making process.

The examiner has stated that it is important **not** to memorise tasks from the sample assessments and that they can and will vary the content and layout of tasks. However, the AAT have provided information about what the various tasks may contain. You should use this table to ensure you are happy with all of the material, putting a tick in the final column when you have completed the work.

*Note that this is only a guideline as to what might come up. The format and content of each task may vary from what we have listed below.

Results will normally be available approximately 6 weeks after the assessment.

Task	Expected Content	Max marks	Chapter Ref	Study complete
Task 1	**Identification of costing information** Information for this task can be given in a variety of forms for this task and students may be required to apply basic costing knowledge in order to arrive at the correct cost or quantity. Students may be asked to do the following: • Prepare a standard cost card for one unit of output • Identify cost behaviour • Prepare a budget for different levels of output • Identify standard cost bases and advantages/disadvantages of different bases	12	Cost classification and behaviour Methods of costing – Activity Based Costing (ABC)	

Task	Expected Content	Max marks	Chapter Ref	Study complete
Task 2	**Direct materials, labour and variable overhead variances** Calculation of direct material and direct labour standard cost variances. Students may be given a budgetary control report and asked to calculate the four material and labour variances, alternatively this task may consist of several shorter tasks, asking for the variances in turn. Tasks may also give a variance and require students to calculate one of the other variables (so called "backward" variances). The variances required for this task are: Direct material price Direct material usage Direct labour rate Direct labour efficiency Variable overhead rate Variable overhead efficiency	16	Variance analysis	
Task 3	**Fixed Overhead variances** Same format as task 2, except here students will be required to calculate the following four variances: • Fixed overhead expenditure • Fixed overhead volume • Fixed overhead capacity • Fixed overhead efficiency • Students may also be asked to calculate standard cost information, or provide reasons for the variances from a drop-down list.	16	Variance analysis	

Task	Expected Content	Max marks	Chapter Ref	Study complete
Task 4	**Standard cost reporting using an operating statement.** This task provides a budgetary control report and variances and requires the completion of an operating statement reconciling the standard cost of actual production with the actual costs. Only some variances will have a sign given, identification of the rest will be required. Students may also be asked to compare operating statements under absorption and marginal costing principles.	12	Variance analysis	
Task 5	**Statistical techniques** The following techniques could be tested in this task: • Seasonal variations • Moving averages • Trend identification • Forecasting using the identified trend and seasonal variation • Index number calculations • Using the regression equation	12	Forecasting data	
Task 6	**Drafting reports on variance analysis or standard costing principles (written)** The requirement here can involve: • Identifying signs for variances • Explaining what they mean	22	Further aspects of variance analysis	

Task	Expected Content	Max marks	Chapter Ref	Study complete
	• Suggesting reasons for each variance • Explaining any links between the variances • Explaining the standards used and behavioural implications of those standards • Ethics and goal congruence issues as a result of standard cost control			
Task 7	**Performance management** Students will be asked to provide a range of information for performance management. The task could include: • Calculations of performance indicators from budgeted financial statements • Identification of value analysis principles • Identification of the different perspectives of the balanced scorecard Calculations of performance indicators feature heavily within this task, so it is important that students know the formulae for each ratio.	20	Performance indicators	
Task 8	**Decision making** This task requires students to use one or more of the key decision making topics: • Breakeven analysis • Margin of safety • Limiting factor decisions • Make or buy decisions	12	Decision making techniques	

Task	Expected Content	Max marks	Chapter Ref	Study complete
	• Assessment of special orders • Re-calculating costs as a result of automation It is essential that contribution theory and cost behaviour are understood for this task.			
Task 9	**Cost management techniques** This tasks covers the following topics: • Lifecycle costing • Target costing • Cost Management Techniques (including NPV) • Activity Based Costing (ABC)	12	Cost management	
Task 10	**Drafting reports on key performance indicators and/or information for decision making (written)** This task is broad and requires students to write a report analysing information including (but not limited to): • The gross profit margin, profit margin and key changes in the business. • The stages of the product lifecycle, commenting on the cost behaviour for different stages of the cycle and how the organisation may change as the product progresses through the cycle.	22	Performance indicators	

Task	Expected Content	Max marks	Chapter Ref	Study complete
	• Discussion of contribution, margin of safety and risk of two different options • Non-financial and ethical considerations of the options presented.			
	Remember to book your CBT! For UK centres call 0845 2262422			

You should ensure with all tasks that you follow any formatting guidelines provided, such as the display of decimals and adverse variances as ignoring this advice will cost you credit for responses.

Skills bank

Our experience of preparing students for this type of assessment suggests that to obtain competency, you will need to develop a number of key skills.

What do I need to know to do well in the assessment?

Management Accounting: Decision and Control is designed to build on your knowledge of costing systems, decision making techniques and the other topics introduced in the unit *Management Accounting: Costing* at Level 3, whilst also complimenting the topics covered in the Level 4 unit *Management Accounting: Budgeting*.

To be successful in the assessment you need to:

- Demonstrate your theoretical knowledge of the different management accounting techniques.

- Apply your knowledge to practical scenarios

Your knowledge will not only be tested in numerical tasks. At least two tasks in the assessment will require a written response. These usually revolve around variance analysis and performance analysis. Examples of written tasks include:

- Explaining the calculation of variances

- Interpreting the outcome of a variance – why has that variance been incurred?

- Assessing the performance of an organisation by explaining the calculation of and interpreting its performance indicators

- Explaining the ethical consequences of actions taken

Assumed knowledge

The following topics were covered in the Level 3 unit *Management Accounting: Costing* and as such form the foundation of *Management Accounting: Decision and Control*:

- Cost classification and behaviour

- Short-term decision making techniques – in particular breakeven analysis, margin of safety and required profit

- Long-term decision making techniques – in particular net present value

Cost classification, cost behaviour and statistical techniques are also covered in *Management Accounting: Budgeting*. However, the focus in *Management Accounting: Decision and Control* is how these techniques can enhance control and decision making within the business rather than help the business plan its resources.

Assessment style

In the assessment you will complete tasks by:

1   Entering narrative by selecting from drop down menus of narrative options known as **picklists**

2   Using **drag and drop** menus to enter narrative

3   Typing in numbers, known as **gapfill** entry

4   Entering **ticks**

5   **Free text** boxes for answering written tasks

You must familiarise yourself with the style of the online questions and the AAT software before taking the assessment. As part of your revision, login to the **AAT website** and attempt their **online practice assessments**.

Introduction to the assessment

The question practice you do will prepare you for the format of tasks you will see in the *Management Accounting: Decision and Control* assessment. It is also useful to familiarise yourself with the introductory information you **may** be given at the start of the assessment. For example:

You have 2 hours and 30 minutes to complete this assessment.

Each task is independent. You will not need to refer to your answers to previous tasks.

Read every task carefully to make sure you understand what is required.

Where the date is relevant, it is given in the task data.

Both minus signs and brackets can be used to indicate negative numbers UNLESS task instructions say otherwise.

You must use a full stop to indicate a decimal point. For example, write 100.57 NOT 100, 57 OR 100 57.

You may use a comma to indicate a number in the thousands, but you don't have to. For example, 10000 and 10,000 are both OK.

Complete all 10 tasks.

Skills practice

1   As you revise, use the **BPP Passcards** to consolidate your knowledge. They are a pocket-sized revision tool, perfect for packing in that last-minute revision.

2   Attempt as many tasks as possible in the **Question Bank**. There are plenty of assessment-style tasks which are excellent preparation for the real assessment.

3   Always **check** through your own answers as you will in the real assessment, before looking at the solutions in the back of the Question Bank.

Answering Written questions

In your assessment there will be written questions on budget submission, budgetary control procedures, motivation of managers to achieve budgets and variance analysis. The main verbs used for these type of question requirements, along with their meaning, are as follows:

Identify – Analyse and select for presentation

Explain – Set out in detail the meaning of

Discuss – by argument, discuss the pros and cons

Analysing the scenario

Before answering the question set, you need to carefully review the scenario given in order to consider what questions need to be answered, and what needs to be discussed. A simple framework that could be used to answer the question is as follows:

- Point – make the point

- Evidence – explain why the point is important. Use evidence in the scenario to help you.

- Explain – explain the relevance or the impact to the business you are discussing

For example if an assessment task asked us to explain a materials variance we could answer as follows:

1. Point – the materials variance is adverse

2. Evidence – the business changed supplier in the period who charged more for materials

3. Explain – meaning that more money was spent on materials than was budgeted generating an adverse variance

Recommendations are normally also required, and are to provide guidance on how to proceed:

1. Recommendation – we should review the standard cost per kg if the new supplier is a permanent change.

This approach provides a formula or framework that can be followed, to answer written questions:

The NPM tells us that (Point) …. in this case the company is (Evidence) ….. which means that (Explain) ….. so we should/should not … (Recommendation).

Key to icons

 Key term — A key definition which is important to be aware of for the assessment

 Formula to learn — A formula you will need to learn as it will not be provided in the assessment

 Formula provided — A formula which is provided within the assessment and generally available as a pop-up on screen

 Activity — An example which allows you to apply your knowledge to the technique covered in the Course Book. The solution is provided at the end of the chapter

 Illustration — A worked example which can be used to review and see how an assessment question could be answered

 Assessment focus point — A high priority point for the assessment

 Open book reference — Where use of an open book will be allowed for the assessment

 Real life examples — A practical real life scenario

AAT qualifications

The material in this book may support the following AAT qualifications:

AAT Professional Diploma in Accounting Level 4, AAT Professional Diploma in Accounting at SCQF Level 8 and Certificate: Accounting (Level 5 AATSA).

Supplements

From time to time we may need to publish supplementary materials to one of our titles. This can be for a variety of reasons, from a small change in the AAT unit guidance to new legislation coming into effect between editions.

You should check our supplements page regularly for anything that may affect your learning materials. All supplements are available free of charge on our supplements page on our website at:

www.bpp.com/learning-media/about/students

Improving material and removing errors

There is a constant need to update and enhance our study materials in line with both regulatory changes and new insights into the assessments.

From our team of authors BPP appoints a subject expert to update and improve these materials for each new edition.

Their updated draft is subsequently technically checked by another author and from time to time non-technically checked by a proof reader.

We are very keen to remove as many numerical errors and narrative typos as we can but given the volume of detailed information being changed in a short space of time we know that a few errors will sometimes get through our net.

We apologise in advance for any inconvenience that an error might cause. We continue to look for new ways to improve these study materials and would welcome your suggestions. Please feel free to contact our AAT Head of Programme at nisarahmed@bpp.com if you have any suggestions for us.

Costing techniques

1

Learning outcomes

1.1	**Distinguish between different cost classifications and evaluate their use in a management accounting function**
	• Calculate direct and indirect costs
	• Calculate variable, fixed and stepped fixed costs
	• Use the high-low technique to extract the fixed and variable elements of a semi-variable cost, including making adjustments for a step up in cost or a quantity discount
	• Calculate the prime cost of a product
	• Understand the differences between cost centres, profit centres and investment centres
1.2	**Discriminate between and use marginal costing and absorption costing techniques**
	• Explain the difference between marginal costing and absorption costing, and how to critically evaluate the differences between the two methodologies
	• Reconcile a marginal costing profit with an absorption costing profit for changes in inventory to demonstrate the differences in the two methodologies

Assessment context

Cost classification and behaviour is essential knowledge used in many of the management accounting techniques.

Qualification context

Cost classification and behaviour is tested in *Management Accounting: Budgeting* and *Management Accounting: Decision & Control* at Level 4.

Business context

Grouping costs together is essential for a business to be able to analyse costs, budget and plan effectively.

Chapter overview

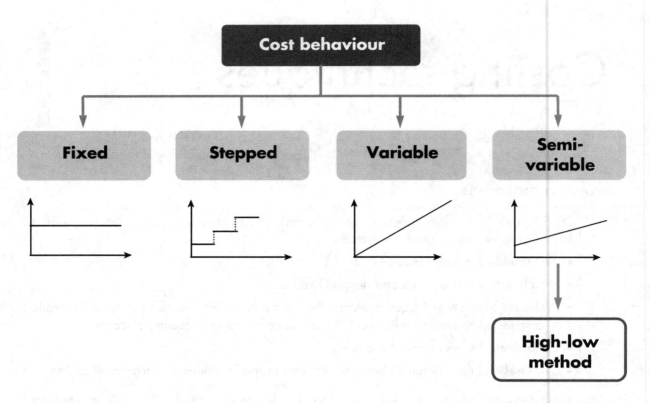

Cost behaviour

- Fixed
- Stepped
- Variable
- Semi-variable

High-low method

- Used to split fixed and variable elements
- Find highest and lowest activity levels
- Subtract Low from High
- Use remainder to calculate variable cost
- Substitute VC back into High or Low total cost formula to calculate fixed cost

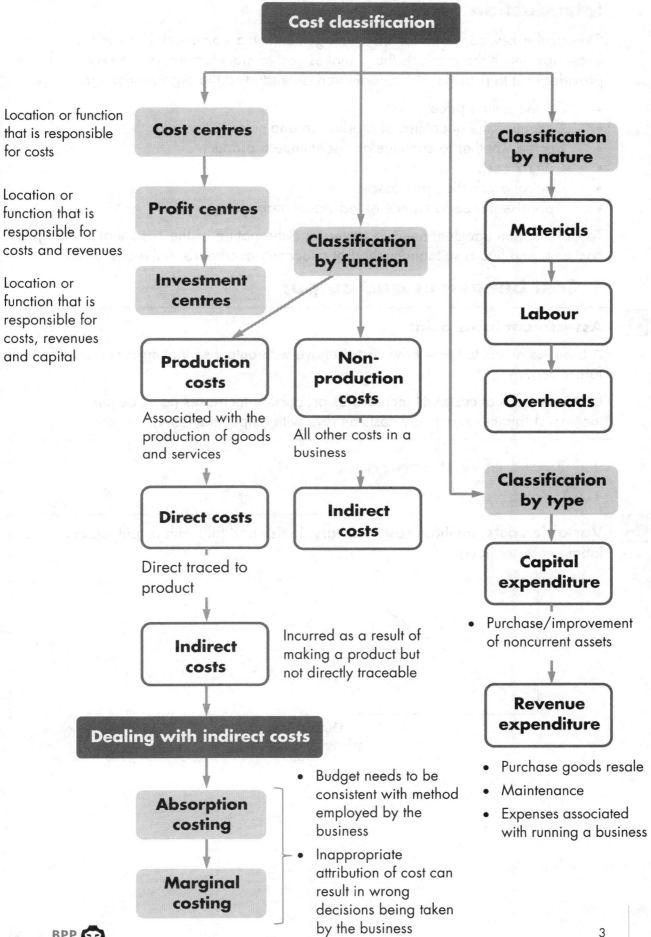

Cost classification

Location or function that is responsible for costs

Cost centres

Location or function that is responsible for costs and revenues

Profit centres

Location or function that is responsible for costs, revenues and capital

Investment centres

Classification by function

Production costs

Associated with the production of goods and services

Non-production costs

All other costs in a business

Direct costs

Direct traced to product

Indirect costs

Indirect costs

Incurred as a result of making a product but not directly traceable

Classification by nature

Materials

Labour

Overheads

Classification by type

Capital expenditure

- Purchase/improvement of noncurrent assets

Revenue expenditure

- Purchase goods resale
- Maintenance
- Expenses associated with running a business

Dealing with indirect costs

Absorption costing

Marginal costing

- Budget needs to be consistent with method employed by the business
- Inappropriate attribution of cost can result in wrong decisions being taken by the business

Introduction

One of the key concerns for the management of a commercial organisation is to know how much the products that it makes cost to manufacture, or the services that it provides cost to provide. This information is needed so the organisation can:

- Set the selling price
- Determine the quantities of production and sales
- Decide whether to continue or discontinue a product
- Control costs
- Control production processes
- Appraise the performance of individual managers

To do this, management need to understand the nature of the costs that make up a cost unit, and find a suitable method of allocating overheads to the cost units.

1 Cost behaviour and output

Assessment focus point

A business needs to know how costs behave with output so that costs can be forecasted.

It is expected that costs will increase as production increases (ie as output increases), but the exact way costs behave with output may vary.

1.1 Types of cost behaviour

1.1.1 Variable costs

Key term

Variable costs are those costs that vary, ie rise and fall, with output (eg materials, labour cost per hour).

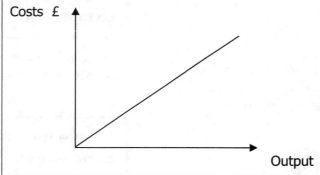

1.1.2 Fixed costs

Key term

Fixed costs are those costs that will not vary with output. These are often referred to as fixed overheads (eg rent and rates).

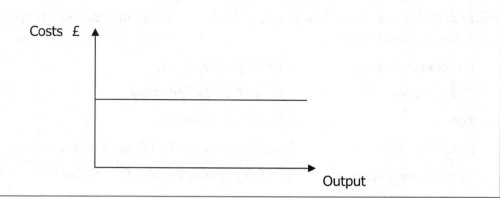

1.1.3 Stepped fixed costs

Key term

Stepped fixed costs are fixed costs in nature within certain levels of activity. These costs remain fixed for a certain level of output and then increase until a further level of output is reached (eg supervisors' costs and rent).

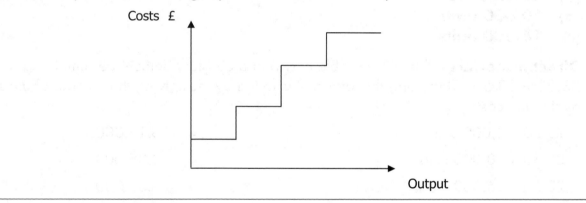

1.1.4 Semi-variable costs

Key term

Semi-variable costs are those costs which are part fixed and part variable and are therefore partly affected by changes in the level of activity (eg telephone).

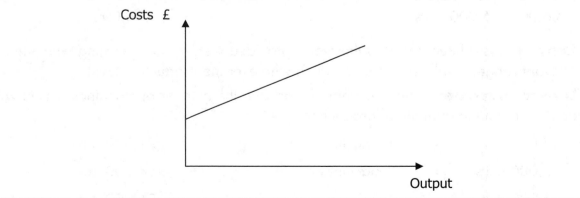

Remember, not all costs follow the textbook profiles. For example, production labour is often described as a variable cost. In reality, basic wages are often fixed and overtime is then paid at a higher rate, should it be required.

Illustration 1: Classification of costs by behaviour

Cameron Ltd produces one product, which requires the following inputs, in the forthcoming quarter:

Direct materials	1 kg @ £3.50 per kg
Direct labour	1 hour @ £6.00 per hour
Rent	£4,000 per quarter
Leased machines	£1,500 for every 4,000 units of production
Maintenance costs	£1,000 per quarter plus £1.00 per unit

Required

Calculate the budgeted total cost of production and the budgeted cost per unit for each of the following production levels for the coming quarter:

(a) 4,000 units
(b) 10,000 units
(c) 16,000 units

Direct materials – this is a variable cost with a constant amount per unit (1 kg × £3.50 = £3.50). Therefore, the total cost is found by multiplying the number of units by the unit cost:

£3.50 × 4,000 units	=	£14,000
£3.50 × 10,000 units	=	£35,000
£3.50 × 16,000 units	=	£56,000

Direct labour – another variable cost, with a unit cost of 1hr × £6 = £6:

£6.00 × 4,000 units	=	£24,000
£6.00 × 10,000 units	=	£60,000
£6.00 × 16,000 units	=	£96,000

Rent – this is a fixed cost and therefore, provided we are still operating within the relevant range, it will remain at £4,000, whatever the production level.

Leased machines – this is a stepped cost and the number of machines leased will depend upon the quantity of production:

4,000 units	=	1 machine	=	£1,500
10,000 units	=	3 machines	=	£4,500
16,000 units	=	4 machines	=	£6,000

Maintenance costs – this is a semi-variable cost with a fixed element of £1,000 and a variable cost of £1 per unit. The total cost for each activity level is:

4,000 units	=	£1,000 + (4,000 × £1.00)	=	£5,000
10,000 units	=	£1,000 + (10,000 × £1.00)	=	£11,000
16,000 units	=	£1,000 + (16,000 × £1.00)	=	£17,000

Thus, the total costs of production are:

| | Production level – units | | |
| | 4,000 | 10,000 | 16,000 |
	£	£	£
Direct materials (variable)	14,000	35,000	56,000
Direct labour (variable)	24,000	60,000	96,000
Rent (fixed)	4,000	4,000	4,000
Leased machines (stepped)	1,500	4,500	6,000
Maintenance costs	5,000	11,000	17,000
Total cost	48,500	114,500	179,000
Number of units	4,000	10,000	16,000
Cost per unit	£12.13	£11.45	£11.19

The cost per unit will decrease if the production quantity increases. This is because the fixed cost and the fixed element of the semi-variable cost will then be spread over a larger number of units.

Variable costs with a discount

Suppose now that the supplier of the materials offers a bulk purchasing discount of 6% for all purchases if an order is placed for more than 8,000 kg.

What is the direct materials cost in total and per unit at each level of production?

4,000 units

| Total cost | 4,000 × £3.50 | = | £14,000 |
| Cost per unit | £14,000/4,000 | = | £3.50 |

10,000 units

| Total cost | 10,000 × (£3.50 × 94%) | = | £32,900 |
| Cost per unit | £32,900/10,000 | = | £3.29 |

16,000 units

Total cost	16,000 × (£3.50 × 94%)	=	£52,640
Cost per unit	£52,640/16,000	=	£3.29

The direct materials are now not a true variable cost, as the cost per unit falls once production is in excess of 8,000 units.

Activity 1: Cost behaviour

A manufacturer of a single product has supplied the budget information for the next quarter end:

Materials per unit	1.5kg at £4.50 per kg
Rent per quarter	£6,500
Supervisor cost	£2,000 for every 2,500 units produced
Electricity	£1,250 per quarter plus £1.30 per unit

Required

Calculate the budgeted quarterly costs of production for the following activity levels to the nearest pound, and classify each cost.

	Quarterly production		Cost classification
Cost	**2,000 units**	**9,000 units**	
	£	**£**	
Direct materials			▼
Rent			▼
Supervisors			▼
Electricity			▼

Picklist:

Fixed
Semi-variable
Stepped
Variable

2 Determining the fixed and variable elements of semi-variable costs

In order to determine the semi-variable costs at a given level of activity, both the fixed element amount and the variable element rate must be known. Splitting out these elements is important as it will help the organisation forecast the cost at a future activity level.

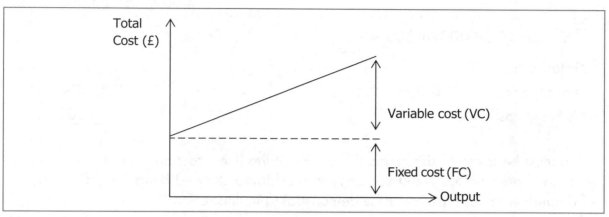

 Formula to learn

Total cost = Fixed cost + VC per unit × Output)

2.1 High-low method for semi-variable costs

 Assessment focus point

This is a four-step method:

(1) Select the highest and lowest activity level and their costs.
(2) Find the difference in the output and costs.
(3) Calculate the variable cost per unit.
(4) Calculate the fixed cost.

 Illustration 2: High-low calculation 1

The total costs of a business for differing levels of output are as follows:

Output (units)	Total Costs
10,000	27,000
12,000	31,000
14,000	35,000

The variable cost/unit and the fixed cost are calculated as follows:

	Output	Cost
Highest	14,000	35,000
Lowest	10,000	27,000
	4,000	8,000

∴ VC/unit = £8,000/4,000 = £2

Total costs	35,000
Variable cost (14,000 units × £2)	(28,000)
∴ Fixed cost	7,000

Care must be taken to determine the nature of the fixed cost base. In the assessment you may be presented with fixed costs that exhibit a stepped behaviour. The process of dealing with this type of cost is demonstrated in Illustration 3.

Illustration 3: High-Low method 2

The following data has been collected from a business:

Units produced	5,000	7,500	10,000
Total costs (£)	54,500	76,500	90,000

Total costs are made up of two elements, a fixed cost (that changes when the units exceed 7,000) and some variable costs, which remain constant per unit.

Here we calculate the total fixed costs at production levels below and above 7,000 units and the variable cost per unit.

High/low method above volume of 7,000 units.

	Output	Cost
Highest	10,000	90,000
Lowest	7,500	76,500
	2,500	13,500

∴ VC/unit = £13,500/2,500 = £5.40

Note. This is constant at all volumes of output.

TC = FC + VC/unit × output

Substitute at lowest (or highest) level:

£76,500 = FC + £5.40 × 7,500

FC = £36,000 above output of 7,000 units.

So at 5,000 units:

TC = FC + VC/unit × output

£54,500 = FC + £5.40 × 5,000

FC = £27,500 below output of 7,000 units.

Activity 2: High-Low Method

You have been supplied with the following information about a factory's overheads.

Units produced	Total overheads £
15,000	250,000
19,000	290,000

The fixed portion of the overheads increases by £5,000 when more than 20,000 units are produced.

Variable costs reduce by £1.50 per unit for units produced in excess of 22,500 units.

Required

Calculate the total fixed and variable overheads for the following production levels.

Enter your answers to the nearest pound.

Units	Fixed £	Variable £
17,000		
25,000		

3 Cost classification

Cost classification is the arrangement of cost items into logical groups, for example, by their **type** (capital and revenue expenditure), their **function** (eg administration, production) or by their **nature** (eg materials, wages).

The eventual aim of costing is to determine the cost of producing a product/service.

3.1 Capital expenditure vs. revenue expenditure

Capital expenditure includes:

- The purchase of non-current assets
- The improvement of the earning capability of non-current assets

Revenue expenditure includes:

- The purchase of goods for resale
- The maintenance of the existing earning capacity of non-current assets
- Expenditure incurred in conducting the business

Capital expenditure is shown as a non-current asset in the statement of financial position, while revenue expenditure is charged as a cost in the income statement.

3.2 Cost classification by function

A company may first arrange cost items into groups by function (ie which part of the business the cost relates to). At the highest level, there could be groups of production costs and groups of non-production costs.

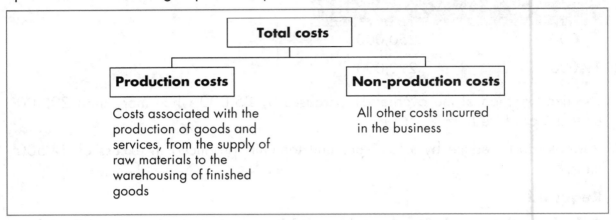

3.3 Cost classification by nature

Production costs can then be broken down further by their nature (ie the category of cost that has been incurred).

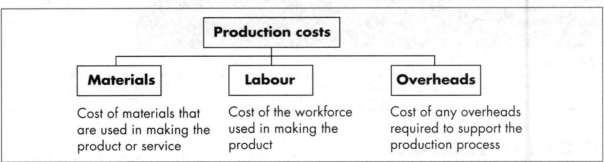

Non-production costs can also be broken down further by their nature to aid analysis.

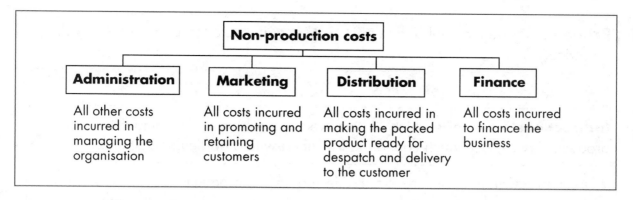

Non-production costs

Administration	Marketing	Distribution	Finance
All other costs incurred in managing the organisation	All costs incurred in promoting and retaining customers	All costs incurred in making the packed product ready for despatch and delivery to the customer	All costs incurred to finance the business

Illustration 4: Classifying costs

The following items of expenditure can be classified by the headings below:

Administration	Marketing and distribution	Capital Expenditure	Cash flow
Depreciation charge of office equipment	Sales staff salaries	Factory extension	Payments to suppliers
Finance director's salary	Advertising	Van purchase	
Accounts staff salaries	Drivers' salaries		
Office staff salaries	Packing materials		
	Lorry repairs		

3.4 Direct and indirect costs

Costs can be further split into direct costs and indirect costs.

3.4.1 Direct costs

Key term

Direct costs are costs which can be specifically identified with, and allocated to, a single cost unit.

Direct costs are often variable (eg materials cost per unit), but can sometimes be fixed (eg tool hire for a specific cost).

The majority of direct costs are production costs, but some non-production costs could also be classified as direct (eg sales commission per unit sold).

Once all of the direct costs are identified for a cost unit, the **prime cost** can them be calculated.

BPP
LEARNING MEDIA

Key term

Prime costs are the total of all direct costs in manufacturing a product/providing a service.

3.4.2 Indirect production costs

Key term

Indirect costs are costs which are incurred in the course of making a product/service, but which cannot be identified with a particular cost unit.

Indirect production costs are often referred to as production overheads. Indirect costs are largely fixed costs, but some variable costs could also be indirect (eg oil for machinery).

Illustration 5: Identifying direct and indirect costs

Here are some of the costs involved in making chocolate bars, grouped by direct and indirect costs:

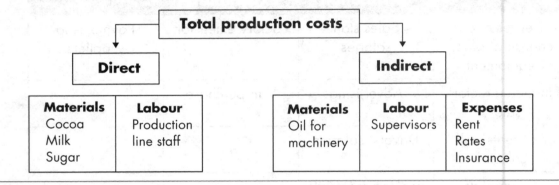

4 Responsibility centres

To assign responsibility for costs and revenues, the various department and functions within an organisation can be classified, in terms of their purpose and responsibilities, into responsibility centres. These can be cost centres, profit centres or investment centres.

Each centre has responsibility for the costs or revenues in its budget, and actual results will then be compared to budgets for each centre in order to monitor and control performance.

4.1 Cost centres

Key term

Cost centre is an area of a business, for example a department such as the factory or canteen, for which costs are incurred.

Each cost centre acts as a collecting place for certain costs before they are analysed further.

Assessment focus point

Cost centres may be set up in any way the business sees appropriate, so in reality the nature and number of cost centres vary from organisation to organisation. However, in the assessment only **factory cost centres** are considered.

In broad terms, factory cost centres can be split in two ways:

- **Production cost centres** – These cost centres are directly involved in the production or provision of the cost unit, eg the assembly department.

- **Service cost centres** – These cost centres are not involved in the production or provision of cost units, but are needed to support or service the production cost centres, eg the canteen.

Activity 3: Classifying factory cost centres

Required

Identify from the following examples which cost centres are production cost centres and service cost centres within a clothes manufacturing factory.

Cost Centre	Type	
Canteen		▼
Stores		▼
Stitching		▼
Maintenance		▼
Packing		▼
Finishing		▼

Picklist:

Production cost centre
Service cost centre

Key terms

Profit centres are areas of the business that are accountable for costs and revenues. For example, a sales department in an organisation can earn revenue from sales, but also incur costs such as a salesperson's salary and commission.

Revenue centres are areas of the business that are accountable for revenues only.

Investment centres are profit centres with additional responsibilities for capital investment. An example might be a separate division of the organisation which has a factory from which it produces goods, sells and despatches them.

Using an example of a solicitors' firm, departments based on their activities (eg corporate law, private client and litigation departments) would be considered profit centres. This is because they incur costs, such as the salaries of the solicitors employed in each centre, but also generate income from charging work to clients.

The firm will also have service departments such as IT, HR (Personnel), Finance teams etc. These would be considered cost centres (or, more specifically, service cost centres) incurring their own costs such as staff salaries but not raising income for the firm.

Let's say the firm had two different offices. One office is in the north and one is in the south of the country. Both offices incur the above costs and generate income, but each office is responsible for the costs of its own building. The separate offices would each be considered investment centres.

Activity 4: Classifying centres

Suggest what types of centres are appropriate for the following list:

Factory canteen
An independent restaurant
Shop in chain
Car dealer

Options

| Cost centre | Revenue centre | Profit centre | Investment centre |

5 Methods of costing

There are three main methods of calculating a cost per unit. These allocate overheads in different ways. You will have covered these in earlier studies, but we will recap these here:

- **Absorption costing** – A method whereby all production costs are included in the costing of a cost unit, both variable and fixed, direct and indirect. This method of costing distinguishes between production and non-production costs.

- **Marginal costing** – Under this method only the variable costs of production are included in the cost per unit. The fixed overheads are treated as period costs and not as part of the cost unit. Instead, the fixed overheads are charged to the statement of profit or loss as an expense for the period.

- **Activity based costing** – This is a method of absorption costing which uses more sophisticated methods of allocating overheads to cost units. This method is covered in Chapter 9.

Assessment focus point

In the assessment you will be required to calculate statements under both absorption and marginal costing principles. You therefore need to be comfortable with the differences between the two costing approaches, and how profit differs between them.

6 Absorption costing

Absorption costing is a method of costing whereby all production costs are included in the costing of a cost unit, ie direct materials, direct labour, variable production overheads and fixed production overheads.

Note that even when applying absorption costing, it is usually only the production overheads of the production and service cost centres that are absorbed. Administrative overheads (eg the salaries of the finance team, the depreciation of the office building) or selling overheads (eg the cost of an advertising campaign) will remain outside the cost units.

Absorption costing calculates an overhead absorption rate (OAR) that can be used to absorb the production overheads into each cost unit.

Key term

Overhead Absorption Rate (OAR) is an estimated amount of fixed overhead used to produce one cost unit.

To calculate the OAR the following method is used:

(1) Allocate and apportion overheads to each production and service cost centre.

(2) Re-apportion service cost centres to production cost centres to find total production cost.

(3) Absorb into production using an overhead absorption rate. This can be calculated as follows:

$$\frac{\text{Total production overheads}}{\text{Total activity level}}$$

The activity level chosen is the one that best reflects how the overhead is incurred, although there is no rule regarding which should be used. The most commonly used activity levels are:

- Total machine hours – This activity level is often used if the production process is machine intensive.

- Total labour hours – This activity level is often used if the production process is labour intensive.

- Budgeted cost units – This activity level is used if the difference between machine and labour hours is negligible, or if only one type of product is manufactured by the organisation.

Assessment focus point

You will not be asked to perform the entire absorption costing exercise in the assessment. Instead, you may be asked to calculate an OAR, and use it to find over- or under-absorption of overheads.

Illustration 6: Absorption costing

Fenton Partners produce one product, the Fenton. The factory has two production departments, assembly and packing.

The expected costs of producing 100,000 units in the next quarter are as follows:

Direct materials	£24.00 per unit
Direct labour	2 hours assembly @ £7.00 per hour
	1 hour packing @ £6.00 per hour
Total assembly production overheads	£470,000
Total packing production overheads	£290,000

Overheads are absorbed on the basis of labour hours.

Production overheads

	Assembly £	Packing £
	470,000	290,000
Absorption rate	200,000	100,000
=	£2.35 per labour hour	£2.90 per labour hour

Interpretation:

For every one hour that the product is worked on in the assembly department, it is charged with a £2.35 share of the overheads incurred.

For every one hour that the product is worked on in the packing department, it is charged with a £2.90 share of the overheads incurred.

Unit cost

	£
Direct materials	24.00
Direct labour – assembly 2 hours × £7.00	14.00
Direct labour – packing 1 hour × £6.00	6.00
Overheads – assembly 2 hours × £2.35	4.70
– packing 1 hour × £2.90	2.90
Unit cost (total absorption costing)	51.60

6.1 Over- and under-absorption of overheads

Overhead absorption rates are usually decided in advance from budgeted overhead costs and activity levels.

However, the problem is that actual overhead costs and activity levels may be different from the overhead costs and activity levels in the budget.

The difference between the budgeted and actual costs and activity levels will give rise to over or under absorption of overheads:

(1) If more overheads are absorbed into actual production than have actually been incurred, this is known as **over-absorption**.

(2) If fewer overheads are absorbed into actual production than have actually been incurred, this is known as **under-absorption**.

Over- or under-absorption is calculated as follows:

	£
Overhead absorbed (Budgeted OAR × actual activity level)	X
Actual overhead incurred	(X)
Over/under-absorbed overhead	X

The profit for the period must be adjusted for the amount of under-absorption or over-absorption as follows:

(1) If there is over-absorption, too many overhead costs have been added to the cost of production, and profit must be adjusted by adding the over-absorbed overhead back to profit.

(2) If there is under-absorption, not enough overhead costs have been added to the cost of production, and profit must be adjusted by subtracting the under-absorbed overhead from profit.

Illustration 7: Over- and under-absorption

Cowslip Limited incurred the following actual overheads and machine hours worked in February and March:

	Units made	Machine hours	£
February	10,000	30,000	140,000
March	9,000	28,000	160,000

The budgeted absorption rate is £5 per machine hour.

In **February**, the actual overheads are £140,000, but 30,000 machine hours were worked. Absorbed overheads are more than actual overhead costs, so we have over-absorption.

	£
Actual overheads	140,000
Absorbed overheads (30,000 hours × £5)	150,000
Over-absorption	10,000

This over-absorption of £10,000 is credited to the statement of profit or loss (income statement), ie it is added back to profit as an adjustment.

In **March** actual overheads are £160,000 and machine hours are only 28,000. This time, there is under-absorbed overhead.

	£
Actual overheads	160,000
Absorbed overheads (28,000 hours × £5)	140,000
Under-absorption	20,000

Under-absorption means that not enough overheads have been charged against the cost of production and profits, so we deduct the under-absorption from profit to make up for this. Profit should therefore be adjusted down by £20,000.

Activity 5: Galaxy

The Galaxy production department produces two types of units. The overheads for the department are as follows:

	£
Supervisors' salaries	10,000
Machine running costs	15,000
Machine maintenance	8,000
Depreciation of machines	5,000
	38,000

The department produces 2,000 units of Pluto. Production uses 5,000 machine hours.

The actual overheads incurred were £40,000, and actual machine hours used was 4,000 hours.

Required

Complete the following statements:

(a) The overhead recovery rate will be £ ☐ per ☐ .

Picklist:

Labour hour
Machine hour

(b) Overheads are ☐ by £ ☐ .

Picklist:

over-absorbed
under-absorbed

7 Marginal costing

Marginal costing (also known as variable costing) is a costing system that measures only the variable (or marginal) cost of cost units – ie direct material, direct labour and variable overheads. This differs from absorption costing which considers both the variable and fixed costs of production.

In marginal costing, fixed costs are treated as a charge against profit in each time period, and are therefore subtracted off in full from profit within the period.

Illustration 8: Marginal costing

Fenton Partners are now considering using marginal costing, and are interested in how the cost per unit will differ under the two costing methods.

In this method, only variable overheads are included in the cost per unit, so these must be ascertained:

	Assembly £	Packing £
Total overhead	470,000	290,000
Variable element (40%)	188,000	116,000
Absorption rate	188,000	116,000
	200,000	100,000
=	£0.94 per labour hour	£1.16 per labour hour

Unit cost

	£
Direct materials	24.00
Direct labour – assembly	14.00
Direct labour – packing	6.00
Variable overhead – assembly (2 hours × £0.94)	1.88
– packing (1 hour × £1.16)	1.16
Unit cost (marginal costing)	47.04

Activity 6: Absorption vs. marginal costing

A business expects to produce 5,000 units of its single product in the next month, with the following costs being incurred:

	£
Direct materials	12,000
Direct labour	15,000
Variable overheads	23,000
Fixed overheads	25,000

Complete the following table to show the cost per unit under both absorption costing and marginal costing methods.

Costing method	Cost per unit £
Absorption costing	
Marginal costing	

7.1 Contribution

A key term in marginal costing is contribution.

Key term

Contribution is the amount of money generated by a cost unit to contribute towards fixed costs incurred in a period in order to make a profit.

Contribution is calculated as follows:

Contribution = Sales revenue – All variable costs

Note that contribution can be calculated either at a unit level, or in total within an accounting period.

Contribution is an important concept, and we will look at the use of contribution for decision making in Chapter 10.

8 Marginal and absorption costing, inventory levels and profit

Under absorption costing inventory is valued at full production cost, including the absorbed fixed overhead.

Under marginal costing the cost per unit only includes variable costs, therefore the value of inventory is lower. Fixed overheads are charged to the statement of profit or loss as an expense for the period.

Due to the differences in the treatment of fixed overhead and the valuation of inventory, absorption costing and marginal costing will not produce the same profit figure.

The rules are that:

(1)   If inventory levels are rising, then absorption costing will give higher profits. This is because the fixed overheads are being carried forward into the next accounting period through the cost of closing inventory, meaning less fixed overhead is incurred in the accounting period.

(2)   If inventory levels are falling, then absorption costing will give a lower profit figure. This is because the fixed overheads from the previous period are brought into the period through the cost of opening inventory, and less fixed overhead is being carried forward into the next period through closing inventory.

(3)   Where inventory levels are constant (provided that unit costs are constant), then absorption costing and marginal costing will give the same level of profit.

BPP
LEARNING MEDIA

Assessment focus point

In the assessment you may be required to compare unit costs and profits under both absorption and marginal costing principles. Therefore, you need to ensure you fully understand the difference in calculating costs and why profits differ under each method.

Illustration 9: Inventory levels and profit

Spa Ltd makes a single product and produces management accounts, including a costing statement of profit or loss each month. In both May and June, 100,000 units of the product were produced.

The production costs in both May and June were:

	£
Direct materials	200,000
Direct labour	300,000
Fixed overheads	300,000
Total production costs	800,000

There were no opening inventories at the start of May and all of the production for May was sold. However, in June only 75,000 units of production were sold, leaving 25,000 units in inventory. Each unit is sold for £10.

(a) Unit cost

   (i) Absorption costing:

   £800,000/100,000 = £8 per unit

   (ii) Marginal costing:

   £500,000/100,000 = £5 per unit

(b) Statements of profit or loss

(i) Absorption costing:

		May		June	
	£	£	£	£	£
Sales		1,000,000			750,000
Less cost of sales					
Opening inventory	–			–	
Cost of production					
100,000 units × £8	800,000			800,000	
	800,000			800,000	
Less closing inventory					
25,000 units × £8	–			(200,000)	
Cost of sales		800,000			600,000
Profit (AC)		200,000			150,000

(ii) Marginal costing:

		May		June	
	£	£	£	£	£
Sales		1,000,000			750,000
Less cost of sales					
Opening inventory	–				
Cost of production					
100,000 units × £5	500,000			500,000	
	500,000			500,000	
Less closing inventory					
25,000 units × £5	–	–		(125,000)	
Marginal cost of sales		500,000			375,000
Contribution		500,000			375,000
Less fixed costs		300,000			300,000
Profit (MC)		200,000			75,000

In May, the profit is the same under both costing methods – £200,000. This is because there is no movement in inventory during the period, since all of the production is sold.

In June, however, profit under absorption costing is £150,000, whereas it is only £75,000 under the marginal costing method. The reason for the £75,000 difference in profit is that the closing inventory, under absorption costing, includes £75,000 (£300,000/100,000 × 25,000 units) of fixed costs that are being carried forward to the next accounting period, whereas under marginal costing, they were all written off in June.

The difference in the two profit figures can be reconciled using the overhead absorption rate per unit, and the increase or decrease in inventory levels. Using the above example, the profit under the two methods can be reconciled as follows:

	May £	June £
Absorption cost profit	200,000	150,000
Increase in inventory × OAR per unit		
(25,000 units × £3 per unit)	0	(75,000)
Marginal cost profit	200,000	75,000

Activity 7: Marginal vs. absorption costing profit

Given below are the budgeted figures for a factory producing a single product. Overheads are absorbed on a production unit basis:

	Month 1	Month 2
Opening inventory (units)	0	
Selling price (£)	100	110
Production (units)	15,000	15,000
Sales (units)	11,000	12,000
Direct materials (£ per unit)	10	10
Direct labour (£ per unit)	8	8
Other variable production costs (£ per unit)	180,000	180,000
Fixed production costs (£)	300,000	300,000

Required

(a) Complete the table below:

	Absorption costing		Marginal costing	
	Month 1	Month 2	Month 1	Month 2
	£	£	£	£
Sales				
Opening inventory				
Production costs				
Closing inventory				
Cost of sales				
Fixed overheads				
Profit/Loss				

(b) Reconcile the absorption costing profit to the marginal costing profit by completing the table below:

	Month 1	Month 2
	£	£
Absorption costing profit		
Change in inventory		
Marginal costing profit		

9 Comparison of absorption and marginal costing

The advantages of using absorption costing are:

(a) Fixed overheads have to be incurred to produce output so it is fair to charge each unit of product with a share of the fixed costs.

(b) Using full absorption cost to value inventory is consistent with the closing inventory value that is required for financial reporting, as it incorporates fixed production cost to inventory valuation.

(c) In the long term, a business needs to cover its fixed costs to be profitable, so when setting selling prices it needs to be aware of the full cost of the product.

The advantages of using marginal costing are:

(a) Fixed costs are the same regardless of output and therefore it makes sense to charge them in full as a period cost.

(b) Marginal costing does not require apportionment of fixed costs which can be arbitrary methods of apportionment and choice of activity for absorption.

BPP
LEARNING MEDIA

(c)   By charging fixed costs as a period cost there is no under- or over-absorption of fixed overheads.

(d)   Marginal costing focuses on variable costs and contribution which can be more useful for decision making (see Chapter 10).

Chapter summary

- The structure of an organisation depends on its activities.

- Different departments or functions can be classified, according to responsibility, as profit centres, investment centres or cost centres.

- These responsibility centres each have a budget associated with them which are combined to form the organisation's budget.

- Costs must be allocated and attributed to the relevant responsibility centre.

- The nature of costs must be determined before budgets can be constructed.

- Costs are either capital or revenue in nature. Revenue expenditure is included in the cost of a product, but capital expenditure is not. Capital expenditure is converted to revenue expenditure in the form of depreciation.

- Direct costs are costs that can be related directly to a cost unit, whereas indirect costs (or overheads) cannot be attributed directly to a cost unit and instead are initially allocated or apportioned to a cost centre.

- Costs are often classified according to their behaviour as activity levels change – the main classifications are variable costs, fixed costs, stepped costs and semi-variable costs.

- There are three main methods of attributing indirect costs to production units – absorption costing, marginal costing and activity based costing (ABC).

- Absorption costing is where the production overheads are included in the cost of each cost unit.

- Under marginal costing, only variable overheads are included in the cost of cost units, with the fixed overheads being charged to the statement of profit or loss as period cost.

- **Activity based costing**: a method of absorption costing which uses more sophisticated methods of allocating overheads to cost units
- **Absorption costing**: a costing method which includes all production overheads within the cost of the cost units
- **Contribution**: the amount of money generated by a cost unit to contribute towards fixed costs and profit in a period
- **Capital expenditure**: purchases of non-current assets or the improvement of the earning capability of non-current assets
- **Cost centre**: an area of the business for which costs are incurred
- **Cost unit**: in a manufacturing business, each unit of production; in service industries such as hospitality, it may be for example, each meal served
- **Direct cost**: cost that can be directly attributed to a cost unit
- **Fixed cost**: cost that remains constant as activity levels change
- **Full production cost**: prime cost plus indirect costs of production
- **Indirect cost** (overhead): cost that cannot be attributed directly to a cost unit but is initially attributed to a cost centre
- **Investment centre**: an area which incurs costs, generates income but also accounts for its own capital employed
- **Marginal costing**: a costing method which includes only variable costs within the cost of the cost units with fixed costs written off as period costs
- **Over-absorption**: where more overheads are absorbed into actual production than were actually incurred
- **Overhead absorption rate**: an estimated amount of fixed overhead used to produce one cost unit
- **Prime cost**: the total of all direct costs
- **Profit centre**: an area of the business which incurs costs, but also generates income
- **Revenue centre**: an area of the business responsible for revenues only
- **Revenue expenditure:**
  - Purchase of goods for resale
  - Maintenance of the existing earning capacity of non-current assets
  - Expenditure incurred in conducting the business
- **Semi-variable cost**: cost which has both a fixed element and variable element
- **Stepped fixed cost**: cost which is fixed over a relatively short range and then increases in steps
- **Under-absorption**: where fewer overheads have been absorbed into actual production that were actually incurred
- **Variable cost**: cost that increases/decreases directly in line with any change in activity level

Test your learning

1   The direct materials cost for 10,000 units is estimated to be £43,600 and for 12,000 it is estimated to be £52,320. This is a variable cost.
   True or false? Tick the correct answer.

   True   ☐

   False   ☐

2   A business expects to incur fixed costs of £64,000 in the following month.

   Complete the table below to show the total fixed cost and the fixed cost per unit at each of the following activity levels.

Activity level	Total fixed cost £	Fixed cost per unit £
3,000 units		
10,000 units		
16,000 units		

3   A business makes 3,500 units per month with the following costs:

Direct materials	£5 per unit
Direct labour	£10 per unit
Rent	£10,000 per month
Supervisor costs	£7,500 per month for every 5,000 units of production

   The marginal cost per month is:

   The full production cost per month is:

4   Given below are the activity levels and production costs for the latest six months for a factory:

	Activity level Units	Production cost £
July	103,000	469,000
August	110,000	502,000
September	126,000	547,000
October	113,000	517,000
November	101,000	472,000
December	118,000	533,000

(a) The variable element of the production cost is:

[   ]

The fixed element of the production cost is:

[   ]

(b) Complete the following table to show the estimated production costs at each of the following levels of production.

Level of production	Production cost £
120,000 units	
150,000 units	

5   A manufacturing business has two production departments P1 and P2. P1 is a labour intensive department, while P2 is highly mechanised with relatively few machine operatives. Budgeted figures are as follows:

	P1	P2
Overheads apportioned	£50,000	£60,000
Machine hours	800	4,000
Labour hours	2,500	600

(a) The overhead absorption rate for department P1 is:

	✓
£62.50	
£20.00	
£15.00	
£100.00	

(b) The overhead absorption rate for department P2 is:

	✓
£62.50	
£20.00	
£15.00	
£100.00	

6 **Complete the following table to show the amount of under- or over-absorption of overheads in each of the three cases below. State in each case whether there is an under- or over-absorption and indicate what adjustment is required in the statement of profit or loss.**

	Amount of under-/over-absorption £	Under- or over-absorption	Add or subtract in statement of profit or loss
An overhead absorption rate of £3 per unit, based on expected production levels of 500 units. Actual overheads turn out to be £1,600, and actual production is 650 units.			
The budget is set at 1,000 units, with £9,000 overheads recovered on the basis of 600 direct labour hours. At the end of the period, overheads amounted to £8,600, production achieved was only 950 units and 590 direct labour hours had been worked.			

7 The budgeted overheads apportioned to two production cost centres, X and Y, together with the budgeted labour hours and machine hours, are given below:

	X	Y
Overheads	£260,000	£380,000
Direct labour hours	20,000	120,000
Machine hours	100,000	10,000

Production cost centre X involves a highly mechanised process, with only a few machine workers. Production Y involves a highly labour intensive process.

(a) **Complete the table to calculate separate departmental overhead absorption rates for each production cost centre using an appropriate basis.**

Department	Overhead absorption rate
X	
Y	

(b) **Each unit of Product A utilises the following hours in each production department.**

	X	Y
Direct labour hours	1	4
Machine hours	5	2

The overhead to be included in the cost of each unit of product A is £ ⬚ .

8 **Explain how fixed production overheads are treated in an absorption costing system and in a marginal costing system.**

9 Given below is the budgeted information about the production of 60,000 units of a single product in a factory for the next quarter:

Direct materials		£12.50 per unit
Direct labour	– assembly	4 hours @ £8.40 per hour
	– finishing	1 hour @ £6.60 per hour
Assembly production overheads		£336,000
Finishing production overheads		£84,000

It is estimated that 60% of the assembly overhead is variable cost and that 75% of the finishing overhead is variable cost.

Complete the table below to show the budgeted cost of the product using each method of costing.

Method of costing	Budgeted cost £
Absorption costing	
Marginal costing	

10 Given below are the budgeted figures for production and sales of a factory's single product for the months of November and December:

	November	December
Production	15,000 units	15,000 units
Sales	12,500 units	18,000 units
Direct materials	£12.00 per unit	£12.00 per unit
Direct labour	£8.00 per unit	£8.00 per unit
Variable production cost	£237,000	£237,000
Fixed production cost	£390,000	£390,000

Overheads are absorbed on the basis of budgeted production and the selling price of the product is £75.

There were 2,000 units of the product in inventory at the start of November.

(a) Prepare the budgeted statements of profit or loss for each of the two months using:

(i)   Absorption costing

(ii) Marginal costing

Absorption costing – statement of profit or loss

	November		December	
	£	£	£	£
Sales				
Less cost of sales				
Opening inventory				
Production costs				
Less closing inventory				
Profit				

Marginal costing – statement of profit or loss

	November			December		
	£	£		£	£	
Sales						
Less cost of sales						
Opening inventory						
Production costs						
Less closing inventory						
Contribution						
Less fixed overheads						
Profit						

(b) **Complete the table below to reconcile the absorption costing profit and the marginal costing profit for each of the two months.**

	November £	December £
Absorption costing profit		
Inventory changes		
Marginal costing profit		

Statistical techniques

2

Learning outcomes

3.1	Calculate key statistical indicators
	• Calculate index numbers, moving averages, seasonal variations and trend information, and use the regression equation
	• Calculate the outputs from various statistical calculations
3.2	Use and appraise key statistical indicators
	• Recommend actions based on the key statistical indicators to forecast income and costs
	• Give reasons for recommendations

Assessment context

Using statistical techniques in order to forecast costs and revenues is likely to form the basis of one task in the assessment.

Qualification context

Forecasting techniques are tested in *Management Accounting: Budgeting* and *Management Accounting: Decision and Control* at Level 4.

Business context

Business will use a variety of models and techniques to help them forecast the performance of their business.

Chapter overview

Reduce by:
- Planning models
- Regular re-forecasting
- Flexible budgets

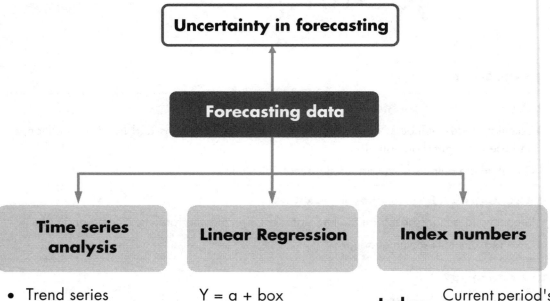

Uncertainty in forecasting

Forecasting data

Time series analysis

- Trend series
- Seasonal variations
- Cyclical
- Random

TS = T + SV

Linear Regression

Y = a + box

Index numbers

$$\text{Index} = \frac{\text{Current period's figure}}{\text{Base period figure}} \times 100$$

Definition

Cash flow deflated to base year
= Actual cash flow in year ×
$$\frac{\text{RPI of base year}}{\text{RPI of year under consideration}}$$

Introduction

A business may collect data about its previous activities, costs and sales revenues and use it to estimate future levels of activity, costs or sales. This data can then be used to forecast future costs and revenues in order to plan and budget forthcoming periods. This chapter considers a number of statistical techniques that can be used to produce forecasts from historical data.

1 Time series analysis

Time series is a series of figures or values recorded over time.

Key term

A time series analysis may be used if an organisation has collected data about costs and revenues over an extended period of time. Examples of this type of data include:

*   Output at a factory each day for the last month
*   Total costs per annum for the last ten years
*   Monthly sales over the last five years

Time series analysis is an analysis of past patterns of demand or sales which will be used to construct expected patterns in the future.

1.1 Components of a time series (TS)

Trend (T)

A trend is the general movement of a time series over a long period of time. It can often be attributed to the impacts of sales growth/decline or inflation. If the trend was plotted on a graph it would show as a smooth line or curve.

The trend can be found through the calculation of moving averages, or through linear regression analysis.

Examples of a trend include a steady decline in the average sales of a national daily newspaper, or a steady increase in sales of a tablet computer.

Seasonal variation (SV)

A seasonal variation is a predicted movement away from the trend. These are due to repetitive events which occur over a short but fixed period of time, for example weekly or quarterly.

Examples of seasonal variations include sales of tabloid newspapers being higher on Mondays and Saturdays than other days due to the extra sports coverage, or sales of ice cream being higher in summer than in winter.

Cyclical variation (C)

A cyclical variation is a recurring pattern over a longer period of time, but not generally of a fixed nature. Because of the variable nature of cyclical variations these can't be predicted with certainty.

Examples of cyclical variations include changes in national unemployment, or movements away from the trend due to variations in the economy, for example from recession to economic growth.

Random variation (R)

A random variation is an irregular variation due to rare or chance occurrences. These occur through circumstances which are beyond the control of the organisation, for example a hurricane or a flood affecting the factory or warehouse.

Examples of random variations include high sales of a tabloid newspaper due to them acquiring exclusive photographs of a celebrity.

Assessment focus point

As cyclical and random variations are not fixed in nature and therefore hard to predict, they are not included in a forecast calculated using time series analysis. You will therefore not be required to include them in your time series calculations, but you may have to identify them in a drop-down list or multiple choice task.

1.2 The additive model

Under the additive model, components are assumed to add together to give the forecast sales.

Due to the unpredictable nature of cyclical and random variations you will only be required to deal with the trend and seasonal variations in calculations. Therefore, to calculate a time series using the additive model the following calculation is used:

Formula to learn

TS = T + SV

Where:

TS = Time series forecast

T = Trend

SV = Seasonal variations

The seasonal variations in time series analysis can be expressed as additions to, or subtractions from, the trend.

1.3 Moving average

The main method for calculating a trend from a time series is the calculation of a **moving average**, which is the average of the results of a fixed number of periods and relates to the mid-point of the overall period.

Let's consider plotting the sales figures generated by a business into a graph:

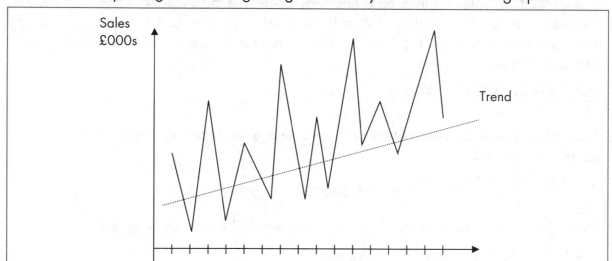

In the above graph, there would appear to be a large seasonal variation in demand, but there is also a basic upward trend. A series of moving averages are therefore calculated to determine what the general movement of the data set is.

Once the trend has been established, a forecast can be determined using the formula TS = T + SV, where TS can be equal to either costs or sales revenue.

Assessment focus point

An assessment task may ask you to calculate the seasonal variation from given actual and trend information. You therefore need to be comfortable with re-arranging the additive formula to find the seasonal variation as follows:

SV = TS – T

Illustration 1: Moving average

The sales figures for a business for the first six months of the year are as follows:

	£
January	35,500
February	37,500
March	34,500
April	40,000
May	42,000
June	39,000

It is felt that the sales cycle is on a quarterly basis – ie the seasonal variations repeat themselves every three months. What is required, therefore, is a three month moving average. This is done by first totalling the figures for January, February and March and then finding the average:

$$\frac{35,500 + 37,500 + 34,500}{3} = £35,833$$

Then we move on by one month, and the average for February, March and April sales is calculated:

$$\frac{37,500 + 34,500 + 40,000}{3} = £37,333$$

Then, the average for March, April and May would be calculated as follows:

$$\frac{34,500 + 40,000 + 42,000}{3} = £38,833$$

Finally the average for April, May and June can be determined:

$$\frac{40,000 + 42,000 + 39,000}{3} = £40,333$$

Now we can show these moving averages, together with the original figures – the convention is to show the moving average next to the middle month of those used in the average.

The seasonal variation can then be calculated by subtracting the moving average from the actual data.

	Actual data	Moving average – Trend	Seasonal variation
	£	£	£
January	35,500		
February	37,500	35,833	+1,667
March	34,500	37,333	–2,833
April	40,000	38,833	+1,167
May	42,000	40,333	+1,667
June	39,000		

Activity 1: Moving averages

Given below are the production costs for a factory for a six month period.

Required

Complete the table to show the three-month moving average for these figures.

Month	Actual £	Three-month moving average £
March	226,504	
April	251,600	
May	238,200	
June	247,600	
July	240,500	
August	262,800	

1.4 Centred moving average

If the moving average is based on an even number of periods, then there is no central time period to place the moving average against. A further average – the centred moving average – is required in order to find the trend.

Illustration 2 – Centred moving average

The quarterly sales figures for Wrigley Partners for the last three years are given below:

		£
20X6	Quarter 1	88,900
	Quarter 2	100,300
	Quarter 3	63,800
	Quarter 4	75,200
20X7	Quarter 1	91,600
	Quarter 2	103,700
	Quarter 3	66,100
	Quarter 4	76,400

The sales figures exhibit seasonal variations over the four quarters of a year. In order to find the trend, a four-quarterly centred moving average must first be calculated.

We start by calculating the average of quarters 1–4 in 20X6:

First average: $\dfrac{88,900 + 100,300 + 63,800 + 75,200}{4} = 82,050$

Next, move on by one quarter, and calculate the moving average for Q2–Q4 20X6 and Q1 20X7:

Second average: $\dfrac{100,300 + 63,800 + 75,200 + 91,600}{4} = 82,725$

Once all moving averages are calculated, they will be displayed as follows:

		Actual £	Moving average £
20X6	Quarter 1	88,900	
	Quarter 2	100,300	
			82,050
	Quarter 3	63,800	
			82,725
	Quarter 4	75,200	
			83,575
20X7	Quarter 1	91,600	
			84,150
	Quarter 2	103,700	
			84,450
	Quarter 3	66,100	
	Quarter 4	76,400	

As the moving average being calculated is an even number, it is shown in between the second and third quarter for each quarterly average – the middle of the four quarters.

In order to obtain a trend line the centred moving average must now be calculated.

To do this we take each consecutive pair of moving average figures and in turn average them, and show them against the third quarter.

First average: $\dfrac{82,050 + 82,725}{2} = 82,388$

Second average: $\dfrac{82,725 + 83,575}{2} = 83,150$

Third average: $\dfrac{83,575 + 84,150}{2} = 83,863$

Fourth average: $\dfrac{84,150 + 84,450}{2} = 84,300$

		Actual £	Moving average £	Centred moving average (Trend) £
20X6	Quarter 1	88,900		
	Quarter 2	100,300		
			82,050	
	Quarter 3	63,800		82,388
			82,725	
	Quarter 4	75,200		83,150
			83,575	
20X7	Quarter 1	91,600		83,863
			84,150	
	Quarter 2	103,700		84,300
			84,450	
	Quarter 3	66,100		
			85,400	
	Quarter 4	76,400		

Activity 2: JB Ltd

JB Ltd is planning ahead and wishes to forecast the cost of its main ingredient used in the manufacture of product X.

Required

(a) **Complete the table below by entering the missing figures. Use minus signs for negative figures.**

2X16 Cost per kg	Jan	Feb	Mar
Underlying cost per kg (£)	180		240
Seasonal variation (£)		12	–18
Seasonally adjusted cost (£)	220	222	

(b) **Assuming the trend and seasonal variations continue as in (a) above, complete the table below to show the projected costs for the first quarter of 2X17. Use minus signs for negative figures.**

2X17 Cost per kg	Jan	Feb	Mar
Underlying cost per kg (£)			
Seasonal variation (£)			
Seasonally adjusted cost (£)			

1.5 The multiplicative model

Assessment focus point

You may be presented with seasonal variations as a percentage movement away from the trend rather than in absolute figures. To find the time series, the multiplicative model is used.

Under the multiplicative model, the components of the time series are multiplied together rather than added together. The time series can then be determined as follows:

Formula to learn

TS = T × SV

Illustration 3: Multiplicative model

The trend figures for sales in units for Earthware Design for the four quarters of 20X0 are given below:

Quarter 1	158,400
Quarter 2	159,900
Quarter 3	161,500
Quarter 4	163,100

The seasonal variations are expressed as follows:

Quarter 1	+8%
Quarter 2	–5%
Quarter 3	–17%
Quarter 4	+14%

Required

What are the forecast sales for each of the quarters of 20X0?

Quarter 1	158,400 × 1.08	=	171,072
Quarter 2	159,900 × 0.95	=	151,905
Quarter 3	161,500 × 0.83	=	134,045
Quarter 4	163,100 × 1.14	=	185,934

2 Linear regression

Linear regression analysis involves the prediction of the value of one variable, for example total cost, given the value of another variable, such as the volume of output. It assumes that there is a linear relationship (straight line on a graph) between the two variables.

2.1 The equation of a straight line

To find the straight line on a graph the following **equation** is used:

$$y = a + bx$$

Both a and b are constants and represent specific figures:

- a is the point on the graph where the line intersects the y axis.
- b represents the gradient of the line (how steep it is).

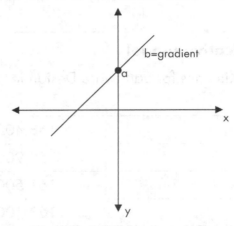

Linear regression can be used for the following purposes:

- Calculation of a future semi-variable cost using historic cost values
- Calculation of a sales trend for use in time series analysis

2.2 Using the equation to forecast semi-variable costs

To forecast the amount of a semi-variable cost at a given production level, the components of the linear regression equation represent the following:

a = Fixed costs

b = Variable cost per unit

y = Total costs

x = Number of units of activity or output

Illustration 4: Linear regression – costs

The linear regression equation for the canteen costs (y) of a business for a month is as follows:

$$y = 20,000 + 45x$$

The variable x represents the number of employees using the canteen.

BPP
LEARNING MEDIA

It is anticipated that the number of employees using the canteen in the next three months will be as follows:

	Number of employees
January	840
February	900
March	875

Required

What are the forecast canteen costs for each period?

		£
January	20,000 + (45 × 840)	57,800
February	20,000 + (45 × 900)	60,500
March	20,000 + (45 × 875)	59,375

2.3 Using the equation to forecast sales

To forecast future sales volumes or sales revenue using the linear regression equation, the components represent the following:

　　y = Total sales

　　x = The time period in the time series (for example, the year number)

　　b = The increase in sales each time period (for example, each year)

　　a = A constant value, which has no specific meaning

Illustration 5: Linear regression – sales revenue

The trend for sales volume for one of Trinket Ltd's products is given:

　　$y = 16.5 + 0.78x$

where y is the volume of sales in thousands in any given time period and x is the time period.

Step 1　Find the values of x for the four quarters in 20X4.

　　　　　Q1　　20X1　　x = 1
　　　　　Q2　　20X1　　x = 2
　　　　　Q3　　20X1　　x = 3
　　　　　Q4　　20X1　　x = 4
　　　　　Q1　　20X2　　x = 5

　　　　　and so on until:

　　　　　Q1　　20X4　　x = 13

Step 2   Calculate the trend for each quarter using the linear regression equation.

20X4	x value	y = 16.5 + 0.78x '000 units
Q1	13	26.64
Q2	14	27.42
Q3	15	28.20
Q4	16	28.98

Assessment focus point

You do not need to commit the equation of a straight line to memory. You will be given this equation in the assessment and asked to find values of its components from given information.

Activity 3: Linear regression – costs

The linear regression equation for production costs (y) for a business is:

   y = 63,000 + 3.20x

Where x = the number of production units.

Required

Calculate the production costs if production is expected to be 44,000 units in the next quarter.

The production costs will be £ ⬚

Activity 4: Linear regression – sales

The linear regression equation for the trend of sales in thousands of units based upon time series analysis of the monthly figures for the last two years is:

   y = 4.8 + 1.2x

Required

Calculate estimated sales trend for each of the first three months of next year.

Month 1 [   ]

Month 2 [   ]

Month 3 [   ]

2.4 Determining a and b

Assessment focus point

If you are asked to calculate the values for a and b in the assessment, you are usually given a range of values for x and y. The a and b variables can then be found by using the high-low method. The high-low method is covered in Chapter 1.

3 Index numbers

Key term

Index is a measurement over time of the average changes in the values, prices or quantities of a group of items.

Like time series analysis, an index can be used to analyse the movement of a trend over a period of time, and therefore to estimate costs and revenues at a specified point in the future.

An example of a price index is the Retail Price Index (RPI), which measures the changes in the costs of items of expenditure of the average household.

3.1 Characteristics

A price index has the following characteristics

- **Base period** – This is a point in time with which current prices/quantities are compared. The index number is the base year is set to 100.

- **Baskets** – These are the items that are included within the index, of which the movement in their price is analysed within the index. For example, the items measured in RPI include food, clothing, heating and lighting, and restaurants and hotels.

- **Weightings** – These are used to give the relative importance of each item. In RPI, for example, each item is given a weighting depending on the proportion it constitutes towards total household expenditure. More weighting is therefore given to heat and light than to restaurants and hotels.

- **Index numbers** – These show the general movement of the data over a period of time and may be used to inflate costs to future periods for forecasting, or deflate costs to a previous period for comparison.

3.2 Calculating an index number

We can get a feel for how data is moving over time by converting the actual figures into a series of index numbers.

This is done by, firstly, determining a base period, which is the period for which the actual figure is equated to an index of 100.

Each subsequent periodic figure (such as a cash flow) is converted to the equivalent index using the following formula:

Formula to learn

Each subsequent periodic figure is converted to the equivalent index using the following formula:

$$\text{Index} = \frac{\text{Current period figure}}{\text{Base period figure}} \times 100$$

If the index for a period is greater than 100, this means that the current period figure is larger than the base period figure. If it is less than 100, the figure is lower than the base period figure. If the index is generally rising then the figures are increasing over the base period but if the index is decreasing, the figures are decreasing in comparison to the base period.

Remember when interpreting an index that it represents the current period figure compared to the base period, not compared to the previous period.

Illustration 6 – Calculating index numbers

The sales figures for a business for the first six months of the year are as follows:

	£
January	136,000
February	148,000
March	140,000
April	130,000
May	138,000
June	145,000

We will set the January figure as the base period, with an index of 100.

This means that the index for February is calculated as:

$$\frac{\text{Current period's figure}}{\text{Base period figure}} \times 100 \quad = \quad \frac{148,000}{136,000} \times 100 \qquad = 109$$

The index for March is: $\qquad \frac{140,000}{136,000} \times 100 \qquad = 103$

The index for April is: $\qquad \frac{130,000}{136,000} \times 100 \qquad = 96$

The index for May is: $\qquad \frac{138,000}{136,000} \times 100 \qquad = 101$

The index for June is: $\qquad \frac{145,000}{136,000} \times 100 \qquad = 107$

From the index numbers we can determine that there is a general trend upwards in the data.

Activity 5: Index numbers

The cost per kg for the materials used in production has been as follows for the last four months.

January X8	February X8	March X8	April X8
£26.20	£26.80	£26.90	£25.80

Required

Convert the costs per kg for January to April into index numbers using January 20X7 as the base period. The price per kg at January 20X7 was £24.95.

Note. Round answers to 2dp.

Month	Cost per kg £	Index number
January	26.20	
February	26.80	
March	26.90	
April	25.80	

3.3 Inflation and deflation of data using index numbers

Key term

Deflation uses index numbers to restate data in terms of the base period.

Deflation states the data at its value if it occurred in the base year. It is an alternative approach to comparing the movement of the data (such as cash flows) without converting costs to index numbers.

Formula to learn

$$\text{Cash flow deflated to base year} = \text{Cash flow to deflate} \times \frac{\text{Index number of base year}}{\text{Index number of year in which cash flow occurs}}$$

Key term

Inflation uses index numbers to restate data to future values.

Inflation states the data at a future value based on the expected index number within a future period. It is an alternative approach to time series analysis and linear regression to forecast future data (such as cash flows).

Formula to learn

$$\text{Cash flow inflated to the current year} = \text{Cash flow to inflate} \times \frac{\text{Index number of future year}}{\text{Index number of year in which cash flow occurred}}$$

Illustration 7 – Inflation and deflation of sales revenue

Index numbers for each of the years 20X1–20X4 are shown below:

	Sales £	RPI
20X1	513,600	100
20X2	516,300	104
20X3	518,400	109
20X4	522,400	113

Required

Restate the sales figures to 20X1 values.

To do this, the sales figures need to be deflated to the base year using the following formula:

$$\text{Sales for current year} \times \frac{\text{Index number in 20X1}}{\text{Index number in year sales occurred}}$$

20X1	Adjusted sales figure	=	513,600 × 100/100	=	£513,600
20X2	Adjusted sales figure	=	516,300 × 100/104	=	£496,442
20X3	Adjusted sales figure	=	518,400 × 100/109	=	£475,596
20X4	Adjusted sales figures	=	522,400 × 100/113	=	£462,301

	Sales £	Adjusted sales £
20X1	513,600	513,600
20X2	516,300	496,442
20X3	518,400	475,596
20X4	522,400	462,596

In 'real' terms, ie without inflationary effects, sales have fallen. This could be due to:

- Falling sales volumes
- Selling prices failing to keep up with general inflation

It could also be due to a combination of these.

Now, let's consider inflation of sales revenue using the same sales figures.

Required

Restate the following figures to 20X4 values.

In order to restate the sales in terms of year 20X4 prices the following formula is applied:

$$\text{Sales in current year} \times \frac{\text{Index number for 20X4}}{\text{Index number for year sales occurred}}$$

The restated figures would appear as follows:

	Actual £	In year 20X8 prices £
20X1	513,600 × 113/100	580,368
20X2	516,300 × 113/104	560,980
20X3	518,400 × 113/109	537,424
20X4	522,400 × 113/113	522,400

We have now shown each year's sales in terms of year 20X8 prices. Again this shows that in real terms annual sales have decreased over the period.

Activity 6: Tees R Us

Tees R Us Ltd makes and packs tea bags. The information below relates to the price of tea.

Required

(a) **Restate the following costs to January 20X7, where January 20X7 is the base period. Give your answer to two decimal places.**

Month 20X7	Actual cost per kg £	Index number	Costs at January prices £
January	4.95	100	
February	4.97	101	
March	4.99	103	
April	5.05	105	
May	5.08	106	
June	5.10	107	

Tees R Us are now forecasting the price of tea for the period July – December 20X8.

(b) **Restate the following costs to future values using January 20X7 as the base period. Give your answer to two decimal places.**

Month 20X8	Index	Actual cost £
July	115	
August	116	
September	119	
October	120	
November	122	
December	123	

3.4 Limitations of index numbers

There are some specific limitations of using price indices:

- The items used to put together the price index (ie the basket of items) may not reflect the cost of items used by the organisation. For example, if an organisation is using RPI then heat and light costs would be relevant to the cost of the organisation, but clothing less so.

- The weightings assigned to the costs need to be evaluated and may not reflect the way in which the costs are incurred by the business.

- Determining the base period can be problematic. The base period needs to be one of relative consistency and stability, but all years will have an aspect of random variation which can skew the index. The base year needs to be reviewed periodically and the index rebased (ie reset to 100).

- New products or items may appear; old ones might get discontinued. Hence, the index needs to be regularly revised.

- The data used in a price index would be collected externally from an organisation using that index to forecast its costs and revenues. Determining the source and accuracy of the data can therefore be problematic.

4 Extrapolation and interpolation

All of the techniques discussed in this chapter aim to derive future forecasts from historical data sets, meaning that both interpolation and extrapolation is used to determine what the future values should be.

Key terms

Interpolation forecasts data within the historical data range.

Extrapolation forecasts data outside of the historical data range.

As an organisation's forecasting looks towards the future, and therefore outside of historical data ranges, extrapolation is the most often used method. This is especially true when extending the trend line in linear regression analysis, and inflating costs using index numbers. When extrapolating data, an underlying assumption is therefore made that current trends will continue into the future.

5 Uncertainties in forecasting

All forecasts are likely to include errors, but be aware of some of the following general limitations in the use of forecasting:

- The more data that is used, the better the results of the forecast will be, so a forecast based on limited data will inevitably be of limited use.

- The further into the future that the forecast considers, the more unreliable it will become as only the short-term can be predicted with relative certainty.

- Forecast figures will often be based upon the assumption that current conditions will continue in the future – ie extrapolation of a trend based upon historical data – which may not be a valid assumption. For example, the company may introduce greater automation in order to generate cost efficiency, which could disrupt the patterns of future costs.

- If the forecast is based upon a trend, there are always random elements or variations which cause the trend to change.

- The forecast produced from the historical data may be quite accurate but the actual future results may be very different from the forecast figures due to changes in the political, economic or technological environment within which the business operates. For example, advancements in technology could introduce a new substitute product to the market, which could potentially disrupt the sales trend.

Uncertainties in forecasting can be addressed by using techniques such as planning models, regular re-forecasting, re-budgeting, rolling budgets and budget flexing.

Assessment focus point

In assessments, the limitations of any income or expenditure forecasts will depend upon each scenario and the task set. Therefore, try to use the information given and consider these general limitations within that context. It is therefore important to consider:

- What the limitation is; and
- Why it is a limitation to that particular company.

Activity 7: YSP Games Ltd

You are employed as an accounting technician at YSP Games Ltd, which manufactures a range of gaming console games. You are attempting to forecast sales demand for the period July–December 20X8.

YSP games uses time series analysis to forecast trends. Trend and seasonal variation information is given below:

Month	Jul	Aug	Sept	Oct	Nov	Dec
(000's) Trend	345	350	355	360	365	370
SV	0	0	150	175	175	350
Forecast sales volume	345	350	505	535	540	720

YSP Games is always looking at technology developments in its industry that it can use within its games. The company also periodically scans the taste of gamers to ensure it is producing games its customers value.

Required

(a) Explain the terms 'trend' and 'seasonal variation'.

(b) Explain the limitations of time series analysis for YSP games.

(a) **Explanation of trend and seasonal variation**

(b) **Limitations of using time series analysis**

Chapter summary

- Statistical techniques can be used to forecast sales revenue and cost data. These forecasts are then use as the basis of planning resources and budgeting.

- Time series analysis can be used to estimate the trend for future periods and then apply seasonal variations to find the forecast sales figures.

- Indexing can also be used to look at trends over time. Index numbers measure the change in value of a figure over time, by reference to its value at a fixed point.

- Linear regression analysis can be used to estimate either semi-variable costs at a particular activity level or future sales volumes at a particular point in time, based on the assumption of a linear trend in sales.

- The linear regression line, $y = a + bx$, will always be given to you in an assessment and you will not need to remember it. However, care should be taken with the variables x and y; x is always the independent variable and y is the dependent variable.

- You may also need to calculate y given values for a, b and x, or a value for x given values for a, b and y. You may also be required to apply the high low method to calculate values for a and b given two pairs of values for x and y.

- All of these methods of forecasting data use a process of extrapolation outside of the historical data set to predict data in future periods.

Keywords

- **Base period:** the period for which the index is expressed as 100 and against which all other period figures are compared

- **Centred moving average:** the average of two consecutive moving averages when the period for the moving average is an even number

- **Cyclical variations:** recurring patterns over a longer period of time, but not generally of a fixed nature

- **Deflation:** using index numbers to restate data in terms of the base period

- **Extrapolation:** forecasting a data set outside of the historical data range

- **Forecast**: an estimate of what may happen in the future based upon historical data and knowledge of future changes

- **Index number:** conversion of actual figures compared to a base year where the base year index is expressed as 100

- **Inflation:** using index numbers to restate data at future values

- **Interpolation:** forecasting a data set within the historical data range

- **Linear regression:** a technique for forecasting semi-variable costs or future sales using the equation for a straight line

- **Linear regression equation:** $y = a + bx$

  where: a is the point on the graph where the line intersects the y axis
               b is the gradient of the line

- **Moving average:** the calculation of an average figure for the results of consecutive periods of time

- **Random variations:** irregular variations due to rare or chance occurrences beyond the control of the organisation

- **Retail Price Index:** a measure of the increase or decrease in general prices in the UK

- **Seasonal variations:** the regular short-term pattern of increases or decreases in figures in a time series

- **Time series:** a series of income or expense figures recorded for a number of consecutive periods

- **Time series analysis:** a method of calculating the trend and other relevant figures from a time series

- **Trend:** the underlying movements of the time series over the period

1   Given below are the production cost figures for a business for the last year.
   Complete the table to calculate a three-month moving average for these figures.

	Actual £	Three-month moving average £
July	397,500	
August	403,800	
September	399,600	
October	405,300	
November	406,100	
December	408,500	
January	407,900	
February	410,400	
March	416,000	
April	413,100	
May	417,500	
June	421,800	

2   Given below are the quarterly sales figures for a business for the last three and a half years.

Complete the table to calculate a four-quarter moving average, the trend using a centred moving average and the seasonal variations.

		Actual £	Four-quarter moving average £	Centred moving average = TREND £	Seasonal variations £
20X5	Quarter 1	383,600			
	Quarter 2	387,600			
	Quarter 3	361,800			
	Quarter 4	328,600			
20X6	Quarter 1	385,900			
	Quarter 2	392,400			
	Quarter 3	352,500			
	Quarter 4	338,800			
20X7	Quarter 1	392,500			
	Quarter 2	410,300			
	Quarter 3	368,900			
	Quarter 4	344,400			
20X8	Quarter 1	398,300			
	Quarter 2	425,600			

3 Given below are the direct materials costs of business operations for the last six months.

Complete the table to calculate the index for each month's costs using January as the base month. Give your answers to one decimal place.

	Cost £	Index
January	59,700	
February	62,300	
March	56,900	
April	60,400	
May	62,400	
June	66,700	

4 Given below are the wages costs of a business for the last six months together with the Retail Prices Index for those months.

(a) **Complete the table to calculate the RPI adjusted wages cost figures for each of the six months, with all costs expressed in terms of June prices.**

	Wages cost £	RPI	Adjusted cost £
January	126,700	171.1	
February	129,700	172.0	
March	130,400	172.2	
April	131,600	173.0	
May	130,500	172.1	
June	131,600	171.3	

(b) **Using the adjusted RPI wages costs, complete the table to calculate an index for the wages costs for each month with January as the base year.**

	Adjusted cost £	Index
January		
February		
March		
April		
May		
June		

5   The total production costs of a business are £15,000 if 1,000 units are produced, and £25,000 if 2,000 units are produced.

The linear regression equation can be used to forecast the production costs where y is the total production cost and x is volume of production:

y = a + bx

Calculate a and b, and then the production costs if 1,400 units are produced.

6   The linear regression equation for costs of the stores department of a business is given as follows:

y = 13,000 + 0.8x

where x is the number of units produced in a period.

The anticipated production levels for the next six months are given below.

Complete the table to calculate the forecast stores department costs for the next six months.

	Production Units	Costs £
January	5,400	
February	5,600	
March	5,700	
April	6,000	
May	5,500	
June	6,100	

7   A time series analysis of sales volumes each quarter for the last three years, 20X6 to 20X8, has revealed that the trend can be estimated by the equation:

y = 2,200 + 45x

where y is the sales volume and x is the time period.

The seasonal variations for each quarter have been calculated as:

Quarter 1	−200
Quarter 2	+500
Quarter 3	+350
Quarter 4	−650

Use the table below to estimate the sales volume for each quarter of 20X9.

	Value of x	Trend	Seasonal variation	Forecast sales
Quarter 1 20X9				
Quarter 2 20X9				
Quarter 3 20X9				
Quarter 4 20X9				

Standard costing

3

Learning outcomes

2.1	Discuss how standard costing can aid the planning and control of an organisation
	• Explain how standard costs can be established and revised
	• Explain the different types of standard (ideal, target, normal and basic)
	• Explain how the type of standard chosen can affect behaviour and variances
	• Explain flexible budgeting and how the standard cost is affected by changes in output
2.2	Calculate standard costing information
	• Prepare a standard cost card from given information
	• Extract information contained in a budgetary control report

Assessment context

Standard costing forms the basis of variance analysis (covered later in the course). It is therefore important that you are able to accurately calculate standard costs. Standard costing can also form a part of the written task on standard costing principles.

Business context

Many manufacturing organisations and some service industries make use of standard costing systems. Standard costs provide management with information to aid planning, decision making and controlling the business operations.

Chapter overview

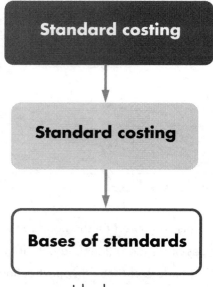

Standard costing

Standard costing

Bases of standards

- Ideal
- Attainable
- Current
- Basic

Introduction

A **standard costing system** is used where a business produces a number of standard products. Every unit of a standard product is expected to use the same quantity of direct materials and requires the same amount of time to make.

The standard cost is the planned unit cost of a standard product or service, and is therefore expected cost of producing one unit of that product or service.

1 Standard cost card

Key term

Standard cost is an estimated unit cost.

A **standard cost** is calculated from management expectations of:

- Usage and efficiency levels on the use of materials and labour
- Prices of materials, labour and overheads
- Budgeted overhead costs and budgeted levels of activity

A standard cost is a predetermined calculation of how much costs should be under specified working conditions. To aid control, it is important that the standard cost is accurate and reviewed regularly.

The standard cost of each unit is set out in a **standard cost card**, which is then used for control within an organisation.

Illustration 1: Standard cost card

The below details a standard cost card for Product A:

	£	£
Direct materials		
Material X – 3 kg at £4 per kg	12.00	
Material Y – 9 litres at £2 per litre	18.00	
		30.00
Direct labour		
Grade A – 6 hours at £7 per hour	42.00	
Grade B – 8 hours at £8 per hour	64.00	
		106.00
Prime cost		136.00
Variable production overhead – 14 hours at £0.50 per hour		7.00
Fixed production overhead – 14 hours at £4.50 per hour		63.00
Standard full production cost		206.00

This cost card can then be used when setting budgets and controlling production of Product A.

Activity 1: Latt

Latt expects to make 5,000 units of production in the coming year.

The following has been estimated:

Each unit will require 3 kg of material with a total cost of £15.

Each unit will require 2 hours of labour paid at £7 per hour.

Fixed overheads are expected to be £50,000.

Required

Complete the standard cost card below:

Unit	Quantity	Cost per unit	Total unit cost
Material			
Labour			
Fixed overheads			
Total			

2 Setting standard costs

Management will use a range of information in order to set the standard usage and price of resources. These are detailed below.

2.1 Information used to set the standard

In order to set an accurate standard cost, the following information can be used:

- **Materials price per unit** – can be obtained from supplier invoices and quotations. This needs to be reviewed regularly for inflation and general increases in the market price.

- **Materials usage per unit** – can be obtained from initial product specifications. If the specification changes this may in turn change the material used per unit.

- **Labour rate per unit** – can be obtained from employee payroll records. This needs to be reviewed regularly for anticipated pay increases and any overtime that is regularly worked.

- **Labour time per unit** – can be obtained from employee timesheets and clock cards. Consideration also needs to be given to the skill level of employees used on the product, as more skilled workers will produce the product in less time.

- **Variable production overhead** – usually assumed to vary with direct labour hours worked.

- **Fixed production overhead** – the Overhead Absorption Rate (OAR) per unit.

2.2 Types of standard

There are a number of different approaches that can be used when determining a standard.

2.2.1 Ideal standard

Key term

Ideal standard is a standard set on the basis that perfect working conditions apply at all times.

Under ideal standards, no allowance is given for wastage, inefficiencies or idle time when setting the standard.

There are two main problems with setting ideal standards:

- The standard is unlikely to reflect the reality of working conditions. Budgets set using this standard are likely to be inaccurate, as in reality the operations are likely to take longer or will require more employees than planned for.

- As there will always be some inefficiency and wastage, variances calculated using ideal standards will usually be adverse. This can de-motivate managers and employees as they feel that these standards can never be met. They may then stop trying to meet them, so any necessary corrective action may not be taken.

2.2.2 Target standard

Key term

Target standard is a standard that incorporates some improvement, but allows for some inefficiency.

A target (sometimes called an attainable) standard is one that is achievable because it better reflects realistic working conditions, making allowances for some wastage and inefficiency. However, the standard can only be met if operations are carried out effectively and efficiently, so a target standard will contain some element of improvement.

Target standards are deemed more motivational for managers and staff as they are not out of reach in the way ideal standards are due to the allowance for wastage and inefficiencies.

2.2.3 Normal standard

Key term

Normal standard is a standard based on current working conditions.

Since normal standards are based on current working conditions, allowing for current levels of wastage and inefficiency, they do not attempt to improve on current levels, so are deemed more short-term. Frequent revisions of the standard are necessary to ensure that current conditions are reflected.

2.2.4 Basic standards

Key term

> **Basic standard** is a standard that has been unaltered over a long period of time.

Basic standards reflect historical working patterns of the organisation. They are very easy to set, but are likely to be out of date as they will not have taken account of changes in inflation or working practices. As a result, variances generated will be large depending on how out-of-date the standard is.

Basic standards are rarely used for variance analysis and budgeting, but may be kept as historical information against more up-to-date standards.

> **Assessment focus point**
>
> Written questions may involve you describing the different ways a standard can be set, why it needs to be regularly reviewed, and the behavioural implications of setting a standard using a certain base. When attempting these questions you need to explain:
>
> * How the standard currently used is being set;
> * Why it is beneficial/inappropriate; and
> * How the standard can be amended to be more appropriate.

> **Illustration 2: Types of standard**
>
> SuperSounds Ltd manufacture a range of headphones. It has provided an extract from its standard costing information:
>
> | Direct cost per unit | £ |
> | --- | --- |
> | Materials | 18.00 |
> | Labour | 12.50 |
> | Packaging | 6.50 |
> | Total prime cost | 37.00 |
>
> The standard for material has been set on the basis that no material is wasted during production. It is estimated that, on average, 2% of material is wasted through production.
>
> The standard for labour was set some time ago when the business first started. Due to automation, there has been improved labour efficiency of 15%.

Required

(a) Explain the behavioural implications of the standards being used.
(b) Calculate appropriately revised standards.

Materials standard

The material standard is based on ideal operating conditions, and doesn't allow for inefficiencies, hence an ideal standard is used. However, this isn't an appropriate standard as material wastage is on average 2%. It appears that no matter what the workforce 2% of materials will always be waste.

The workforce may see this standard as being unfair because, due to the wastage, they will never achieve the standard. This can demotivate the workforce, and this demotivation may have a further detrimental impact on SuperSounds's performance.

A more appropriate standard would be to incorporate the 2% waste. We would therefore need to adjust the £18.00 material standard cost by 2% in order to reflect this wastage.

Currently the standard is set at 98% of what it should be. We would need to gross this standard back up to 100% to get to the standard that should be set.

A more appropriate standard for materials would, therefore, be:

£18 × 100/98 = £18.37

Labour

The labour standard has been set on an historical basis, and is therefore a basic standard. This does not reflect current working conditions, especially seeing that labour efficiency has improved by 15%.

This basic standard does not give the workforce an incentive to improve efficiency further, so meaningful performance improvements will not be achieved.

A more appropriate standard needs to be set to incorporate the 15% efficiency that the organisation has achieved.

Currently the standard is set at 115% of what it should be. We would need to net this back down to 100% to get to the standard that should be set.

A more appropriate standard would, therefore, be:

£12.50 × 100/115 = £10.87

Activity 2: GreenGrass Ltd

GreenGrass Ltd have always used ideal standards when setting standard costs. Recently, the managers at GreenGrass have been complaining that the standards that they are monitored against are unrealistic and unachievable. This has led to increased demotivation throughout GreenGrass.

The Finance Director is now considering using target standards in order address this demotivation.

Required

Explain how setting target standards can improve motivation within GreenGrass Ltd.

Standard costing can aid management in planning, decision making and controlling business operations in the following ways:

- **Planning** – Standard costing allows for prediction of the use of resources so that budgets can be set. For example, the standard quantities of materials and labour can help the construction of the production budget. Standard costing can therefore improve the accuracy of budgets set.

- **Control** – Standards allow for detailed variance analysis to be performed; a vital control technique which compares actual with standard costs and revenues. Decisions can be made regarding remedial action to be taken, or areas of the business that require monitoring.

- **Decision making** – Standards can be used to make decisions in, for example, setting selling prices or comparing the cost of two products.

 Assessment focus point

Some assessment questions will ask you to extract information from standard cost cards and budget control reports as the basis of variance analysis. This usually takes the form of a numerical task.

Activity 3: Press Co

The budgeted and actual results for Press Co for the month of February 20X1 are as follows:

		Budget		Actual
Production (units of C06)		12,000		15,000
Direct materials	21,000 kg	£63,000	26,000 kg	£79,000
Direct labour	2,400 hours	£36,000	3,100 hours	£47,000
Fixed overheads (absorbed on a unit basis)		£54,000		£60,000
Total		£153,000		£186,000

Required

Complete the following sentences:

(a) The standard quantity of labour per unit is ⬚ minutes.

(b) The budgeted quantity of materials needed to produce 15,000 units of C06 is ⬚ kg.

(c) The budgeted labour hours to produce 15,000 units of C06 is ⬚ hours.

(d) The budgeted labour cost to produce 15,000 units of C06 is £ ⬚ .

(e) The budgeted overhead absorption rate per unit is £ ⬚ .

(f) The fixed production overheads were £ ⬚ ⬚ .

Picklist:

Over-absorbed
Under-absorbed

Chapter Summary

- In a standard costing system, all output is valued at a standard cost per unit.

- The direct materials standard cost is set by determining the estimated quantity of material to be used per unit and the estimated price of that material.

- The direct labour standard cost is set by determining the estimated labour time per unit and the estimated rate per hour.

- The fixed overhead standard cost is determined by finding a realistic estimate of each of the elements of the fixed overhead.

- The standards that can be set are an ideal standard, attainable standard, current standard and basic standard.

Keywords

- **Standard costing system:** a costing system where costs of production are recorded at a standard cost as set out in a standard cost card. Actual costs are compared in detail with this standard cost card and variances (differences) are recorded and reported

- **Standard cost card:** document detailing the standard cost of a unit of a product

- **Ideal standards:** standards based on perfect working conditions

- **Target standards:** realistically achievable standards into which are built elements of normal wastage and inefficiency

- **Normal standards:** standards based on current working conditions

- **Basic standards:** historical standards that are normally set when the product is initially produced

1 Explain where the information for setting the standard direct labour cost would be found and what factors should be taken into consideration when setting it.

2 Explain where the information for setting the standard direct material cost would be found and what factors should be taken into consideration when setting it.

3 Explain the difference between ideal standards, target standards and basic standards.

4 Explain the motivational impact of setting an ideal standard.

Variance analysis

4

Learning outcomes

2.3	Calculate standard costing variances
	• Raw materials variances (total raw material, price and usage)
	• Labour variances (total, rate, idle time and efficiency)
	• Variable overhead variances (total, rate and efficiency)
	• Fixed production variances (total, expenditure, volume, capacity and efficiency)
	• Actual and standard costs derived from variances (backward variances)

Assessment context

Variance analysis will be frequently examined in the assessment, and is split between two tasks – one on variable cost variances and one on fixed costs variances.

Business context

Variance calculations are universally performed to enable management to understand which areas of the business are/are not performing well.

Chapter overview

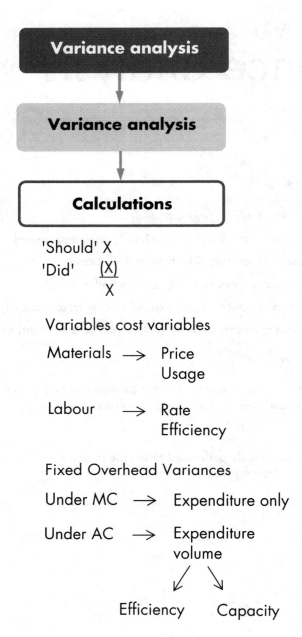

Variance analysis

Variance analysis

Calculations

'Should' X
'Did' <u>(X)</u>
X

Variables cost variables

Materials $\longrightarrow$ Price
Usage

Labour $\longrightarrow$ Rate
Efficiency

Fixed Overhead Variances

Under MC $\longrightarrow$ Expenditure only

Under AC $\longrightarrow$ Expenditure
volume

Efficiency   Capacity

Introduction

As we discussed in Chapter 3, one use of standard costing is to control business operations as it enables an organisation to perform variance analysis.

Variances explain the difference between actual results and expected results generated by the standard. They can either be **favourable** (F) – better than the standard allows – or **adverse** (A) – worse than the standard allows.

Each standard cost is made up of a quantity element and an expenditure element. Differences in quantities are known as efficiency, usage or volume variances. Differences in expenditure are known as rate, price or expenditure variances.

The variances are performed in order to flex the budget to actual levels, so that a like-for-like comparison can be made.

Assessment focus point

Different assessment variants will assess different variances. Whilst you may not be asked to calculate all of the variances detailed below, it is important that you learn how to calculate each to fully prepare yourself for the assessment.

1 Direct cost variances

The direct cost variances cover direct materials, direct labour and variable overhead. Each of the total variances can be broken down as follows:

Summary of variances: standard absorption costing

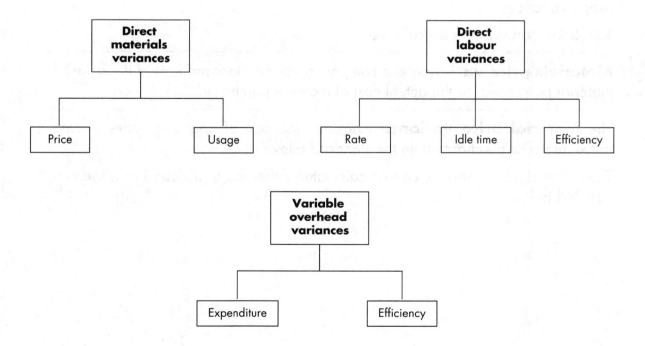

1.1 Materials variances

1.1.1 Total direct materials variance

Key term

Total materials variance is a comparison of the total standard cost of materials for actual production, to the total actual cost of materials.

The total materials cost variance measures the cost of spending more or less on materials for actual production units than the standard allows.

The total direct materials variance is based on the actual number of units produced – the budgeted production units are ignored. Calculating the standard cost of actual production units is known as flexing the budget.

The total direct materials variance can, therefore, be calculated as follows:

Formula to learn

		£
'Should'	**Actual units** should cost (Act units × std kg per unit × std £ per kg)	X
'Did'	Actual material used did cost	(X)
		X

The total material variance can then be split into the material price and material usage variances.

1.1.2 Materials price variance

Key term

Materials price variance is a comparison of the standard cost of the actual material purchased, to the actual cost of material purchased.

The **material price variance** measures the cost of spending more or less on actual material purchases than the standard allows.

The material price variance can be calculated either via a proforma or a formula, as detailed below.

Formula to learn
Proforma method

		£
'Should'	**Actual purchases** should cost (Act kg × std £ per kg)	X
'Did'	Actual purchases did cost	(X)
		X

Formula method

Material price variance = AQM × (AP – SP)

Where:

AQM is the actual quantity of materials used

AP is the actual price paid per unit of direct materials

SP is the standard price paid per unit of direct materials

1.1.3 Materials usage variance

Key term

Materials usage variance is a comparison of the standard usage of material for actual production units, to the actual usage of material for actual production units, valued at standard cost per unit of material.

The **materials usage variance** measures the cost of using more or less material to produce actual production units than the standard allows.

To calculate the usage variance the actual and standard material usage for actual production is compared, and the difference is converted into a cost variance by applying the standard price per unit of direct material.

The materials usage variance can be calculated by either using a proforma or formula as detailed below.

Formula to learn

Proforma method

		Kg
'Should'	**Actual production** should use (Act units × std kg per unit)	X
'Did'	Actual production did use	(X)
		X
	Difference valued at standard cost	£X

Formula method

Materials usage variance = (AQM – SQM) × SP

where:

AQM is the actual quantity of materials used

SQM is the standard quantity of materials for the units produced

SP is the standard price per unit of direct materials

The sum of the price and usage variances should equal the total materials cost variance as follows:

	£
Materials price variance	X
Materials usage variance	X
Total materials cost variance	X

Illustration 1: Direct materials variances

The standard cost card for one of Lawson Ltd's products, the George, is shown below:

	£
Direct materials 4 kg @ £2.00 per kg	8.00
Direct labour 2 hours @ £7.00 per hour	14.00
Fixed overheads 2 hours @ £3.00 per hour	6.00
Total standard absorption cost	28.00

The budgeted level of production for July was 20,000 units but in fact only 18,000 units were produced.

The actual quantity of materials used in July was 68,000 kg. The total cost of the materials was £142,800.

Calculate the following variances:

(a) Direct materials total variance
(b) Direct materials price variance
(c) Direct materials usage variance

(a) Direct materials total variance

	£
18,000 units should have cost (18000 units × 4 kg × £2.00)	144,000
But did cost	142,800
Total materials cost variance	1,200 (F)

The actual price is less than the standard, so the price variance is favourable.

(b) Direct materials price variance

	£
68,000 kg of materials should have cost (68,000 kg × £2.00)	136,000
But did cost	142,800
Materials price variance	6,800 (A)

The actual price paid for the materials is more than the standard price, so the price variance is adverse.

(c) Direct materials usage variance

	Kg
18,000 units should have used (× 4 kg)	72,000
But did use	68,000
Materials usage variance in kg	4,000 (F)
× Standard price per kg of materials	× £2
Material usage variance in £	£8,000 (F)

The actual quantity of materials used is less than the expected or standard quantity, so the usage variance is favourable.

The materials variances can be reconciled as follows:

	£
Materials price variance	6,800 (A)
Materials usage variance	8,000 (F)
Total materials cost variance	1,200 (F)

Activity 1: News Co

News Co operates a standard costing system. It purchases and uses 53,000 kg of material at a cost of £2.38 per kg.

The budgeted production was 25,000 units which requires 50,000 kg of material at a total standard cost of £125,000. The actual production was 27,000 units.

Required

Calculate:

(a) The total materials variance
(b) The material price variance
(c) The material usage variance

(a)   The total materials variance is   £ [   ] [▼]

(b)   The material price variance is   £ [   ] [▼]

(c)   The material usage variance is   £ [   ] [▼]

Picklist:

Adverse
Favourable

1.2 Labour variances

1.2.1 Total labour cost variances

Key term

Total labour variance is a comparison of the standard labour cost of actual production units, to the actual labour cost of actual production units.

The total labour cost variance measures the cost of spending more or less on labour for actual production units than the standard allows.

As with the total direct materials cost variance, the total direct labour cost variance is based on the actual number of units produced, therefore flexing the budget to actual production levels.

The total direct materials variance can be calculated as follows:

Formula to learn

		£
'Should'	**Actual units** should cost (Act units × std hrs per unit × std £ per hour)	X
'Did'	Actual labour used did cost	(X)
		X

The total labour cost variance can then be split into the labour rate, labour efficiency and idle time variances.

1.2.2 Labour rate variance

Key term

Labour rate variance is a comparison of the standard cost of actual hours paid to the actual cost of actual hours paid.

The **labour rate variance** measures the cost of spending more or less on actual labour hours paid than the standard allows.

The labour rate variance can be calculated either via a proforma or a formula, as detailed below.

Formula to learn

Proforma method

		£
'Should'	**Actual hours paid** should cost (Act hrs paid × std £ per hour)	X
'Did'	Actual hours paid did cost	(X)
		X

Formula method

Direct labour rate variance = AH × (AR – SR)

where

AH is the actual hours worked and paid for

AR is the actual rate paid per direct labour hour

SP is the standard rate per direct labour hour

1.2.3 Labour efficiency variance

Labour efficiency variance is a comparison of the standard hours worked for actual production units, to the actual hours worked for actual production units, valued at standard rate per hour.

Key term

The **labour efficiency variance** measures the cost of the workforce working more or less efficiently than the standard allows.

To calculate the usage variance, the actual and standard labour hours for actual production is compared, and the difference is converted into a cost variance by applying the standard rate per labour hour.

The labour efficiency variance can be calculated by either using a proforma or formula as detailed below.

Formula to learn

Proforma method

		Hrs
'Should'	**Actual production** should take (Act units × std hrs per unit)	X
'Did'	Actual production did take	(X)
		X
	Difference valued at standard rate per hour	£X

Formula method

Labour efficiency variance = (AH – SH) × SR

where

AH is the actual hours worked (excluding idle time)

SH is the standard hours of actual units produced

SR is the standard rate of pay per direct labour hour

1.2.4 Idle time variance

Idle time variance is a comparison of actual hours worked and actual hours paid, valued at the standard rate per labour hour.

Key term

The **idle time variance** measures the cost of the workforce being unproductive in the period. When idle time occurs, the labour force is still paid but no actual work is done.

Idle time could occur as a result of machine breakdowns, bottlenecks in production, a shortage of materials, or a shortage of customer orders.

As the workforce is paid for idle time, the amount of hours paid is compared to the actual hours worked in production, and the difference is converted into a cost variance by applying the standard rate per labour hour.

Idle time can therefore be calculated as follows:

Formula to learn

	Hrs
Hours worked	X
Hours paid	(X)
	X
Difference valued at standard rate per hour	£X

The sum of the price and usage variances should equal the total materials cost variance as follows:

	£
Labour rate variance	X
Labour efficiency variance	X
Idle time variance	X
Total materials cost variance	X

Illustration 2: Direct Labour Variances

The standard direct labour cost of product X is as follows:

2 hours of labour at £5 per hour = £10 per unit

During the period, 1,500 units of product X were made. The cost of labour was £17,500 for 3,080 hours, however 2,980 hours were worked.

Calculate the following variances:

(a)   **The direct labour total variance**
(b)   **The direct labour rate variance**
(c)   **The direct labour efficiency variance**
(d)   **The idle time variance**

(a)   **The direct labour total variance**

	£
1,500 units of product X should have cost £10 per unit	15,000
But did cost	17,500
Direct labour total variance	2,500 (A)

Actual cost is greater than standard cost. The variance is therefore adverse.

(b) Direct labour rate variance

	£
2,980 hours should have cost (2,980 hours × £5 per hour)	14,900
But did cost	17,500
Direct labour rate variance	2,600 (A)

Actual cost is greater than standard cost. The rate variance is therefore adverse.

(c) Direct labour efficiency variance

	Hrs
1,500 units should take (1,500 units × 2 hours)	3,000
But did take	2,980
Direct labour efficiency variance in hours	20 (F)
× Standard rate per hour	× £5
Direct labour efficiency variance in £	£100 (F)

20 fewer hours were worked to produce 1,500 units, so the variance is favourable

(d) Idle time variance

	Hrs
Hours worked	2,980
Hours paid	3,080
Idle time variance in hours	100 (A)
X Standard rate per hour	× £5
Idle time variance in £	£500 (A)

The variances can be reconciled as follows:

	£
Direct labour rate variance	2,600 (A)
Direct labour efficiency variance	100 (F)
Idle time	500 (A)
Direct labour total cost variance	2,500 (A)

Activity 2: Yard Co

Yard Co, operating a standard costing system, expects to produce 3,000 units of Y using 12,000 hours of labour. The standard cost of labour is £12.50 per hour.

Last month the company actually made 2,195 units. The actual labour cost was £110,750 for the 9,200 hours worked.

Required

Calculate:

(a) The total labour variance
(b) The labour rate variance
(c) The labour efficiency variance

(a) The total labour variance is   £ ☐ ☐▼

(b) The labour rate variance is   £ ☐ ☐▼

(c) The labour efficiency variance is £ ☐ ☐▼

Picklist:

Adverse
Favourable

Activity 3: Flight Co

Flight Co expected to produce 200 units of its product. Actual production was 260 units. The standard labour cost per unit was £70 (10 hours at a rate of £7 per hour).

During the period the workforce worked 2,200 hours, but was paid for 2,300 hours.

Required

Calculate the idle time variance.

The idle time variance is £ ☐ ☐▼

Picklist:

Adverse
Favourable

1.3 Variable overheads variances

1.3.1 Total variable overhead variance

Key term

Total variable overhead variance is a comparison of the standard variable overhead cost for actual production units, to the actual variable overhead cost for actual production units.

The total variable overhead variance measures the cost of spending more or less on variable overhead for actual production units than the standard allows.

The total variable overhead cost variance is calculated as follows:

Formula to learn

		£
'Should'	**Actual units** should cost	X
'Did'	Actual variable overheads did cost	(X)
		X

The total variable overhead variance is then split into variable overhead expenditure and variable overhead efficiency variances.

1.3.2 Variable overhead expenditure variance

Key term

Variable overhead expenditure variance is a comparison of the standard variable overhead cost of actual hours worked, to the actual variable overhead cost of actual hours worked.

The variable overhead expenditure variance measures the cost of spending more or less on variable overheads than the standard allows.

To calculate the variable overhead expenditure variance, it is assumed that the amount of variable overhead incurred varies with the number of direct labour hours actually worked (total direct labour hours less idle time).

The variable overhead expenditure variance is calculated as follows:

Formula to learn

		£
'Should'	**Actual hours paid** should cost (Act hrs paid × std £ per hour)	X
'Did'	Actual hours paid did cost	(X)
		X

This will measure whether the actual hours worked have cost more or less in overhead than expected.

1.3.3 Variable overhead efficiency variance

Key term

Variable overhead efficiency variance is a comparison of the standard hours for actual production units, to the actual hours for actual production units, valued at the standard variable overhead per hour.

The variable overhead efficiency variance is calculated in the same way as the labour efficiency variance, but to convert it into a monetary variance the hourly difference is multiplied by the standard variable overhead rate per hour rather than the standard labour rate per hour.

The variance is calculated as follows:

Formula to learn

		Hrs
'Should'	**Actual production** should take	X
'Did'	Actual production did take	(X)
		X
	Difference valued at standard variable overhead rate per hour	£X

Activity 4: Bee Co

Bee Co uses the following standard cost card for product H:

2 hours of labour at £15 per hour = £30 per unit

During the period, 1,000 units of product Z were made in 1,960 hours. The cost of variable production overhead was £30,750.

Required

Calculate:

(a)   The total variable overhead variance
(b)   The variable overhead expenditure variance
(c)   The variable overhead efficiency variance

(a)   The total variable overhead variance is £ [   ] [▼]

(b)   The variable overhead expenditure variance is £ [   ] [▼]

(c)   The variable overhead efficiency variance is £ [   ] [▼]

Picklist:

Adverse
Favourable

2 Fixed overhead variances (under absorption costing)

As discussed in Chapter 1, under absorption costing all of the production overheads (both fixed and variable) are included in the cost of producing a cost unit. In order to include an estimated amount of fixed overhead per unit, an overhead absorption rate (OAR) is calculated. To control overheads, the OAR is used with actual production units to calculate over- or under-absorption of overheads.

Over- or under-absorption occurs because:

(1)   The overhead incurred cost more or less than expected or;
(2)   Greater or fewer units were produced than expected.

To understand the reasons behind the over- or under-absorption, the total fixed overhead variance is broken down as follows:

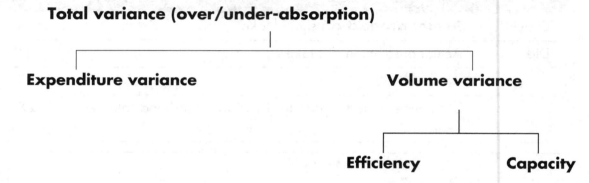

2.1 Fixed overhead expenditure variance

Key term

Fixed overhead expenditure variance is a comparison of budgeted and actual fixed overhead incurred.

The **fixed overhead expenditure variance** measures whether the over- or under-absorption was caused by a difference in the level of spending on fixed overheads.

For example, if actual fixed overhead is higher than budgeted fixed overhead, this indicates that under-absorption has occurred.

The fixed overhead expenditure variance is, therefore, calculated as follows:

Formula to learn

		£
'Should'	Budgeted fixed overhead	X
'Did'	Actual fixed overhead	(X)
	Fixed overhead expenditure variance	X

2.2 Fixed overhead volume variance

Key term

Fixed overhead volume variance is a comparison of budgeted and actual units produced, valued at standard OAR per unit.

The **fixed overhead volume variance** measures whether the over- or under-absorption was caused by a difference in production volumes:

- If actual units produced was higher than budgeted units, more units have been produced to spread the fixed cost over. This can therefore lead to over-absorption of overheads and a favourable volume variance.

- If actual units produced was lower than budgeted units, then there are fewer units to spread the fixed cost over. This can therefore lead to under-absorption of overheads and an adverse volume variance.

The volume variance is calculated as follows:

Formula to learn

		Units
'Should'	Budgeted production units	X
'Did'	Actual production units	(X)
		X
	Difference valued at standard OAR per unit	£X

The volume variance is then broken down into efficiency and capacity variances.

2.3 Fixed overhead efficiency variance

Key term

Fixed overhead efficiency variance is a comparison of the standard hours of actual production to the actual hours of actual production, valued at standard OAR per hour.

The **fixed overhead efficiency variance** measures whether the volume variance was generated due to the workforce working more or less efficiently than the standard allows.

This variance is calculated in the same way as the direct labour efficiency variance, but uses standard OAR per hour to convert it into a monetary variance.

Formula to learn

		Hrs
'Should'	**Actual production** should take (Act units × std hrs per unit)	X
'Did'	Actual production did take	(X)
		X
	Difference valued at standard OAR per hour	£X

2.4 Fixed overhead capacity variance

Key term

Fixed overhead capacity variance is a comparison of actual hours worked and actual hours paid, valued at the standard OAR per hour.

The **fixed overhead capacity variance** considers whether the volume variance occurred due to the workforce working for greater or fewer hours than budgeted.

This variance is calculated in the same way as labour idle time, but uses standard OAR per hour to convert it into a monetary variance.

Formula to learn

Hours worked	X
Hours paid	(X)
	X
Difference valued at standard OAR per hour	£X

With the capacity variance, it is important to remember that if more hours are achieved out of the workforce than budgeted, the organisation made good use of its capacity. More units should have been produced to spread fixed costs over, so a favourable variance is generated.

As the efficiency and capacity variances are sub-divisions of the volume variance, the sum of these variances should reconcile back to the volume variance as follows:

	£
Fixed overhead efficiency variance	x
Fixed overhead capacity variance	x
Fixed overhead volume variance	x

BPP
LEARNING MEDIA

Likewise, the expenditure and volume variances are sub-divisions of the total over- or under-absorption of fixed overheads. The sum of these variances should reconcile back to under- or over-absorption as follows:

	£
Fixed overhead expenditure variance	x
Fixed overhead volume variance	x
Fixed overhead over- or under-absorption	x

Illustration 3: Fixed Overhead Variances

Below is the standard cost card for one of Kettle Ltd's products, T:

	£
Fixed overheads 2 hours @ £3.00 per hour	6.00

Actual production was 18,000 units rather than the budgeted figure of 20,000 and the production work took a total of 38,000 labour hours.

The actual fixed overhead incurred in the period was £115,000.

Calculate:

(a) **The total fixed overhead cost variance**
(b) **The fixed overhead expenditure variance**
(c) **The fixed overhead volume variance**
(d) **The fixed overhead efficiency variance**
(e) **The fixed overhead capacity variance**

(a) **Fixed overhead cost variance**

	£
Fixed overhead expenditure incurred	115,000
Fixed overhead absorbed (18,000 units × £6.00 per unit)	108,000
Total cost variance = Fixed overhead under-absorbed	7,000 (A)

There is under-absorption of overhead and under-absorption is an adverse variance.

(b) Fixed overhead expenditure variance

	£
Budgeted fixed overhead	120,000
Actual fixed overhead	115,000
Fixed overhead expenditure variance	5,000 (F)

As the actual fixed overhead expenditure is less than the budgeted amount, this is a favourable variance.

(c) Fixed overhead volume variance

	Units
Actual production in units	18,000
Budgeted production in units	20,000
Fixed overhead volume variance in units	2,000 (A)
Standard fixed overhead cost **per unit**	£6
Fixed overhead volume variance in £	12,000 (A)

The variance is adverse, as actual production is less than budgeted production.

(d) Fixed overhead efficiency variance

	Hours
18,000 units should take (18,000 units × 2 hours)	36,000
But did take	38,000
Fixed overhead efficiency variance in hours	2,000 (A)
× Standard fixed overhead absorption rate **per hour**	× £3
Fixed overhead efficiency variance in £	6,000 (A)

As the actual production of 18,000 units took more hours than the standard hours for 18,000 units, this is an adverse efficiency variance.

(e) Fixed overhead capacity variance

	Hours
Budgeted hours of work	40,000
Actual hours of work	38,000
Fixed overhead capacity variance	2,000 (A)
× Standard fixed overhead absorption rate **per hour**	× £3
Fixed overhead capacity variance in £	6,000 (A)

Only 38,000 hours were worked, although 40,000 hours were budgeted for. This is therefore an adverse capacity variance, since actual hours worked were less than budget and not all the productive capacity has been used.

The variances can be reconciled as follows:

	£	£
Fixed overhead expenditure		5,000 (F)
Fixed overhead efficiency	6,000 (A)	
Fixed overhead capacity	6,000 (A)	
Fixed overhead volume		12,000 (A)
Total fixed overhead variance		7,000 (A)

Activity 5: Armour

Armour Ltd has budgeted to make 1,100 units of a product called Soul during the month of April 20X3. The budgeted fixed overhead cost is £33,000 and the standard time to make a unit of Soul is 3 hours.

The actual fixed overhead cost during the month turns out to be £33,980. 1,000 units of Soul were produced and the labour force worked for 3,500 hours.

Required

Calculate the following variances:

(a) Fixed overhead total variance

(b) Fixed overhead expenditure variance

(c) Fixed overhead volume variance

(d) Fixed overhead efficiency variance

(e) Fixed overhead capacity variance

Select the appropriate answer from the following:

£3,980 A	£3,980 F	£980 F
£980 A	£3,000 A	£3,000 F
£2,000 F	£5,000 F	£1,000 A
£2,000 A	£5,000 A	£1,000 F

3 Fixed overheads variances (under marginal costing)

Under marginal costing, the standard cost card includes only the variable cost of production. The fixed overheads are not included in the cost of the cost units, and are written off as period costs.

As no OAR is calculated under marginal costing, no over- or under-absorption of overhead is incurred. Therefore, the difference in budgeted and actual fixed overhead incurred is due to the difference in the level of spend on fixed overheads. Therefore the only fixed overhead variance calculated in marginal costing is the fixed overhead expenditure variance.

4 Backward variances

Assessment focus point

Sometimes an assessment question may be set that requires you to work back from a set of variances in order to derive budgeted or actual data.

Illustration 4: Backward Variances

The direct labour cost data relating to last month was as follows:

Actual hours	28,000
Total direct labour cost	£117,600
Direct labour rate variance	£8,400 (A)
Direct labour efficiency variance	£3,900 (A)

Required

To the nearest 1,000, what were the total standard hours last month?

To answer this question we need to take the following steps:

(1) Work the labour rate variance backwards to find actual hours paid at standard cost. We need this in order to work out the standard labour cost per hour. This is done as follows:

Labour rate variance	£
Actual hours paid (28,000) should cost (balancing figure)	109,200
Actual hours paid did cost	(117,600)
	(8,400) A

The standard labour cost per hour is therefore £109,200/28,000 = £3.90.

(2) Use the standard labour cost per hour to work out the total standard labour hours.

The variance is currently £3,900 adverse. We can convert this to hours by taking £3,900/£3.90 = 1,000 hours.

(3) Work the labour efficiency variance backwards to find total standard hours. This is done as follows:

Efficiency variance	Hrs
Actual production should use (balancing figure)	27,000
Actual production did use	28,000
	(1,000) A

Activity 6: Grace

Grace manufactures product WT. Grace operates a standard cost system in which production overheads are fixed and absorbed on a unit basis.

The budgeted activity is for the production of 66,000 units at a total fixed production cost of £726,000.

The actual volume of production was 60,000 units and the fixed overhead expenditure variance was £70,000F.

Complete the following sentences:

(a) The fixed overhead volume variance is £ _____ .

(b) The actual fixed production overheads incurred were £ _____ .

Chapter summary

- For this unit materials, labour, variable overhead and fixed overhead variances must be calculated.

- The total direct materials cost variance can be split into a materials price variance and a materials usage variance.

- The total direct labour cost variance can be split into the labour rate variance and the labour efficiency variance.

- The total variable overhead variance can be split into an expenditure and an efficiency variance.

- The total fixed overhead cost variance in an absorption costing system is the amount of fixed overhead that has been under- or over-absorbed in the period.

- The total fixed overhead variance can then be analysed into the fixed overhead expenditure variance and fixed overhead volume variance.

- The fixed overhead volume variance can be split into a fixed overhead efficiency variance and a fixed overhead capacity variance.

- In a standard marginal costing system there is only one fixed overhead variance, the fixed overhead expenditure variance.

Keywords

- **Adverse variance:** where the actual cost is higher than the standard cost, or where actual performance is worse than expected

- **Favourable variance:** where the actual cost is less than the standard cost, or where actual performance is better than expected

- **Fixed overhead capacity variance:** the difference between the actual hours worked and the hours budgeted to be worked, valued at the standard fixed overhead absorption rate per hour

- **Fixed overhead efficiency variance:** the difference between the standard hours for the actual production and the actual hours, valued at the standard fixed overhead absorption rate per hour

- **Fixed overhead expenditure variance:** the difference between the budgeted fixed overhead and the actual fixed overhead expenditure

- **Fixed overhead volume variance:** the difference between actual production level and budgeted production level in units, valued at the standard absorption rate per unit

- **Idle time variance:** the difference between hours worked and hours paid, multiplied by standard OAR per labour hour

- **Labour efficiency variance:** the difference between the standard hours for the actual production and the actual hours worked, valued at the standard labour rate per hour

- **Labour rate variance:** the difference between the standard rate of pay for the actual hours paid for and the actual cost of those hours

- **Materials price variance:** the difference between the standard price of the materials purchased and their actual purchase cost

- **Materials usage variance:** the difference between the standard quantity of material for the actual production and the actual quantity used, valued at the standard price of the material

- **Total fixed overhead variance:** the total under- or over-absorbed fixed overhead for the period

- **Total labour variance:** the difference between the standard labour cost for the actual production and the actual cost of the labour

- **Total material variance:** the difference between the standard materials cost for the actual production and the actual cost of the materials

- **Variances:** the difference between the standard costs and the actual costs for a period

The following budgeted and actual information is provided by Crispy PLC for their product YG:

	Budget	Actual
Production	1,600	1,800
Materials – kg	11,200	12,000
Materials – £	67,200	70,800
Direct labour – hrs	4,000	5,000
Direct labour – £	27,200	25,000
Total hours paid	4,000	5,500

1 **Using the information in the table above, calculate the following variances:**

   (a) The total materials cost variance

   Total materials cost variance £

   (b) The materials price variance

   Materials price variance £

   (c) The materials usage variance

   Materials usage variance £

2 **Using the information in the table above, calculate the following variances:**

   (a) The total labour cost variance

   Total labour cost variance £

   (b) The labour rate variance

   Labour rate variance £

   (c) The labour efficiency variance

   Labour efficiency variance £

The table below shows management accounting information for a chocolate manufacturer:

		Budget		Actual
Units		7,000		6,400
Machine hours		21,000		20,000
		£		£
Materials	5,500 kg	16,500	4,750	13,300
Labour	10,000 hrs	70,000	12,800	76,800
Fixed overheads		52,500		56,000

Fixed overheads are absorbed on the basis of machine hours

3 **Using the information in the above table, calculate the following:**

  (a) Standard materials for 6,400 units

  (b) Standard labour hours for 6,400 units

  (c) Standard machine hours for 6,400 units

4 **Using the information in the above table, calculate the following variances:**

  (a) Total fixed overhead variance

  (b) Fixed overhead volume variance

  (c) Fixed overhead efficiency variance

  (d) Fixed overhead capacity variance

Operating statements

5

Learning outcomes

2.4	**Prepare and reconcile standard costing operating statements**
	• Prepare a standard costing operating statement reconciling budgeted cost with actual cost of actual production
	• Explain the differences between marginal costing and absorption costing operating statements
	• Reconcile the difference between the operating statement under marginal costing and absorption costing

Assessment context

Operating statements will form one question within the assessment.

Business context

As part of the control process, managers frequently use operating statements to show the link between budgeted and actual performance. These are regularly referred to as a 'profit bridge' or a 'profit reconciliation statement'. Managers use these statements to make decisions to ensure the organisation remains on track to its profit target.

Chapter overview

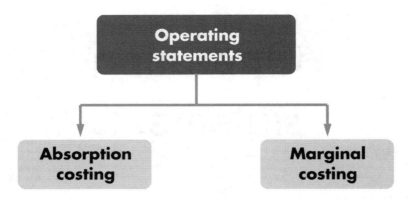

Operating statements

Absorption costing

- Preparation of operating statements under an absorption costing system

Marginal costing

- Preparation of operating statements under a marginal costing system

Introduction

All the cost variances together explain the difference between actual costs of production and the standard cost of production.

A reconciliation between the standard cost and actual cost of production can be presented in a management report known as an **operating statement**.

It is usual practice to start with the total standard cost for the actual production, then adjust this for the variances calculated in order to finish with the total actual cost of production. This can be illustrated as follows:

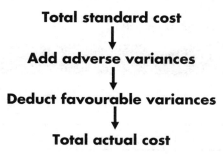

Total standard cost
↓
Add adverse variances
↓
Deduct favourable variances
↓
Total actual cost

Assessment focus point

Read the assessment task carefully. Sometimes you are asked to reconcile actual cost back to standard cost. To do this you will need to reverse the above calculation, ie add favourable variances and subtract adverse variances.

1 Reconciling total standard cost to total actual cost under absorption costing

Under absorption costing, variances for both variable and fixed costs will be included.

Illustration 1: Operating statement under absorption costing

The standard cost card for Product X is given below:

	£
Direct materials 4 kg @ £2.00 per kg	8.00
Direct labour 2 hours @ £7.00 per hour	14.00
Fixed overheads 2 hours @ £3.00 per hour	6.00
Total standard absorption cost	28.00

Budgeted fixed overheads were £120,000 in the period.

The actual production costs and units during March were as follows:

Production units	18,000 units
	£
Direct materials	142,800
Direct labour	254,600
Fixed overhead	115,000
Total actual production cost	512,400

The following variances were generated:

	£
Materials price variance	6,800 (A)
Materials usage variance	8,000 (F)
Labour rate variance	11,400 (F)
Labour efficiency variance	14,000 (A)
Fixed overhead expenditure variance	5,000 (F)
Fixed overhead efficiency variance	6,000 (A)
Fixed overhead capacity variance	6,000 (A)
Fixed overhead volume variance	12,000 (A)

The standard cost of actual production is:

	£
Direct materials 18,000 × £8.00	144,000
Direct labour 18,000 × £14.00	252,000
Fixed overhead 18,000 × £6.00	108,000
Total standard production cost	504,000

(The figure for total standard cost of production can also be calculated as 18,000 × £28, ie standard cost per unit × actual units)

The standard cost of actual production can be reconciled with the actual cost of actual production as follows:

Operating statement under absorption costing – March

	Favourable (Subtract) £	Adverse (Add) £	£
Standard cost of actual production			504,000
Variances			
Materials price		6,800	
Materials usage	8,000		
Labour rate	11,400		
Labour efficiency		14,000	
Fixed overhead expenditure	5,000		
Fixed overhead efficiency		6,000	
Fixed overhead capacity		6,000	
Total variance	24,400	32,800	8,400 (A)
Actual cost of actual production			512,400

As the net total variance is adverse this is added onto the standard cost of actual production to arrive at actual cost of actual production.

Note. The fixed overhead volume variance is not included in the operating statement. This is because it has been broken down into the efficiency and capacity variances, so the volume variance does not need to be included.

Activity 1: Tivvel

Tivvel plc manufactures plastic bottles at various locations in the UK. It has recently set up a plant in Tayside to provide plastic bottles to the local spring water distributors.

The standard cost card for each bottle is as follows:

	Units	Unit cost £	Cost/bottle £
Materials	4 kg	4.50	18.00
Labour	5 hrs	5.00	25.00
Fixed overheads	5 hrs	3.00	15.00
			58.00

The new plant's actual results for the first four weeks of operations are shown below:

Production (bottles)	8,900
	£
Material 36,490 kg	156,907
Labour 51,620 hrs	252,938
Fixed overheads	134,074
Cost of production	543,919

Other information relating to the new factory:

- The plastic bottle is the only product made.

- Budgeted fixed overheads total £1,566,000 per year.

- Fixed overheads are charged to production on the basis of labour hours.

- There are 48 operating weeks in the year.

- Production is budgeted to take place evenly throughout the 48 operating weeks.

You are employed in the central accounts department of Tivvel plc. One of your responsibilities is to prepare and monitor standard costing variances at the new plant.

Required

(a) Calculate the following information relating to the new plant:

(i)   **Actual price of material per kg**

(ii) **Actual labour rate per hour**

(iii) **Actual labour hours per bottle**

(iv) **Budgeted production of bottles for the year**

(v)   **Budgeted production of bottles for the first four weeks of operation**

(vi) **Budgeted fixed overheads for the first four weeks of operation**

(b) Calculate the following variances for bottle production at the new plant:

(i)   **Material price variance**

(ii) **Material usage variance**

(iii) **Labour rate variance**

(iv) **Labour efficiency variance**

(v)   **Fixed overhead expenditure variance**

(vi) **Fixed overhead volume variance**

(vii) Fixed overhead capacity variance [ ]

(viii) Fixed overhead efficiency variance [ ]

(c) **Prepare a statement reconciling the standard cost of actual production to the actual cost of actual production for the first four weeks of the year (under absorption costing).**

			£
Standard cost of actual production			
	£(F)	£(A)	
Cost variances:			
Materials price			
Materials usage			
Labour rate			
Labour efficiency			
Fixed overhead expenditure			
Fixed overhead capacity			
Fixed overhead efficiency			
Actual cost of actual production			

2 Reconciling total standard cost to total actual cost under marginal costing

Under marginal costing the way in which the total standard cost of actual production units is calculated, and the presentation of the operating statement, is different to under absorption costing in the following ways:

- The total standard cost of actual production is calculated by flexing the variable costs only. Fixed costs are not flexed, but are instead subtracted in full from the total variable cost.

- The operating statement does not show all of the fixed overhead variances. Instead, only the fixed overhead expenditure variance is shown.

Illustration 2: Operating statement under marginal costing

Let's assume that Product X is now being produced under marginal costing principles.

The standard cost of actual production is now calculated by flexing the direct material and direct labour costs to actual levels, and adding on the fixed cost in full as follows:

	£
Direct materials 18,000 × £8.00	144,000
Direct labour 18,000 × £14.00	252,000
Marginal cost of production (18,000 × £22)	396,000

The total standard cost is the marginal cost of production plus budgeted fixed costs:

	£
Marginal cost of production	396,000
Budgeted fixed overhead	120,000
Standard cost of production	516,000

The marginal costing operating statement includes all of the direct cost variances and the fixed overhead expenditure variance. The fixed overhead capacity and efficiency variances are not included.

The operating statement will be presented as follows:

			£
Standard cost of actual production			516,000
Variances	**Favourable (Subtract)** £	**Adverse (Add)** £	
Materials price		6,800	
Materials usage	8,000		
Labour rate	11,400		
Labour efficiency		14,000	
Fixed overhead expenditure	5,000		
Total variance	24,400	20,800	3,600 (F)
Actual cost of actual production			512,400

Activity 2: Blast Co

Blast Co uses a standard marginal costing system. The following budgetary control report has been provided together with the variances calculated below:

	Budget	£	Actual	£
Production units		20,000		20,500
Direct material A1	50,000 kg	500,000	51,000 kg	616,000
Direct material A2	70,000 kg	490,000	72,000 kg	168,000
Direct labour	45,000 hrs	450,000	51,000 hrs	700,000
Fixed Overhead		720,000		680,000
Total cost		2,160,000		2,164,000

Variance	£	
A1 material price	–106,000	A
A1 material usage	2,500	
A2 material price	336,000	F
A2 material usage	–1,750	
Fixed overhead expenditure	40,000	
Direct labour rate	–190,000	
Direct labour efficiency	–48,750	A

Required

Insert the correct variance into the correct column and enter the standard cost for actual production, the total variance and the actual cost for actual production in the appropriate boxes.

Enter minus signs where necessary.

Options:

£106,000	£2,500	£336,000
£1,750	£40,000	£190,000
£96,000	£78,000	£48,750

Variance	Fav	Ad	£
Standard cost of actual production			
A1 material price			
A1 material usage			
A2 material price			
A2 material usage			
Direct labour rate			
Direct labour efficiency			
Fixed overhead expenditure			
Total variance			
Actual cost of actual production			

3 Reconciling standard cost of production to actual cost of production for a single direct cost

In the previous chapter we considered the reconciliation of detailed variances back to a total variance (eg the materials price and usage variances back to the total materials variance). This reconciliation, alongside with the approach taken in this chapter to reconcile standard to actual costs, can be used to reconcile the standard direct cost to the actual direct cost for a single cost type.

Illustration 3: Reconciliation of a single cost type.

Rohan Ltd manufacture office items. The information in the table below shows the budgeted variable costs for the manufacture of 250 filing cabinets:

	Cost per unit £	Budgeted cost £
Materials	15.00	3,750
Direct labour	25.00	6,250
Variable overhead	9.00	2,250
Total cost		12,250

Actual production for the period was 200 filing cabinets and the total variances incurred were as follows:

	Total variance £
Materials	960 Favourable
Labour	40 Favourable
Variable overhead	900 Adverse

During the period, the actual purchases of material was 1,200 kg costing £3.30 per kg. The standard kg per unit is 4 kg.

Actual hours worked were 1,100 hours. Standard hours per unit was 5 hours.

Required

(a) Reconcile the actual material cost to the standard material cost of production by calculating the material price and material usage variances.

(b) Reconcile the actual labour cost to the standard labour cost of production by calculating the labour rate and labour efficiency variances.

(a) Materials

To reconcile actual cost of materials to the standard cost of materials, we need to take note of the information presented to us. We have the information to calculate the materials price variance, but not the materials usage variance.

The materials price variance is calculated as follows:

	£
1,200 kg should cost (1,200 kg × £15/4kg)	4,500
1,200 kg did cost (1,200 kg × £3.30)	3,960
	540 F

Remember that the sum of the materials price and usage variances add back to the total materials variance. We can use this reconciliation to calculate the materials usage variance, as this is the difference between the materials price and total materials variance:

	£
Materials price variance	540 F
Materials usage variance (Balancing figure)	420 F
Total materials variance	960 F

Finally, we can use the information in the materials price variance alongside the materials usage variance to reconcile actual cost of materials for actual production to standard cost of materials for actual production:

	£
Actual material cost (from materials price variance)	3,960
Materials price variance	540
Materials usage variance	420
Standard material cost of production	3,000

(b) Labour

To reconcile actual cost of labour to the standard cost of labour, we have the information to calculate both the labour efficiency variance but not the labour rate variances. We also can't calculate the actual cost of labour as no information is provided about the actual labour rate.

The labour efficiency variance is calculated as follows:

	Hrs
200 units should take (200 units × 5 hrs)	1,000
200 units did take	1,100
	100 A
Difference valued at standard rate per hour ∴ 100 hrs × £25/5 hrs	£500 A

Remember that the sum of the labour efficiency and rate variances add back to the total labour variance. We can use this reconciliation to calculate the labour rate variance, as this is the difference between the labour efficiency and total labour variance:

	£
Labour rate variance (Balancing figure)	540 F
Labour efficiency variance	500 A
Total labour variance	40 F

We can work out the standard labour cost of production by taking the standard cost per unit and the actual units produced as follows:

Standard labour cost per unit = £25 per unit × 200 units = £5,000

Finally, we can combine all of the above information to calculate the actual cost of labour:

	£
Actual labour cost (Balancing figure)	4,960
Labour rate variance	540
Labour efficiency variance	(500)
Standard labour cost of production	5,000

Activity 3: Colin's Cakes

Colin's Cakes manufacture a range of different styles of cake. The below information relates to a birthday cake that they produce for a supermarket:

	Budget	Actual
Production - units	10,000	12,000
Flour (kg)	30,000	33,000
Flour – £	18,000	17,000
Direct labour – hours	20,000	23,000
Direct labour – £	160,000	175,000

Required

(a) For each variance below, show the variance amount and whether the variance is adverse, favourable or whether there is no variance.

Variance	Variance amount £	Adverse/favourable/ no variance
Flour price		
Direct labour rate		

Picklist:

Adverse
Favourable
No variance

(b) Complete the reconciliation statement below. Indicate any negative figures by using a minus sign.

	£
Standard direct cost of actual production	
Flour price variance	
Flour usage variance	
Direct labour rate variance	
Direct labour efficiency variance	
Actual direct cost of production	

Chapter Summary

- The operating statement is sometimes referred to as a reconciliation statement.

- A reconciliation of the standard cost for the actual production to the actual cost of production can be performed by adding the adverse variances to the standard cost and deducting the favourable variances.

- In an absorption costing operating statement all variances except the fixed overhead volume variance are included.

- In a marginal costing operating statement the only fixed overhead variance that is included is the fixed overhead expenditure variance.

- The format for an operating statement is slightly different for standard marginal costing from an operating statement for standard absorption costing, to allow for the differing treatments of fixed costs.

- **Operating statement or reconciliation statement:** a statement which uses the variances for the period to reconcile the standard cost for the actual production to the actual cost

Test your learning

1   The standard cost card for a business's product, the MU, is shown below:

	£
Direct materials 4.2 kg @ £3.60 per kg	15.12
Direct labour 1.5 hours @ £7.80 per hour	11.70
Fixed overheads 1.5 hours @ £2.80 per hour	4.20
	31.02

The budgeted production was for 1,800 units of MU. The actual costs during the month of June for the production of 1,750 units of the MU were as follows:

	£
Direct materials 7,500 kg	25,900
Direct labour 2,580 hours	20,600
Fixed overheads	8,100

Required:

(a) Calculate the materials price and usage variances.

Materials price variance £ [   ]

Materials usage variance £ [   ]

(b) Calculate the labour rate and efficiency variances.

Labour rate variance £ [   ]

Labour efficiency variance £ [   ]

(c) Calculate the fixed overhead expenditure, efficiency and capacity variances.

Fixed overhead expenditure variance £ [   ]

Fixed overhead efficiency variance £ [   ]

Fixed overhead capacity variance £ [   ]

(d) **Complete the table to prepare a reconciliation statement reconciling the standard cost of the production to the total cost.**

Operating statement – Absorption costing

			£
Standard cost of production			
Variances	**Favourable variances**	**Adverse variances**	
Materials price			
Materials usage			
Labour rate			
Labour efficiency			
Fixed overhead expenditure			
Fixed overhead efficiency			
Fixed overhead capacity			
Total variance			
Actual cost of production			

2 A business operates a marginal standard costing system and the cost card for its single product is given below:

	£
Direct materials 12 kg @ £4.80	57.60
Direct labour 3 hours @ £8.00	24.00
	81.60

The budgeted output for the period was 2,100 units and the budgeted fixed overhead was £95,000.

The actual production in the period was 2,400 units and the actual costs were as follows:

	£
Direct materials 29,600 kg	145,000
Direct labour 6,900 hours	56,200
Fixed overhead	92,000

You are to:

(a) Calculate the total direct materials cost variance and the materials price and usage variances.

Direct materials cost variance £ ⬚

Materials price variance £ ⬚

Materials usage variance £ ⬚

(b) Calculate the total direct labour cost variance and the labour rate and efficiency variances.

Direct labour cost variance £ ⬚

Labour rate variance £ ⬚

Labour efficiency variance £ ⬚

(c) Calculate any relevant fixed overhead variances.

Fixed overhead expenditure variance £ ⬚

(d) Complete the table to produce an operating statement reconciling the standard cost of the production to the actual cost.

			£
Standard variable cost of actual production			
Budgeted fixed overhead			
Variances	**Favourable variances**	**Adverse variances**	
Materials price			
Materials usage			
Labour rate			
Labour efficiency			
Fixed overhead expenditure			
Total variances			
Total actual cost			

Interpreting variances

6

Learning outcomes

2.5	Analyse and effectively present a report to management based on standard costing information
	• Identify the nature of variances
	• Identify what causes standard costing variances such as wastage, economies of scale, learning effect, inflation and skills mix
	• Identify possible action that can be taken to reduce adverse variances and increase favourable variances
	• Identify elements of a variance that are controllable and non-controllable
	• Effectively communicate what the standard costing variance means in report format

Assessment context

Explaining why variances have arisen and the interrelationship of variances will form a written task in the assessment. It is important that you are able to describe how each variance has been generated, and explain what has caused each variance.

Business context

Once variances have been calculated businesses need to understand why those variances have arisen. This will help manages control the operations of the business. Variance reporting is therefore an important part of an organisation's control process – indeed many businesses still use variance reporting as their primary control tool.

Chapter overview

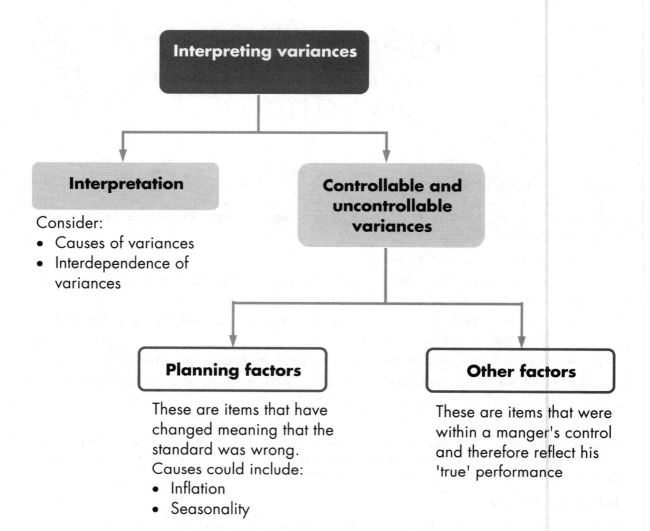

Interpreting variances

Interpretation

Consider:
- Causes of variances
- Interdependence of variances

Controllable and uncontrollable variances

Planning factors

These are items that have changed meaning that the standard was wrong.
Causes could include:
- Inflation
- Seasonality

Other factors

These are items that were within a manger's control and therefore reflect his 'true' performance

Introduction

When reporting variances to management, a simple operating statement as illustrated in the previous chapter is a useful starting point. However, management will also need to understand why variances occurred so that control action can be taken to either prevent them happening again, or to achieve similar results in the future.

1 Causes of variances

Assessment focus point

Having calculated variances, the cause of the variance must then be determined before appropriate action can be taken. This will form the basis of a written task within the assessment. When putting together your answer you need to consider:

- What has caused the variance to occur; and
- The impact this has had on the performance of the organisation.

The following table may help you to think about some of the operational causes of variances:

Variance	Favourable	Adverse
Material price	<ul><li>Unforeseen bulk/trade discounts received. This can either be due to a change in supplier, or more units being produced meaning that a bulk discount could be obtained. This is known as generating **economies of scale**.</li><li>Negotiating better prices with suppliers</li><li>Cheaper materials used in production. This could have a negative impact on quality.</li></ul>	<ul><li>A general market price increase and all suppliers have consequently increased their prices.</li><li>An unexpected change to a more expensive supplier.</li><li>More expensive materials used in production. This could also have a positive impact on the quality of material used.</li></ul>
Material usage	<ul><li>Material used of higher quality than standard, generating less wastage.</li><li>More experienced labour used, meaning fewer mistakes were made and less wastage.</li></ul>	<ul><li>Excessive waste due to defective material, inexperienced labour or machinery malfunction.</li><li>Theft of material, meaning more material was purchased, increasing the usage per unit.</li><li>Stricter quality control leading to more rework and more materials being used in production.</li></ul>

Variance	Favourable	Adverse
Labour rate	• Cheaper, less experienced/skilled labour was used. This could have an impact on labour hours worked and materials used. • Less overtime worked, meaning overtime premiums were not paid.	• Use of higher paid workers than standard. This could have a positive impact on labour hours worked and materials used. • A shortage of staff meaning that more expensive, temporary staff were used in the period. • More overtime worked, increasing overtime premiums in the period.
Idle time	The idle time variance is always adverse.	The workforce may be unproductive in the period due to: • Machine breakdown • Illness or injury to worker • Materials delivered late
Labour efficiency	• Increased worker motivation, meaning the workforce worked quicker on each production unit. • Better quality materials used meaning less rework of production units was required • Higher skilled staff used who were experienced in production, therefore producing units in fewer hours than expected. • More efficient machinery used making the production process less labour intensive than expected. • Greater production volumes means that staff find techniques to produce units more quickly. This is known as the **learning effect** and helps to facilitate economies of scale.	• Lack of training making staff inexperienced in the production process, increasing the amount of time spent in production. • Less skilled staff who were less experienced in production, therefore producing units in more hours than expected. • Inefficient machinery used, meaning that more labour hours were required to meet production requirements. • Lower quality materials used leading to more rework and more time spent in production.

Variance	Favourable	Adverse
Fixed overhead expenditure	• Unexpected savings in cost, for example a re-negotiation of rent or an unexpected market decrease in the price of utilities. • Change of supplier of the type of service used eg a change in electricity provider.	• An overall market increase in the cost of the service used eg telephone line rental charges.
Fixed overhead volume	• Production or level of activity greater than budgeted, increasing the amount of production units that fixed costs can be spread over, so economies of scale have been achieved.	• Production or level of activity less than budgeted, meaning there are fewer production units that fixed overheads can be spread over.
Fixed overhead efficiency	Reasons for this tie in exactly to labour efficiency.	
Fixed overhead capacity	• More overtime worked, meaning more hours were worked by the workforce than expected. • Greater employee motivation. Employees were therefore happy to work more hours. • Temporary resources used, increasing the total amount of hours worked.	• Greater absenteeism eg holidays/sickness. Fewer staff members were therefore available, meaning that fewer hours were worked than budgeted. • Machine breakdown leading to workers being unproductive in the period.

Activity 1: Causes of variances

Complete the following sentences:

Which of the following situations would probably cause a favourable labour rate variance?

Picklist:

Higher grade of labour used
Lower grade of material used
More overtime worked
Lower grade of labour used

Which of the following situations would probably cause a favourable materials usage variance?

[   ]

Picklist:

Stricter quality control
More experienced staff used
Excessive wastage of materials
Machine breakdowns

1.1 Interdependence of variances

You may have noticed from the above table that some causes of variances are likely to be connected, eg a lower grade of material can cause a favourable material price variance, but an adverse materials usage variance. This is known as the **interdependence of variances**.

Assessment focus point

You will be given hints in a short scenario about what may have caused each variance. Make sure you read the scenario carefully, spotting any instances where the variances may interrelate. In your answer, it's important to 'tell the story' of how the variances occurred, so consider how the variances presented are linked, and provide a logical flow when you put your answer together.

Illustration 1: Interdependence of variances

The following direct cost variances were generated in January for Armada Ltd:

	£
Materials price variance	6,300 (F)
Materials usage variance	6,000 (A)
Labour rate variance	5,040 (A)
Labour efficiency variance	2,400 (F)
Idle time	1,500 (A)
Fixed overhead expenditure variance	3,200 (F)
Fixed overhead volume variance	900 (A)

Upon investigation of the variances, the following is discovered:

- A new supplier was used in the period, which provided materials at a cheaper price than the old supplier.

- More material wastage was reported through the period as some of the materials received onto the production line was defective and had to be replaced.

- The defective material caused problems with production machinery, resulting in increased machinery maintenance and production downtime. However, due to the downtime, the power costs were lower than anticipated.

- To attempt to overcome this downtime, Armada employed a higher grade of labour than normal. These production operatives were highly experienced in the production process, resulting in production that was just below that which was budgeted.

Required

Explain why each variance has occurred.

The causes of these variances can be explained by referring to the interdependence of the variances.

The materials provided by the new supplier were cheaper than those obtained by the old supplier. This would mean that actual materials purchased would cost less than the standard cost of materials, causing a favourable materials price variance.

However, some material used in production was defective and had to be replaced. This would have caused more material being used to produce each unit than the standard allowed. The result of this is an adverse materials usage variance.

The defective material could also explain the idle time and fixed overhead volume variances. Since production was halted as a result of the machine downtime, this has led to production operatives being unproductive in the period, leading to the idle time variance. This has also led to an adverse fixed overhead volume variance – as workers were unable to produce units, production was just below that which was budgeted.

It is important to note that should more highly skilled workers not have been used, the fixed overhead volume variance could have been even more adverse than the £900 reported.

Due to the defective materials, Armada employed a higher grade of labour than planned. This higher grade of labour were more skilled, so commanded a higher wage than normal labour. This resulted in actual labour cost per hour being more than standard cost per hour, and an adverse labour rate variance.

However, this higher grade of labour was skilled in the production process, and efficiently worked to bring production just below that budgeted. The increased efficiency resulted in each unit being produced quicker than the standard allowed, causing the favourable labour efficiency variance.

BPP
LEARNING MEDIA

Activity 2: Shoebox Ltd

Shoebox Ltd is a manufacturer of trainers. It operates a standard absorption costing system. It has provided the following operating statement and information relating to its operations during the previous month:

	£
Standard cost of actual production	588,000
Variances	
Material price variance	21,740
Material usage variance	(11,760)
Labour rate variance	27,930
Labour efficiency variance	13,230
Fixed overhead expenditure variance	(2,000)
Fixed overhead capacity	3,330
Fixed overhead efficiency	4,410
Actual cost of production	644,880

Recent Events

Supplier

One of our suppliers went out of business during the month. We had to unexpectedly change to a new supplier who was more expensive, but provided a higher quality material.

Machinery

A machine on the production line was upgraded during the month. Production was halted for 4 days whilst the machinery was installed. Overtime then had to be worked in order for us to meet our production target for the month.

Warehouse

During the month our warehouse rent contract was renewed. We unexpectedly managed to negotiate our rent down for the coming year. This was so unexpected that we even estimated a rental increase when we set the budget.

Required

Write a memo to a colleague explaining what impact each of the events described above has had on the variances in the operating statement.

To: Colleague	Subject: Variance explanations
From: Accounting Technician	Date: xx/xx/20xx

Supplier

Machinery

Warehouse

2 Controllable and uncontrollable variances

Causes of variances can fall into the following categories:

(a) Controllable expenditure, eg incorrect buying decisions

(b) Uncontrollable expenditure, eg a market price rise of raw materials

(c) Inaccurate standard due to:

- Poor planning
- Use of unrealistic standard

In assigning the responsibility for the variances, managers should only be held accountable for factors that are within their control. In order to establish these areas, the traditional variances can be split into uncontrollable and controllable variances.

An **uncontrollable variance** is driven by an error in the planning of the standard. Standards are set through an element of forecasting, which sometimes proves to be wrong, so to an extent changes to the standard are uncontrollable by managers. This is sometimes referred to as a planning variance.

A **controllable variance** is the element that was within the manager's control, as the factors that give rise to this part of the variance is attributable to factors experienced in actual operations. Management decisions therefore have direct impact on this part of the variance. This is sometimes referred to as a control variance.

For example, a materials price variance can be broken down as follows:

	£	
Actual kg should have cost	X	
But did cost	X	
Materials price variance	X	

This can be analysed into:

Price variance due to known price change (non-controllable variance)	£	Price variance due to other factors (controllable variance)	£
Standard price for actual quantity used	X	Price-adjusted cost for actual quantity used	X
Price-adjusted cost for actual quantity used	X	Actual cost	X
Non-controllable price variance	X	Controllable price variance	X

Illustration 2: Controllable and uncontrollable variances

The standard direct materials cost for Tiger Ltd's product is:

> 4 kg @ £5.00 per kg = £20.00

During the month, Tiger generated a materials price variance of £20,000 adverse. However, it was later recognised that the standard should have been set at a price per kg of £5.50.

Required

Calculate the non-controllable and controllable elements of the materials price variance.

The non-controllable variance is calculated by comparing the original standard against the revised standard. Therefore we need to compare the original total cost for actual kg against the revised total cost for actual kg as follows:

	£
Standard price for actual quantity 45,600 kg × £5.00	228,000
Adjusted price for actual quantity 45,600 kg × £5.50	250,800
	22,800 (A)

The controllable variance is calculated by comparing the revised standard against the actual cost that was incurred. Therefore we need to compare revised total cost for actual kg against the actual cost for actual kg as follows:

	£
Adjusted price for actual quantity 45,600 × £5.50	250,800
Actual quantity at actual price	248,000
	2,800 (F)

We can now reconcile these variances back to the materials price variance as follows:

	£
Non-controllable variance	22,800 (A)
Controllable variance	2,800 (F)
Materials price variance	20,000 (A)

Activity 3: Tivvel

Tivvel plc manufactures plastic bottles at various locations in the UK. It has recently set up a plant in Tayside to provide plastic bottles to the local spring water distributors.

The material element of the standard cost card for each bottle is as follows:

	Units	Unit cost	Cost/bottle
Materials	4 kg	£4.50	£18.00

The new plant's actual results for the first four weeks of operations are shown below:

Production (bottles)	8,900
Material 36,490 kg	£156,907

You are informed by the production manager that the standard price for materials on the cost card was incorrect and should have been £5 per kg.

Required

Calculate the non-controllable and controllable elements of the materials price variance.

(a) **The non-controllable element of the materials price variance is**

[   ] .

(b) **The controllable element of the materials price variance is**

£ [   ] .

2.1 Seasonal variations in price

Sometimes material prices will fluctuate at different times of the year. It may therefore be useful to analyse the price variance into the element due to seasonality and the element due to other factors.

Activity 4: Patch

The material used in making Patch is subject to seasonal price variations.

The seasonal variations are:

Month 1–3   −10%

Month 4–6   +5%

Month 7–9   +15%

Month 10–12   −10%

The standard cost is £10/kg and each Patch uses 3 kg.

During month 8, 10,000 units were made. 34,000 kg were bought at a price of £355,000.

Required

(a) **Calculate the materials price variance.**

(b) **Calculate the non-controllable variance as a result of seasonality, and the controllable variance as a result of other factors.**

(a)

	£
Actual purchases should cost	
Actual purchases did cost	
Material price variance	

(b)

	£
Actual purchases should cost	
Actual purchases at revised standard cost	
Price variance due to difference in index value	

	£
Actual purchases at revised standard cost	
Actual purchases did cost	
Price variance due to other reasons	

If a company analyses its variances into non-controllable and controllable elements, some managers may try to suggest that any adverse variances that occur are not controllable and are due to errors when setting the standard.

Activity 5: Blossom

Blossom Ltd manufactures and sells garden statues. You work as an Accounting Technician reporting to the Finance Director. The company uses a standard cost stock system.

The actual and budgeted results for the production department for November are as follows:

Production department: Extract of actual and budgeted results for November 20X4

	Actual		Budget	
Production	6,500 units		7,500 units	
	£		£	
Materials 20,800 kg	91,520	22,500 kg	90,000	
Labour 7,150 hours	44,330	7,500 hours	45,000	

The following variances have been calculated for the period:

	£
Material price	8,320 A
Material usage	5,200 A
Labour rate	1,430 A

139

At a meeting of senior management, the validity of the November variance data was questioned. Particular comments were as follows:

Purchasing Manager

'I don't think it's fair to measure my performance against the standard materials cost. This was set in January 20X4 when the price index for materials was 110. In November, the same price index was 123.2.'

Personnel Manager

'We have had real difficulties recruiting production labour and we're seeing the result in overtime working.'

Required

(a) Calculate the uncontrollable part of the material price variance.

(b) Calculate the controllable part of the material price variance.

(c) Respond to the comments made by the purchasing and personnel manager, explaining whether their comments fully account for the labour and material variances given.

(a) The uncontrollable part of the materials price variance is [   ].

(b) The controllable part of the materials price variance is [   ].

(c) Response to the purchasing manager

Response to the personnel manager

Chapter summary

- Each type of variance can have a variety of causes. Often the variances are interdependent, meaning that a factor that caused one variance is also the factor that causes other variances.

- Information about standard costs and usage can be derived by working a variance backwards.

- Variances can be split into the non-controllable element caused by inaccurate standards (ie a planning variance) and the controllable variance caused by other variances (ie a control variance).

- A manager may be tempted to manipulate departmental results and variances. This will give rise to both ethical and goal congruence issues.

Keywords

- **Economies of scale:** cost savings achieved due to the production of a greater amount of cost units. This can be due to the learning effect, bulk discounts, and more efficient use of fixed overhead.

- **Interdependence of variances:** this is where the reasons for two or more variances may be the same, so that the variances are interrelated: the factor which causes one variance can also be the cause of another variance

- **Uncontrollable variances:** the part of a variance that is due to a cause outside the control of the manager responsible for the aspect of performance to which the variance relates

- **Controllable variances:** the part of a variance that is due to controllable operational factors or decisions

1   Given below is the operating statement for one of the factories of a business for the month of November, reconciling the total standard cost to the total actual cost for the month.

Operating statement – November

| | Variances | | |
| | **Adverse** | **Favourable** | |
	£	**£**	**£**
Total standard cost			634,200
Variances:			
Materials price	9,200		
Materials usage	14,600		
Labour rate		15,400	
Labour efficiency	13,200		
Fixed overhead expenditure	7,200		
Fixed overhead efficiency	11,500		
Fixed overhead capacity		6,000	
	55,700	21,400	
Add adverse variances			55,700
Less favourable variances			(21,400)
Total actual cost			668,500

You also discover the following information:

* Due to staff shortages a more junior grade of labour than normal, from one of the other factories, had to be used in the production process, giving rise to inefficiencies and additional wastage.

* The material price has been increased by all suppliers and it is doubtful that the materials can be purchased more cheaply than this in future.

* Due to its inventory-holding policy the factory has had to rent some additional space but this has not been recognised in the standard fixed overhead cost.

* Due to the inefficiencies of labour, more hours had to be worked than normal in the month.

Write a report to the Managing Director explaining:

(a) Possible reasons for the variances
(b) Future actions that could be taken

2 **What possible effect will the following scenarios have on variances? (You will need to create a table on a separate sheet of paper.)**

Scenarios	Possible effects
A business replaces machinery with new equipment	
A company has supply issues with a raw material	

3 The following information has been given for Ballpoint Ltd:

	£	Hours
Favourable material price variance	268	
Standard cost per kg of material	22	
Actual cost of material	1,000	
Adverse labour rate variance	636	
Actual labour hours		768
Actual cost of labour	22,560	

Complete the following two sentences:

The actual quantity of material purchased is ⬚ kg.

The standard labour rate is £ ⬚ .

4 Mugshot Ltd absorbs its fixed production overheads on a labour hour base. It has provided the following information:

	£
Favourable fixed overhead expenditure variance	8,500
Adverse fixed overhead volume variance	12,900
Actual units produced	49,500
Standard OAR per labour hour	4.20
Budgeted fixed overheads	78,000

Complete the following sentence:

The standard labour hours for the period were ⬚ hrs.

5 Eggcup has provided the following standard cost information:

	Budget	Actual
Production units	500	400
Actual hours worked		800
Labour cost per hour	£5.00	
Adverse labour rate variance		£900
Actual cost of labour		£4,900

The production manager has since informed you that, due to a general wage increase, the standard cost per labour hour should have been £6.50.

Required

Calculate:

(a) The uncontrollable part of the labour rate variance
(b) The controllable part of the labour rate variance

(a) The uncontrollable variance is ☐.

(b) The controllable variance is ☐.

Performance indicators

7

Learning outcomes

4.1	**Identify and calculate key financial and non-financial performance indicators**
	• Identify a range of and select key performance indicators
	• Calculate a range of key performance indicators and manipulate them
4.2	**Evaluate key financial and non-financial performance indicators**
	• Explain what the performance indicator means
	• Explain how the various elements of the indicator affect its calculation
	• Explain the impact of various factors on performance indicators including learning effect and economies of scale
	• Explain how some performance indicators interrelate with each other
	• Explain how proposed actions may affect the indicator
	• Explain what actions could be taken to improve the indicator
	• Explain how lack of goal congruence can affect the overall business objectives when managers are attempting to maximise a given indicator
	• Explain how ethical and commercial considerations can affect the behaviour of managers aiming to achieve a target indicator
4.4	**Make recommendations and effectively communicate to management based on analysis**
	• Explain how analysis and calculations lead to recommendations
	• Use the analysis to make reasoned recommendations and communicate them effectively

Assessment context

Performance indicators are likely to form one question in the assessment. Be prepared not just to calculate the performance indicator, but explain what the indicator tells the organisation about their performance.

Business context

Performance measurement is an important control tool within organisations, and organisations produce regular reports about their performance. This will include calculated performance indicators alongside written analysis of them.

Organisations need a range of indictors to fully understand their performance. Therefore organisations produce a performance report containing both financial and key non-financial performance indicators that qualify the financial performance.

Chapter overview

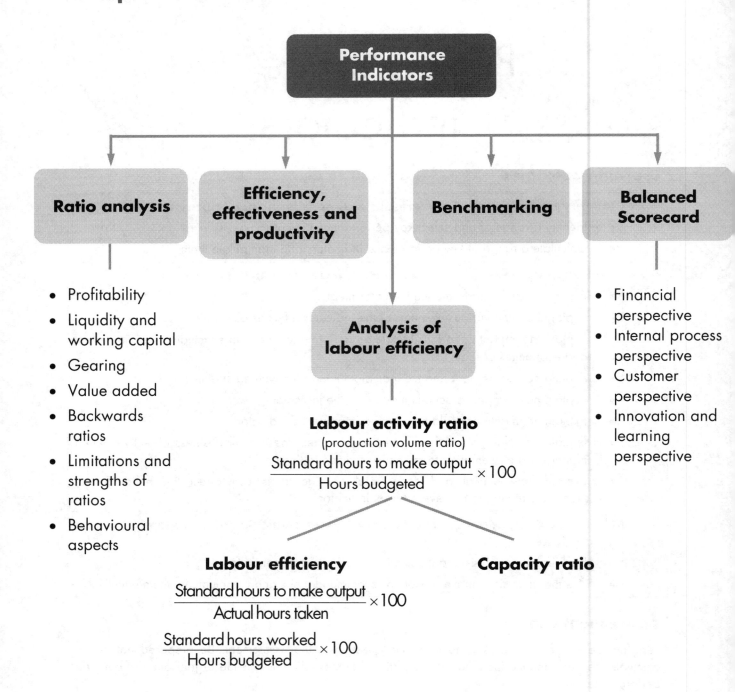

Performance Indicators

Ratio analysis

Efficiency, effectiveness and productivity

Benchmarking

Balanced Scorecard

- Profitability
- Liquidity and working capital
- Gearing
- Value added
- Backwards ratios
- Limitations and strengths of ratios
- Behavioural aspects

Analysis of labour efficiency

Labour activity ratio
(production volume ratio)

$$\frac{\text{Standard hours to make output}}{\text{Hours budgeted}} \times 100$$

Labour efficiency

$$\frac{\text{Standard hours to make output}}{\text{Actual hours taken}} \times 100$$

$$\frac{\text{Standard hours worked}}{\text{Hours budgeted}} \times 100$$

Capacity ratio

- Financial perspective
- Internal process perspective
- Customer perspective
- Innovation and learning perspective

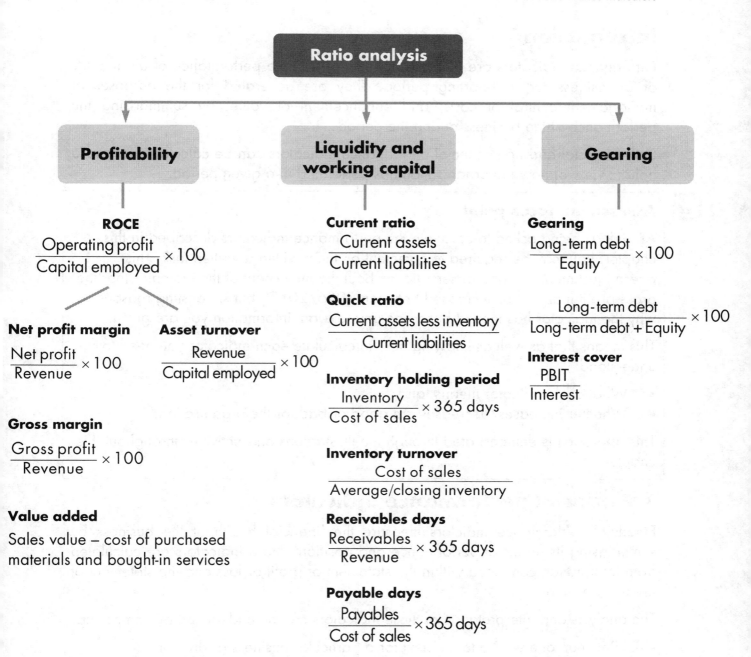

Ratio analysis

Profitability

Liquidity and working capital

Gearing

ROCE

$$\frac{\text{Operating profit}}{\text{Capital employed}} \times 100$$

Net profit margin

$$\frac{\text{Net profit}}{\text{Revenue}} \times 100$$

Asset turnover

$$\frac{\text{Revenue}}{\text{Capital employed}} \times 100$$

Gross margin

$$\frac{\text{Gross profit}}{\text{Revenue}} \times 100$$

Value added

Sales value – cost of purchased materials and bought-in services

Current ratio

$$\frac{\text{Current assets}}{\text{Current liabilities}}$$

Quick ratio

$$\frac{\text{Current assets less inventory}}{\text{Current liabilities}}$$

Inventory holding period

$$\frac{\text{Inventory}}{\text{Cost of sales}} \times 365 \text{ days}$$

Inventory turnover

$$\frac{\text{Cost of sales}}{\text{Average/closing inventory}}$$

Receivables days

$$\frac{\text{Receivables}}{\text{Revenue}} \times 365 \text{ days}$$

Payable days

$$\frac{\text{Payables}}{\text{Cost of sales}} \times 365 \text{ days}$$

Gearing

$$\frac{\text{Long-term debt}}{\text{Equity}} \times 100$$

$$\frac{\text{Long-term debt}}{\text{Long-term debt + Equity}} \times 100$$

Interest cover

$$\frac{\text{PBIT}}{\text{Interest}}$$

Introduction

Performance indicators are methods of summarising the performance of all or parts of a business for a reporting period. They are generated for the purposes of management control of costs, and enhancement of value, by summarising the performance of the business during the period.

Both financial and non-financial performance indicators can be calculated to give a holistic view of how the organisation has performed in a given period.

Assessment focus point

As well as being asked to calculate the performance indicators described in this chapter, you may be required to comment on them within a written task. This doesn't just mean making observations about the movement of the indicator (eg 'the gross profit margin has increased between 20X6/20X7') but suggesting reasons why the indicator has moved based on any relevant information you are given.

This means that as well as knowing how to calculate each indicator you need to understand:

- What each indicator means; and
- Whether increases/decreases are good or bad for the organisation.

This approach is demonstrated through the illustrations and activities throughout this chapter.

1 Financial performance indicators

Financial performance indictors measure the financial health of the business by summarising its financial performance and position. These indicators are calculated from information contained within the statement of profit or loss and the statement of financial position.

The analysis and interpretation of these indicators can be undertaken by comparing:

- Between one year and the next for a particular business or division; or
- Between one business or division and another.

1.1 Profitability indicators

The aim of most businesses is to make a profit, therefore management will be interested in profitability performance indicators. The profitability indicators could also be described as efficiency indicators, as they are measuring the efficiency with which the business has used its assets to earn profits.

1.1.1 Return on capital employed

The **return on capital employed** (ROCE) is an indicator of investment efficiency, as it looks at how well a business has invested the capital available to it. It is calculated as:

Formula to learn

Return on capital employed = $\dfrac{\text{Profit before interest and tax}}{\text{Capital employed}} \times 100$

where

Capital employed = Total assets – Current liabilities or;

Equity or capital + Non-current liabilities

(**Note.** Sometimes net profit is used instead of profit before interest and tax.)

ROCE relates the profit that has been earned for the period to the equity/capital from the statement of financial position to determine what return has been made on the owners' investment in the business.

An alternative approach to calculating the returns to owners is to just use the equity figure from the statement of financial position in replacement of capital employed. This is known as the **return on net assets** (RONA) and is calculated as:

Formula to learn

Return on net assets = $\dfrac{\text{Operating profit}}{\text{Equity}} \times 100$

Assessment focus point

Read the assessment task carefully for the ratio you are being asked to calculate, and make sure you are using the correct formula.

1.1.2 Gross profit margin

The **gross profit margin** shows the gross profit for the period as a percentage of sales. It is calculated as:

Formula to learn

Gross profit margin = $\dfrac{\text{Gross profit}}{\text{Revenue}} \times 100$

The gross profit margin shows the amount of gross profit that has been made for every £1 of sales revenue. It gives an indication as to whether sufficient sales revenue is being achieved, or whether cost of sales are being adequately controlled.

When comparing the gross profit margin over different periods, any changes are likely to be caused by:

- Changes in the selling price of goods

- Changes in the mix of the goods sold

- Changes in the price of the production cost (ie changes in the price of materials, production labour and production overheads)

- A combination of these factors

The gross profit margin can therefore be improved by increasing selling prices or decreasing cost of sales. This will help to improve the overall profitability of the business.

1.1.3 Operating profit margin

The **operating profit margin** is the operating profit as a percentage of sales revenue for the period. It is calculated as follows:

Formula to learn

$$\text{Operating profit margin} = \frac{\text{Profit from operations}}{\text{Revenue}} \times 100$$

Operating profit is the profit generated by the business before interest and tax. It is therefore sometimes referred to as profit before interest and tax (PBIT).

Sometimes you are asked for the net profit margin. This can be calculated as:

$$\text{Net profit margin} = \frac{\text{Net profit}}{\text{Revenue}} \times 100$$

The operating profit margin shows the amount of operating profit generated for every £1 of sales revenue. It gives an indication of how well expenses have been controlled in the business.

Changes in the operating profit margin will be partly explained by changes in the gross profit margin, alongside changes in the volume of other expenses incurred.

The steps discussed above to improve the gross profit margin can also help to improve the operating profit margin. However, improving sales volumes is another way of improving the operating profit margin, especially if the operating overheads of the business are mostly fixed.

1.1.4 Expenses

It is also sometimes useful to express individual items of expense as a percentage of the sales figure to determine how these expenses have changed. This is done by the following calculation:

Formula to learn

$$\textbf{Expenses as a percentage of revenue} = \frac{\text{Item of expense}}{\text{Revenue}} \times 100$$

If sales and production are increasing over accounting periods:

- The percentage change in variable costs will increase in line with the percentage change in volume of production and sales

- The percentage change in fixed costs will decrease as fixed costs are spread over more production volume.

1.1.5 Asset turnover

Asset turnover compares the sales revenue of the business to the capital employed. It is calculated as:

> **Formula to learn**
>
> **Asset turnover** $= \dfrac{\text{Revenue}}{\text{Capital employed}}$
>
> where
>
> Capital employed = Total assets – Current liabilities or;
>
> Equity or capital + Non-current liabilities
>
> (**Note.** Sometimes net profit is used instead of profit before interest and tax.)

Asset turnover shows the revenue that is generated from each £1 of capital employed, or every £1 of investment in assets and liabilities. It may be expressed as 'x times' – for example, if sales are £200,000 and capital employed is £100,000, the asset turnover is 2 times.

Asset turnover is an important figure as it is one of the elements that make up ROCE, as can be seen below:

$$\boxed{\text{ROCE}} \quad = \quad \boxed{\text{Asset turnover}} \quad \times \quad \boxed{\text{Net profit margin}}$$

If we look at how each of these ratios are calculated you will see how this works:

$$\boxed{\frac{\text{Operating profit}}{\text{Capital employed}}} \quad = \quad \boxed{\frac{\text{Turnover}}{\text{Capital employed}}} \quad \times \quad \boxed{\frac{\text{Operating profit}}{\text{Turnover}}}$$

The importance of this relationship is that we can explain any change in ROCE by changes in asset turnover and changes in the operating profit margin.

Illustration 1: Profitability ratios

Below are the summarised statements of profit or loss and statement of financial position for the years ended 31 October 20X7 and 31 October 20X8 for Jamboree Ltd, a manufacturing organisation which produces a range of plastic tricycles for children:

Summarised statements of profit or loss (income statements)

	Y/e 31 Oct 20X8 £000	Y/e 31 Oct 20X7 £000
Revenue	420	320
Cost of sales	256	180
Gross profit	164	140
Expenses	100	89
Operating profit	64	51
Interest payable	10	10
Profit before tax	54	41
Tax	16	12
Profit after tax	38	29

Summarised statements of financial position

	31 Oct 20X8		31 Oct 20X7	
	£000	£000	£000	£000
Non-current assets		394		369
Current assets:				
Inventory	50		30	
Receivables	69		44	
Cash	2		12	
	121		86	
Payables	52		30	
Net current assets		69		56
		463		425
Long-term loan		100		100
		363		325
Capital		250		250
Retained earnings		113		75
		363		325

Required

Calculate the following ratios and, comment on the performance of the company over the last two years in the light of these ratios:

(a) **Gross profit margin**
(b) **Operating profit margin**
(c) **Expenses to sales**
(d) **ROCE**
(e) **Asset turnover**

The ratios are calculated as follows:

	20X8	20X7
(a) Gross profit margin		
164/420 × 100	39.0%	
140/320 × 100		43.8%
(b) Operating profit margin		
64/420 × 100	15.2%	
51/320 × 100		15.9%
(c) Expenses to sales		
100/420 × 100	23.8%	
89/320 × 100		27.8%
(d) ROCE		
64/463 × 100	13.8%	
51/425 × 100		12.0%
(e) Asset turnover		
420/463	0.91	
320/425		0.75

In order to explain the performance of the company over the last two years, look at the change in each ratio and how the changes in each ratio may relate to each other.

Gross profit margin

The gross profit margin has decreased. Whilst total revenue has increased during the period, the gross profit margin may be explained by a reduction in the selling price per unit in order to increase sales volumes. The reduced selling price would have generated less contribution per unit, impacting adversely on the gross profit margin.

Operating profit margin

Whilst the operating profit margin has decreased slightly, it hasn't decreased in line with the gross profit margin. This indicates better cost control of expenses, evidenced by the decrease in the percentage of expenses to sales revenue. Some of the expenses are likely to be fixed costs and therefore have not increased in line with sales revenue.

ROCE

ROCE has increased despite the fall in profit margins. This is directly linked to the improvement in asset turnover.

Asset turnover

Asset turnover has increased between the two years despite the lower profit margins reported. There has been investment in non-current assets, as these have increased between the two years. The increasing asset turnover may therefore be due to efficiencies as a result of the new non-current assets.

1.2 Liquidity ratios

Liquidity is a measure of how safe the business is in terms of the availability of cash. Even if a business is profitable, it must still have enough cash to be able to pay its trade payables and long-term liabilities when they fall due.

1.2.1 Current ratio

The **current ratio** is the ratio of current assets to current liabilities. It is calculated as follows:

Formula to learn

$$\textbf{Current ratio} = \frac{\text{Current assets}}{\text{Current liabilities}}$$

It can be expressed as either a ratio (eg 2.4:1) or as a single number (eg 2.4). In the assessment, enter your answer as a single number.

If the current ratio is low, there is a risk that the business may be unable to pay its payables on time. A ratio of 2:1 is often considered safe, but this depends on the type of business. For example, retailers often have low volumes of receivables and rapid inventory movement, but high payables, so they tend to have low current ratios. However, this is considered normal for the industry.

1.2.2 Quick ratio

Inventory is not a particularly liquid current asset – it could take some organisations many months for them to convert it into cash. Therefore, a more immediate method of assessing the liquidity of a business is to calculate the **quick ratio** as follows:

Formula to learn

$$\textbf{Quick ratio} = \frac{\text{Current assets less inventory}}{\text{Current liabilities}}$$

The quick ratio is similar to the current ratio, but excludes inventory from current assets.

Illustration 2: Liquidity ratios

Let's revisit the statement of profit or loss and the statement of financial position for Jamboree Ltd.

Required

Calculate the following ratios, and comment on the performance of Jamboree Ltd over the last two years.

(a) Current ratio
(b) Quick ratio

The ratios are calculated as follows:

	20X8	20X7
(a) Current ratio		
121/52	2.3	
86/30		2.9
(b) Quick ratio		
71/52	1.4	
56/30		1.9

Again, in order to explain the performance of the company over the last two years, look at the change in each ratio and how the changes in each ratio may relate to each other.

Current ratio

The current ratio has fallen between 20X8 and 20X7. This is due to the decreasing cash balance and the increasing payables balance, putting strain on the cash position of Jamboree Ltd.

Quick ratio

The quick ratio has fallen in line with the current ratio, indicating that immediate liquidity within Jamboree has also fallen, despite the increase in inventories.

To investigate these ratios further, further working capital ratios need to be calculated and analysed.

1.3 Working capital ratios

Working capital is the total of the current assets of a business less its current liabilities.

It can be used to monitor the working capital (or cash) cycle – that is, the speed with which a business can complete the cycle of making payments to suppliers, converting inventory into sales, and then receiving cash from its customers from that sale.

To monitor this cycle, the business will need to monitor the length of time inventories are held for, the average time taken to collect cash in from customers, and the average time to make payments to suppliers.

1.3.1 Inventory holding period

The **inventory holding period** (also known as inventory days), measures the length of time that inventory is held in the business. It is calculated as follows:

Formula to learn

Inventory holding period in days $= \dfrac{\text{Inventory}}{\text{Cost of sales}} \times 365 \text{ days}$

This indicates the number of days that inventory is held before it is used or sold.

In some assessment variants you will be given opening and closing statement of financial position balances. In this case, average inventory should be use instead of closing inventory. Average inventory can be calculated as follows:

Formula to learn

Average inventory $= \dfrac{\text{Opening inventory} + \text{closing inventory}}{2}$

Monitoring inventory days is an important element of working capital management as cash is tied up in inventory while it is waiting to be sold.

1.3.2 Inventory turnover

An alternative to measuring the inventory holding period is to calculate **inventory turnover**. Instead of expressing inventory in terms of the number of days inventory is held, inventory turnover expresses inventory as the number of times a year it is turned over.

Inventory turnover is calculated as follows:

Formula to learn

Inventory turnover $= \dfrac{\text{Cost of sales}}{\text{Average/closing inventory}}$

1.3.3 Receivables collection period

The **receivables collection period** (also known as receivables days) measures how long it takes credit customers to pay for the goods or services they buy. It is calculated as follows:

Formula to learn

Receivables collection period $= \dfrac{\text{Receivables}}{\text{Credit sales}} \times 365 \text{ days}$

The receivables collection period can be monitored over time in order to assess how well receivables are being managed. For example, if the average collection period is getting longer, this may be a sign of inefficient credit control, or customers contravening their agreed credit period.

1.3.4 Payables payment period

The **payables payment period** (also known as payables days) measures how long the business takes to pay its credit suppliers. It is calculated as follows:

Formula to learn

$$\text{Payables payment period} = \frac{\text{Payables}}{\text{Credit purchases}} \times 365 \text{ days}$$

Assessment focus point

Sometimes in the assessment, credit purchases is not given to you. In this instance, use total purchases or total cost of sales from the statement of profit or loss.

The payables payment period can be monitored against the receivables collection period to ensure it is not significantly shorter. For example, if customers are taking 75 days to pay, but the business is paying its payables within 15 days, this would mean that money is being paid out of the business more rapidly than it is being received.

Assessment focus point

In the assessment you may be asked to calculate inventory holding period, receivables' collection period or payables' payment period in months rather than in days. In these situations substitute 12 months for 365 days in the formulae.

Illustration 3: Working capital ratios

Let's revisit the statement of profit or loss and the statement of financial position for Jamboree Ltd.

Required

Calculate the following ratios, and comment on the performance of Jamboree Ltd over the last two years.

(a) Inventory days
(b) Receivables collection period
(c) Payables payment period

The ratios can be calculated as follows:

	20X8	20X7
(a) Inventory days		
50/256 × 365	71 days	
30/180 × 365		61 days
(b) Receivables' collection period		
69/420 × 365	60 days	
44/320 × 365		50 days
(c) Payables' payment period		
52/256 × 365	74 days	
30/180 × 365		61 days

The ratios can be interpreted as follows:

Inventory days

Inventory days have increased and inventories are now being held for 71 days rather than 61 days. This is reflected by the increasing investment in inventories between 20X7 and 20X8. More information is required, but Jamboree could be stocking a wider range of tricycles.

Receivables collection period

The receivables collection period has increased by 10 days to 60 days. Jamboree could either be extending credit terms to new customers, or there is inefficient credit control. Either way, cash is not being collected as efficiently, reducing the cash balance and putting a strain on the current ratio.

Payables payment period

The payables payment period has increased by 13 days to 74 days. This may be due to cash being further tied up in both inventories and receivables, indicating that less cash is available for Jamboree to use to pay suppliers. The increase in payments payment period is, however, not enough to offset the increases in both inventory holding and receivables collection periods, putting further strain on Jamboree's current ratio.

1.4 Gearing

Gearing considers the capital structure of a business. Many companies are financed by both long-term debt and equity, but a significant amount of long-term debt brings with it certain financial risks:

- The company may not be able to pay the interest on loans they possess.
- The company may not be able to repay the loan when repayments fall due.

To ensure these risks are controlled, management should monitor the amount of debt in their capital structure.

1.4.1 Gearing ratio

The **gearing ratio** measures the amount of loan capital a company has compared to its equity sources of finance. It is calculated as follows:

> **Formula to learn**
>
> $$\text{Gearing} = \frac{\text{Long-term debt}}{\text{Equity}} \quad \text{or} \quad \frac{\text{Long-term debt}}{\text{Long-term debt} + \text{Equity}} \times 100$$

> **Assessment focus point**
>
> In the assessment both calculations are valid – the marking for both computer- and human-marked tasks will accept answers based on either calculation.

The gearing ratio measures the financial risk of a company. If the ratio is high then it means that the company is mostly financed by long-term debt, increasing risk of default on that debt.

1.4.2 Interest cover

Interest cover is a measure of whether the company can make the interest payments on its debt capital out of annual profits. It is calculated as follows:

> **Formula to learn**
>
> $$\text{Interest cover} = \frac{\text{Operating profit (PBIT)}}{\text{Interest}}$$

Interest cover measures how many times the interest payment is covered by profits, measuring the company's ability to service its debt.

> **Illustration 4: Gearing**
>
> Let's revisit the statement of profit or loss and the statement of financial position for Jamboree Ltd.
>
> **Required**
>
> **Calculate the following ratios, and comment on the performance of Jamboree Ltd over the last two years.**
>
> (a) **Gearing**
> (b) **Interest cover**

The ratios are calculated as follows:

	20X8	20X7
(a) Interest cover		
64/10	6.4	
51/10		5.1
(b) Gearing ratio (total debt/equity)		
100/363	27.5%	
100/325		30.8%

We can interpret the ratios as follows:

Gearing

Gearing has decreased between the two years, and remains at a relatively low percentage. It appears that further investment within Jamboree has been met by increasing equity, as long-term loans have remained the same. This indicates low financial risk within Jamboree, as it is mostly financed by equity rather than long-term debt.

Interest cover

Interest cover has increased between the two years. This is due to the increasing profit, as more profit is available to service the same amount of loan finance and interest charge. This further indicates low financial risk within Jamboree.

Assessment focus point

The range of indicators detailed here are not exhaustive. In the assessment you may be asked to calculate non-standard financial indicators, for example revenue per employee. These indicators should be straightforward to calculate.

Activity 1: LNG Ltd

Extracts from the latest operating statements of LNG Ltd and certain performance indicators from its competitor Ads Ltd are shown below.

Statement of profit or loss extract for the year ended 30 November 20X5

LNG Ltd	£000
Advertising revenue	4,200
Less: Cost of sales:	
Materials	(1,900)
Direct labour	(430)
Fixed production overheads	(880)
Gross profit	990
Sales and distribution costs	(540)
Administration costs	(240)
Profit from operations	210
Finance charges	(60)
Profit for year	150

Statement of financial position

LNG Ltd	£000
Non-current assets	3,265
Receivables	1,050
Cash and cash equivalents	85
Payables	(600)
Net assets	3,800

Other operating data

LNG Ltd	
Newspapers produced	7,500,000
Number of employees	70
Advertising transactions	40,000

Performance indicators for Ads Ltd

Ads Ltd	
Gross profit margin	33.2%
Operating profit margin	10.0%
ROCE	15.4%
Administration costs as % of sales	4.0%
Receivables age (in months)	2.0
Payables age (in months)	1.5
Current ratio	2.0
Average advertising revenue per newspaper	£0.75
Advertising revenue per employee	£88,500.00
Advertising revenue per advertising transaction	£120.00
Interest cover	3.5 times

Required

(a) Calculate the following performance indicators for LNG. Where rounding is required, give your answer to one decimal place:

(i) **Gross profit margin**
(ii) **Operating profit margin**
(iii) **Administration costs as a percentage of sales**
(iv) **ROCE**
(v) **Average advertising revenue per newspaper produced**
(vi) **Advertising revenue per employee**
(vii) **Average advertising revenue per advertising transaction**
(viii) **Current ratio**
(ix) **Average receivables collection period in months**
(x) **Average payables payment period in months**
(xi) **Gearing**

(b) **Write a memo to LNG's managing director which explains why the following indicators are different to those of Ads:**

(i) **Gross profit margin**
(ii) **Operating profit margin**
(iii) **ROCE**
(iv) **Current ratio**
(v) **Interest cover**

(a)

Gross profit margin	
Operating profit margin	
Administration costs as a percentage of sales	
ROCE	
Average advertising revenue per newspaper produced	
Advertising revenue per employee	
Average advertising revenue per advertising transaction	
Current ratio	
Average age of receivables in months	
Average age of payables in months	
Interest cover	

(b)

Memo

To: Managing Director   From: Accounting Technician

Subject: Performance Indicators

(i)   Gross profit margin

(ii)   Operating profit margin

(iii) ROCE

(iv) Current ratio

(v)   Interest cover

Assessment focus point

An assessment task may ask you to describe the impact that certain decisions may have on the financial indicators you have initially calculated. This may require you to:

- Recalculate the indicators

- Interpret the likely impact that these decisions would have on financial indicators in a written part of the task

Illustration 5: Improving financial performance at LNG

At LNG Ltd, a management meeting was held to discuss the annual results. In a bid to increase profits and be more competitive, the following improvements were identified:

- Average advertising revenue per advertising transaction could be increased by 5%.

- Wastage of paper could be reduced which would result in a saving of 3% in total materials costs.

- A credit controller could be employed at an annual cost of £25,000. As a result, receivables would be reduced to £850,000.

Required

Explain the impact that these decisions have had on the following ratios, making appropriate calculations:

(a) Gross profit margin
(b) Operating profit margin
(c) ROCE
(d) Receivables collection period

Firstly, we need to consider the instruction of 'making appropriate calculations'. It would be appropriate to re-calculate the ratios taking into account the decisions that have been made. We can then compare the results to the original ratios calculated.

The above decisions would have the following effect on the ratios:

Gross profit margin

The gross profit margin can now be calculated as follows:

Revised revenue: 4,200 × 1.05 = £4,410

Revised cost = (1,900 × 0.97 + 430 + 880) = £3,153

Revised gross profit margin:

$$\frac{(4,410-3,153)}{4,410} \times 100 = 28.5\%$$

The gross profit margin has improved from an original 23.6%. This is due to both the increased advertising revenue and the 3% reduction in material wastage. Since revenue has gone up and variable costs have decreased, more contribution is being earned by LNG. The additional contribution has improved the gross profit margin.

Operating profit margin

The operating profit margin can now be calculated as follows:

Revised profit: 4,410 – 3,153 – 540 – 240 – 25 = £452

Revised operating profit margin:

$$\frac{452}{4,410} \times 100 = 10.2\%$$

Despite the fact that the additional cost of the credit controller has added additional overhead cost to LNG, the operating profit margin has improved. This is as a direct result of the improvements in the gross profit margin, as more contribution is now being generated towards overheads and operating profit.

ROCE

The increase in profit will lead to an overall increase in capital employed as follows:

- The increase in revenue will increase cash in LNG by £210,000.

- The decrease in materials cost will either decrease payables or increase cash by £57,000.

- The employment of the credit controller will decrease cash in the business by £25,000.

Revised net assets is therefore calculated as follows:

3,800 + 210 + 57 – 25 = £4,042

The revised return on capital employed can be calculated as follows:

$$\frac{452}{4,042} \times 100 = 11.2\%$$

Like the operating profit margin, the increase in cost generated by the credit controller is not enough to offset the savings made in materials cost or the additional advertising revenue generated. Therefore, the improvement in operating profit does not offset the additional capital employed to generate the profit, so ROCE improves.

Receivables collection period

The revised receivables collection period can be calculated as:

$$\frac{850}{4,410} \times 12 = 2.3 \text{ months}$$

The receivables collection period has improved from the original three months. This is due to efficient working of the credit controller, despite the fact that they had more revenue to collect due to the 5% increase in advertising revenue. This has improved LNG's liquidity position.

Activity 2: Seat Co

The actual and budgeted operating results for the sales and production of leather chairs at Seat Co for the year ended 31 December 20X2 are as follows:

	Actual £	Budget £
Revenue	2,750,000	3,000,000
Cost of sales		
Opening finished goods inventory	200,000	200,000
Cost of production	2,329,600	2,400,000
Closing finished goods inventory	(240,000)	(200,000)
	2,289,600	2,400,000
Gross profit	**460,400**	**600,000**
Distribution and administration costs	345,000	360,000
Profit from operations	**115,400**	**240,000**
Net assets	£1,075,400	£1,200,000

Required

(a) **Calculate the following performance indicators:**

   (i) **Gross profit margin**
   (ii) **Operating profit margin**
   (iii) **ROCE**
   (iv) **Inventory turnover (in months)**

(b) **Write a memo to the Finance Director. Your memo should include one course of action the company could take to improve each performance indicator.**

(a)

	Actual	Budget
Gross profit margin		
Operating profit margin		
ROCE		
Inventory turnover		

(b)

Memo	
To: Finance Director	From: Accounting Technician
Subject: Performance Indicators	Date: xx/xx/xxxx

(i)   **Gross profit margin**

(ii)   **Operating profit margin**

(iii)   **ROCE**

(iv)   **Inventory turnover**

Assessment focus point

An assessment task may require you to make recommendations about options to grow the business, based on calculated financial ratios. When making recommendations, you need to explain two things:

- What your recommendation is, and
- Why you are making the recommendation.

When giving the reason for your recommendation, find the most important points from your initial discussion and summarise them in a succinct sentence.

Activity 3: Grippit

Grippit manufacturers domestic wind turbines. A colleague has prepared forecast information based upon two scenarios. The forecast profit and loss account and balance sheet for both scenarios are shown below.

- Scenario 1 is to set the price at £1,250 per unit with sales of 10,000 units per year.

- Scenario 2 is to set the price at £1,000 per unit with sales of 14,000 units per year.

The following information has been provided for each scenario:

	Scenario 1	Scenario 2
Gross profit margin	36.00%	28.57%
Net profit margin	17.20%	11.79%
Direct materials cost per unit	£300	£300
Direct labour cost per unit	£200	£200
Fixed production cost per unit	£300	£214.29
Gearing	58.82%	57.36%
Interest cover	4.58	3.75

Required

Draft an email for the Finance Director covering the following:

(a) **An explanation of why the gross profit margin is different in each scenario. Your answer should refer to the following:**

    (i) **Sales price per unit**
    (ii) **Materials, labour and fixed cost per unit**

(b) **An assessment of the level of gearing and interest cover under each scenario**

(c) **A recommendation of which scenario the managers should choose**

Email

To: Finance Director   Date: xx/xx/20xx

From: Accounting Technician   Subject: Analysis of scenarios

(a) Gross profit margin

   (i)   Sales price per unit

   (ii)   Materials

   (iii) Labour

   (iv) Fixed costs

(b) Gearing and interest cover

(c) Recommendation

As well as calculating various ratios, you may need to work backwards through a ratio. To do this, you need to have good working knowledge of how each ratio is calculated to find the figure you are asked for.

Illustration 6: Backwards ratios

A company has current assets of £650,000 capital employed of £2.25m.

Required

Calculate:

(a) The revenue required to give an asset turnover of 4

(b) The operating profit required to give a ROCE of 20%

(c) The amount of current liabilities required to give a current ratio of 2.3

Give your answer to the nearest whole £.

Let's work through each requirement in turn:

(a)   To work out the amount of revenue required for an asset turnover of 4, we need to work backwards through the asset turnover ratio.

If we worked forwards, the asset turnover ratio is:

$$\text{Asset turnover} = \frac{\text{Revenue}}{\text{Capital employed}}$$

Re-arranging this formula, revenue can therefore be calculated as:

Revenue = Asset turnover × capital employed

We know that the asset turnover is 4, and capital employed is £2.25m, so revenue is therefore:

£2,250,000 × 4 = £9,000,000

(b)   To work out the operating profit required for a ROCE of 20%, we need to work backwards through the ROCE formula.

ROCE is calculated as:

$$\text{ROCE} = \frac{\text{Profit from operations}}{\text{Capital employed}}$$

Re-arranging this formula, profit can therefore be calculated as:

Profit from operations = ROCE × Capital employed

We know that ROCE is 20% and capital employed is £2.25m. Profit can therefore be calculated as:

£2,250,000 × 0.2 = £450,000

(c)   To work out the amount of current liabilities required to give a current ratio of 2.3, we need to work backwards through the current ratio formula.

The current ratio formula is:

$$\text{Current ratio} = \frac{\text{Current assets}}{\text{Current liabilities}}$$

Re-arranging this formula, current liabilities are therefore calculated as:

$$\text{Current liabilities} = \frac{\text{Current assets}}{\text{Current ratio}}$$

We know that current assets are £650,000, and the current ratio is 2.3. Current liabilities can therefore be calculated as:

$$\frac{650,000}{2.3} = £282,609$$

2 Limitations of financial performance indicators

Whilst financial performance indicators are useful tools to summarise performance over a number of periods and to identify patterns over time, there are several limitations in the use of them:

- **Comparator needed** – Financial indicators are meaningless on their own. A suitable, like-for-like comparator needs to be found, eg between accounting periods or between organisations. Finding a suitable comparator can be problematic, as changes in accounting policies by an organisation or between organisations will be reflected in the ratios themselves. Adjustments may need to be made to the figures before the ratios are calculated and compared.

- **Inflation** – Adjustments may need to be made to the figures using, for example, an appropriate index, so that all figures are stated at one price level. Not inflating or deflating figures can skew the ratios calculated.

- **Representative figures** – Ratios are often based on year-end figures, which may not be representative of future costs or the average value for the year.

- **Other factors** – As ratios use the financial results from the statement of profit or loss and statement of financial positions, they do not convey the full picture of the organisation. Factors that relate to organisational success, eg customer satisfaction and quality, are ignored. Additional non-financial indicators may need to be calculated in order to 'tell the story' of the financial indicators.

- **Short-termisim** – Financial indicators can lead to managers excessively focussing on profit. A profit focus is short-term, as other factors may need to be controlled in order to ensure long-term success.

3 Behavioural aspects

Another limitation of financial performance indicators is that they can encourage managers to act in a dysfunctional way. Managers may take actions for the good of one area or their division which are not in the interests of the company as a whole. This is known as acting in a non-goal congruent manner.

Illustration 7: ABC

The key performance indicator for the production department of ABC is ROCE.

Results for the production department for the year 20X9 were:

	£
Profits	90,000
Net assets	500,000

The company is now considering investing in a new labour-saving piece of equipment which will cost £10,000 and have an annual profit of £1,200. This piece of equipment will not only save labour, but will also ensure a more consistent product and should help increase quality and, therefore, customer satisfaction.

Required

(a) Explain whether the manager will choose to invest in the new machinery.

(b) Explain the goal congruence implications of the manager's decision.

(a)   Current ROCE = 90,000/500,000 = 18%

ROCE of equipment = 1,200/10,000 = 12%

As the ROCE of the new equipment is below that of current departmental ROCE the manager will choose not to invest. This is because ROCE is likely to be the manager's key performance target. Investing in the new machinery will drag down the department's ROCE, making it appear like the manager is making poor operating decisions.

(b)   If the manager chooses not to invest in the machinery this is not goal congruent. This is because the machinery will drive future efficiency improvements within ABC, as well as improving product quality attracting more customers and driving more revenue. The investment in the machine is therefore a good long term investment for ABC which will drive long-term profit improvements.

Activity 4: Blossom

Blossom Ltd manufactures and sells garden statues. The managers receive a profit based bonus – if their department's ROCE 5% or more above their target ROCE, then that manager receives a bonus equal to 2% of total department profit.

Required

Explain the ethical and goal congruence consequences of that may arise as a result of the bonus scheme in Blossom.

4 Non-financial performance indicators

One of the major limitations of financial performance indicators is that it ignores other factors vital to the organisation's success. **Non-financial performance indicators** may need to be calculated and monitored to explain a company's financial performance.

Two specific groupings of non-financial performance indicators are:

- **Effectiveness** – These indictors measure the extent to which the organisation is achieving its overall strategy. These indictors can include measurements of quality, market share, customer satisfaction, employee satisfaction and research and development.

- **Productivity** – These indicators measure how productive the workforce is. Examples of productivity indicators include the number of units produced per employee, the number of hours spent in production, or the average amount of customers served per hour.

Activity 5: Baker's Biscuits

Baker's Biscuits is a premium biscuit manufacturer. It aims to provide good quality biscuits to the market whist maintaining efficiency in the production process.

Required

Suggest a range of non-financial performance measures to measure effectiveness and productivity with Baker's Biscuits.

4.1 Value added

Value added is a specific measure of productivity. It is the difference between the purchase costs of external materials and services, and the selling prices of an organisation's own goods or services. It can be calculated as follows:

Formula to learn

Value added = Sales value – cost of purchased materials and bought-in services

Value added is the extra value that the business has created through the work of its employees, as the employees add value to the bought-in goods and services in order to create value in the finished goods the business eventually sells.

Total value added can be converted into a measure of productivity by calculating value added per employee.

Illustration 8: Value Added

You are given the following information about a small manufacturing business for the year ending 30 June.

Sales revenue	£835,400
Cost of materials used	£466,700
Cost of bought-in services	£265,000
Number of employees	12

Required

What is the total value added and the value added per employee in the month?

Value added	=	Sales revenue – (cost of materials and bought-in services)
	=	£835,400 – (466,700 + 265,000)
	=	£103,700
Value added per employee in the month	=	£103,700/12
	=	£8,642

4.2 Labour control ratios

In order to control the productivity of the workforce the following control ratios can also be calculated.

4.2.1 Labour activity ratio

The **labour activity ratio** is an indicator of how actual output compares to budgeted output. It is calculated as:

Formula to learn

Labour activity ratio $= \dfrac{\text{Standard hours to make output}}{\text{Hours budgeted}} \times 100\%$

The labour activity ratio is sometimes referred to as the production volume ratio. This ratio can be calculated as follows:

Formula to learn

Production volume ratio $= \dfrac{\text{Actual output}}{\text{Budgeted output}} \times 100\%$

4.2.2 Labour efficiency ratio

The labour efficiency ratio is a measure of how efficiently the workforce has operated during a period. It is calculated as:

Formula to learn

Labour efficiency ratio $= \dfrac{\text{Standard hours to make output}}{\text{Actual hours taken}} \times 100\%$

If the ratio is more than 100% this means that the workforce has worked more efficiently than expected.

4.2.3 Labour capacity ratio

The **labour capacity ratio** is a measure of the hours worked compared with budgeted hours, and is calculated as:

Formula to learn

Capacity ratio $= \dfrac{\text{Actual hours worked}}{\text{Hours budgeted}} \times 100\%$

The capacity ratio measures whether the workforce has worked more or fewer hours than that budgeted. If the outcome is more than 100% then the workforce worked more hours than budgeted, and therefore should have produced more units than budgeted.

The three ratios are related to each other as follows:

Activity/Production volume ratio	=	Efficiency ratio	×	Capacity ratio

This relationship demonstrates that the volume of output actually achieved depends on a combination of efficiency and the number of hours worked.

Illustration 9: Labour control ratios

The production figures for June for Factory C are as follows:

	Factory C
Budgeted production in units	4,800
Actual production in units	4,500
Labour hours worked	10,000
Standard hours for each unit	2

Efficiency ratio

$$\text{Efficiency ratio} = \frac{\text{Standard hours for actual production}}{\text{Actual hours worked}} \times 100\%$$

$$= \frac{4,500 \text{ units} \times 2 \text{ hours per unit}}{10,000} \times 100\%$$

$$= \frac{9,000}{10,000} \times 100\%$$

$$= 90\%$$

The workforce has worked well below standard levels, taking 10,000 hours to produce output that should have taken only 9,000 hours.

Capacity ratio

$$\text{Capacity ratio} = \frac{\text{Actual hours worked}}{\text{Budgeted hours}} \times 100\%$$

$$= \frac{10,000}{4,800 \text{ units} \times 2 \text{ hours}} \times 100\%$$

$$= \frac{10,000}{9,600} \times 100\%$$

$$= 104.17\%$$

The capacity ratio shows that more hours have been worked than were budgeted.

Activity ratio

$$\text{Activity ratio} = \frac{\text{Standard hours for actual production}}{\text{Budgeted hours}} \times 100\%$$

$$= \frac{4,500 \text{ units} \times 2 \text{ hours}}{4,800 \text{ units} \times 2 \text{ hours}} \times 100\%$$

$$= \frac{9,000}{9,600} \times 100\%$$

$$= 93.75\%$$

This shows that actual output was only 93.75% of the budgeted output.

These ratios are related as follows:

Efficiency ratio	×	Capacity ratio	=	Activity ratio
90%	×	104.17%	=	93.75%

The activity ratio shows production was only 93.75% of the budgeted level. We can now explain that this was due to the significantly lower level of efficiency than budgeted for, despite the workforce working for more hours than budgeted.

Activity 6: Barnes

Barnes Ltd budgeted to make 12,000 standard units of output during a budget period of 36,000 hours (each unit should take 3 hours each).

During the period, the company actually made 14,000 units which took 40,000 hours.

Required

Calculate the following labour ratios to the nearest whole number:

(i)   Efficiency
(ii) Capacity
(iii) Activity

(i)   [   ]

(ii)   [   ]

(iii) [   ]

5 The Balanced Scorecard

The **balanced scorecard** is a framework that can be used to determine a number of different performance indicators that are important to a business.

The balanced scorecard recognises that there are four different perspectives of a business, all of which must be monitored to ensure the business remains competitive and financially successful in the long-term.

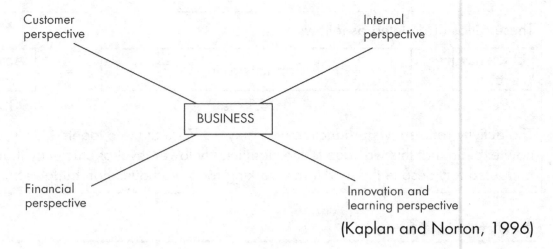

(Kaplan and Norton, 1996)

A description of each perspective, and performance indicators that could be used to monitor them, is given in the table below:

Perspective	Concerned with:	Possible performance measures:
Customer	Giving satisfaction to customers and meeting their needs by monitoring loyalty, quality, delivery, after-sales service.	• Number of repeat orders • Average delivery period • Number of complaints
Internal	Operational performance and efficient and effective management of resources.	• Value added • Number of units rejected in quality inspections
Innovation and Learning	The business's capacity to maintain its competitive position by acquiring new skills and developing new products	• Training costs per employee • Percentage of sales from new products
Financial	Achieving the financial objectives of the organisation, especially profitability and meeting the needs of shareholders.	• ROCE/RONA • Profit margins

Activity 7: The Balanced Scorecard

Suggest a range of possible indicators that an organisation could use in each area of the balanced scorecard.

- Performance indicators can be calculated to summarise productivity, profitability and resource utilisation – some of the performance indicators are financial measures and some are non-financial measures.

- The gross profit margin measures the profitability of the trading element of a business and the operating and net profit margins give a measure of profitability after deduction of expenses.

- The return on capital employed relates the operating profit to the amount of capital invested in the business to give an overall return to the providers of that capital – the return on capital employed is made up of the asset turnover multiplied by the operating profit margin.

- Return on net assets is a similar measure to ROCE and assesses the efficiency with which shareholders' funds have been used by the business to generate profits.

- Asset turnover which shows the amount of revenue earned for each £1 investment.

- The liquidity of a business is its ability to make payments to payables when these are due. Liquidity can be monitored by means of the current ratio and the quick ratio. Individual elements of working capital can be controlled by monitoring and managing inventory days, the receivables' collection period and the payables' payment period.

- The gearing level (amount of debt finance) can be measured using the gearing ratio and the interest cover ratio. Gearing considers the ability of a business to service its debt.

- Productivity can be measured as units produced per hour or units produced per employee. Productivity can also be measured by considering the value added per employee.

- A further method of measuring productivity is to use the three control ratios – efficiency, capacity and activity ratios.

- Performance indicators must also be interpreted. In order to do this comparative figures are required.

Keywords

- **Activity ratio:** an indicator of how the actual output compares to budgeted output

- **Asset turnover:** the amount of sales revenue earned for each £1 invested in the capital of the business

- **Balanced scorecard:** a framework that can be used to determine a number of different performance indicators to be used from a financial, customer, internal and innovation and learning perspective

- **Capacity ratio:** a measure comparing actual hours worked with budgeted hours

- **Control ratios:** the productivity measures of efficiency, capacity and activity

- **Current ratio:** ratio of current assets to current liabilities

- **Efficiency ratio:** a measure of how efficiently the employees have worked compared to standard efficiency

- **Gearing ratio:** a measure of the percentage of total debt (long- and short-term loan capital) in the capital structure

- **Gross profit margin:** gross profit as a percentage of sales

- **Interest cover:** the number of times that the annual interest charge is covered by the annual profit before interest

- **Inventory holding period:** number of days inventory is held (on average)

- **Inventory turnover:** the number of times inventory is turned over within a year

- **Labour activity ratio:** an indicator of how actual output compares to budgeted output

- **Labour capacity ratio:** a measure of the actual hours worked compared with budgeted hours

- **Labour efficiency ratio:** a measure of how efficiently the workforce has operated during a period

- **Liquidity:** how much cash the business has or can access within a fairly short time

- **Non-current asset turnover:** the amount of sales revenue earned for each £1 invested in non-current assets

- **Non-financial performance indicators:** performance indicators which measure the effectiveness and productivity of an organisation, but are not expressed in monetary terms

- **Operating profit margin:** operating profit as a percentage of sales

- **Payables' payment period:** the number of days before suppliers are paid (on average)

- **Performance indicators:** ways of summarising elements of performance using a formula

- **Productivity:** a measure of how efficiently employees are working

- **Quick ratio:** ratio of current assets less inventory to current liabilities

- **Receivables' collection period:** the number of days it takes customers to pay (on average)

- **Return on capital employed:** operating profit as a percentage of total capital (shareholders' capital plus debt capital)

- **Return on net assets:** net profit as a percentage of net assets (shareholders' funds)

- **Value added:** sales value less the cost of materials and bought-in services

- **Working capital:** current assets less current liabilities

- **Working capital (cash) cycle:** the speed with which a business can complete the cycle of making payments to suppliers, converting inventory into sales, and receiving cash from customers

Test your learning

1   Given below are the production figures for a factory for the last three months.

	April	May	June
Production costs	£418,300	£424,500	£430,500
Production wages	£83,700	£86,000	£86,300
Output in units	121,700	123,500	128,000
Hours worked	11,200	11,500	11,500
Budgeted output	120,000	125,000	125,000
Sales revenue	£625,000	£634,000	£656,000
Number of employees	81	83	83

Production costs are made up of the materials for production and the bought-in services required in the month. It is estimated that 11 units should be produced each hour.

Required

Calculate the following performance indicators:

(a)   Productivity per labour hour
(b)   Efficiency ratio
(c)   Capacity ratio
(d)   Activity ratio
(e)   Value added per employee

	April	May	June	Total
Productivity per labour hour				
Efficiency ratio				
Capacity ratio				
Activity ratio				
Value added per employee				

2 Given below is a summary of a business's performance for the last three months:

	Mar £000	Apr £000	May £000
Revenue	450	510	560
Cost of sales	260	320	340
Expenses	141	136	157
Total assets	396	413	467
Current liabilities	69	85	99

Required

(a) For each month of the year, complete the table to calculate the following performance indicators:

(i)   **Gross profit margin**
(ii) **Operating profit margin**
(iii) **Percentage of expenses to revenue**
(iv) **Return on capital employed**
(v)   **Asset turnover**

	Mar	Apr	May
Gross profit margin			
Net profit margin			
% expenses to revenue			
Return on capital employed			
Asset turnover			

(b) Comment on the movement in the gross profit margin and return on capital employed by referring to the following:

(i)   **Sales revenue**
(ii) **Cost of sales**
(iii) **Total assets**

3   Given below is a summary of the performance of a business for the last three years:

	20X6 £000	20X7 £000	20X8 £000
Revenue	820	850	900
Cost of sales	440	445	500
Expenses	290	305	315
Interest	–	3	3
Capital and reserves	500	560	620
Long-term loan	–	50	50
Non-current assets	385	453	498
Receivables	85	112	128
Inventory	50	55	67
Payables	30	34	41
Bank balance	10	24	18

For each of the three years complete the table to calculate the following performance measures and comment on what the measures indicate about the performance of the business over the period:

(a)   Gross profit margin
(b)   Operating profit margin
(c)   Return on capital employed
(d)   Asset turnover
(e)   Non-current asset turnover
(f)   Current ratio
(g)   Quick ratio
(h)   Receivables' collection period
(i)   Inventory days
(j)   Payables' payment period
(k)   Interest cover
(l)   Gearing ratio

	20X6	20X7	20X8
Gross profit margin			
Operating profit margin			
Return on capital employed			
Asset turnover			
Non-current asset turnover			
Current ratio			
Quick ratio			
Receivables' collection period			
Inventory days			
Payables' payment period			
Interest cover			
Gearing ratio			

4   A retail business has two small department stores in Firmwell and Hartfield. The figures for the first six months of 20X8 are given below:

	Firmwell £	Hartfield £
Financial details		
Revenue	540,000	370,000
Opening inventory	51,000	45,000
Direct costs	210,000	165,000
Closing inventory	56,000	50,000
Expenses	270,000	175,000
Net assets	550,000	410,000
Payables	25,800	27,500
Non-financial details		
Floor area	2,400 sq m	1,700 sq m
Employees	28	13
Hours worked	30,500	14,100

(a) **Complete the table to calculate the following performance indicators for each store:**

    (i) **Gross profit margin**
    (ii) **Operating profit margin**
    (iii) **Return on net assets**
    (iv) **Inventory days**
    (v) **Payables' payment period**
    (vi) **Sales per square metre of floor area**
    (vii) **Sales per employee**
    (viii) **Sales per hour worked**

	Firmwell	Hartfield
Gross profit margin		
Operating profit margin		
Return on net assets		
Inventory days		
Payables' payment period		
Sales per sq m		
Sales per employee		
Sales per hour worked		

(b) **Write a report to the sales director of the chain comparing the performances of the two stores for the six-month period.**

5   **Explain the limitations of financial performance indicators.**

6   **Calculate the following:**

(a) **A business operates on a gross profit margin of 44% and sales for the period were £106,500. What is the gross profit?**

£ [   ]

(b) **A business operates on a gross profit margin of 37.5% and the gross profit made in the period was £105,000. What was the figure for revenue for the period?**

£ [   ]

(c) **A business had revenue of £256,000 in a month, with a gross profit margin of 41% and an operating profit margin of 13.5%. What were the expenses for the month?**

£ [   ]

BPP
LEARNING MEDIA

(d) A business has a return on capital employed of 12.8% and made an operating profit for the period of £50,000. What is the capital employed?

£ [ ]

(e) A business has an operating profit percentage of 10% and a return on capital employed of 15%. What is the asset turnover of the business?

[ ] times

(f) A business has opening inventory and closing inventory of £118,000 and £104,000 respectively and made purchases during the year totalling £465,000. How many times did inventory turn over during the year?

[ ] times

(g) A business has a receivables' collection period of 64 days and the closing receivables figure is £64,000. What is the figure for revenue for the year?

£ [ ]

7   **Identify the four perspectives of the Balanced Scorecard.**

Cost management

8

Learning outcomes

5.1	Use lifecycle cost to aid decision making
	• Identify the components of the lifecycle cost of a product, machine or business unit
	• Calculate the discounted and non-discounted lifecycle cost of a product, machine or business unit
	• Interpret the results of calculations of lifecycle costs
5.2	Use target costing to aid decision making
	• Analyse and evaluate target costs
	• Identify the components of a target cost
	• Explain the concepts behind target costing, including value analysis and value engineering
5.4	Evaluate the commercial factors that underpin the life cycle of a product
	• Identify the stages of the product lifecycle
	• Explain how costs change throughout the product lifecycle
	• Explain the concepts of economies of scale, mechanisation, learning effect, and how costs can switch between variable and fixed through the stages of the product lifecycle
5.5	Take account of ethical considerations in the decision making process
	• Explain how ethical considerations can be included in the design of a product and packaging in order to promote good corporate citizenship
	• Explain how ethical considerations can be included in the value analysis/engineering of a product in order to promote good corporate citizenship
	• Explain how ethical considerations can be included in the achievement of goal congruence of an organisation

Assessment context

Cost management will form part of a task in the assessment. It will take the form of either a numeric or written question.

Business context

Modern business is radically different from that of 80 years ago. As such new techniques have emerged, many coming from Japanese companies, such as Toyota, which are more appropriate for today's environment.

Product lifecycles are becoming shorter and shorter. Organisations increasingly reassess product lifecycle costs and revenues as the time available to sell the product and recover the investment shrinks.

Target costing was developed in Japan in response to the problems of controlling and reducing costs over a product's lifecycle.

Chapter overview

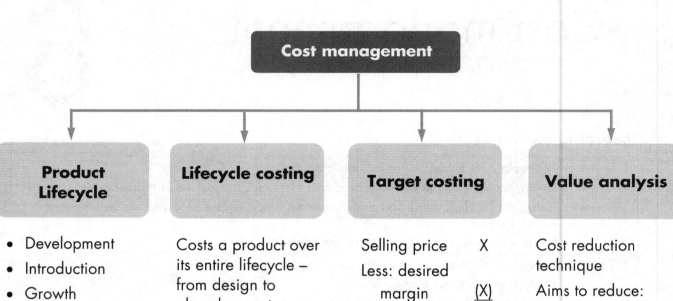

Cost management

Product Lifecycle

- Development
- Introduction
- Growth
- Maturity
- Decline

Lifecycle costing

Costs a product over its entire lifecycle – from design to abandonment

Stages of product lifecyle:

- Development
- Introduction
- Growth
- Maturity
- Decline

Net present value

The sum of discounted life cycle cash flows

Target costing

Selling price	X
Less: desired margin	(X)
Target cost	X

Value analysis

Cost reduction technique

Aims to reduce:

- Cost value

Maintain/improve:

- Exchange value
- Use value
- Esteem value

Value Engineering

Used for new products

Introduction

Managing costs effectively is important to an organisation in order to control its profitability. Managers can therefore adopt a range of techniques in order for them to manage costs effectively, in particular:

- Being aware of how costs change within the product lifecycle, and ensuring that all costs have been considered in the lifecycle of products and services

- Considering cost reductions in products using target costing, value analysis and value engineering

1 Product Lifecycle

A product lifecycle consists of different phases or stages in the commercial life of the product. At each stage sales volumes, costs and profitability are different.

1.1 Stages of the product lifecycle

The stages of the product lifecycle, as identified by Raymond Vernon in 1966, are detailed on the below graph:

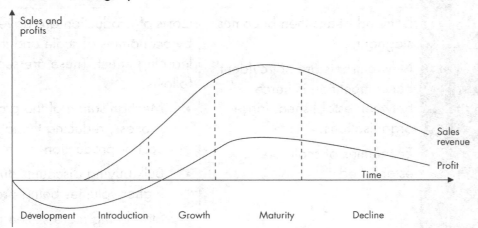

The nature of the market and costs incurred will change as the product progresses through the product lifecycle, as demonstrated in the below table.

Stage	Nature of market	Costs
Development	No external market.	High level of capital development costs, eg purchase of non-current assets.
Introduction	Little to no competition. Customers have few alternative products to switch to.	Advertising and promotion and continuing development costs. Direct costs (materials, labour and overheads) start to be incurred.
Growth	Demand for the product increases leading to a rapid increase in sales. New competitors enter the market attracted by the success and profitability of the product.	Fixed promotion cost can remain high to combat the new entrants into the market. Direct material, labour and overheads become biggest proportion of cost as production is increased to satisfy demand.
Maturity	Demand peaks then becomes stagnant. New entrants are not evident, but competition is fierce between established, large organisations. Economies of scale are established.	Costs of production are driven down by economies of scale and the learning effect. These are secured as follows: • Mechanisation of the production process, reducing the labour cost or production • Bulk buying discounts due to higher volumes being produced • Staff being more skilled in production producing greater efficiencies. This learning effect reduces labour costs • Lower fixed production overheads spread over more units Mechanisation generates more fixed production overheads.
Decline	Market saturation reached. Eventual drop in demand. The business will consider whether production of the product should continue.	Production costs reduce. Increased obsolescence cost (eg lost contribution on discounted products, wastage costs of unsold inventory).

Activity 1: Product lifecycle costs

At each stage of the product lifecycle, explain whether the costs incurred will be mostly fixed or variable.

It is important to note that the product lifecycle varies from industry to industry. For example, a chocolate cake may not ever reach the decline phase unless social tastes for chocolate change. In contrast, a tablet computer can have a very short lifecycle due to rapid changes in technology.

1.2 Lifecycle costing

Traditional costing methods analyse the cost of a product once production of the product has begun. However, the product lifecycle demonstrates that product costs are incurred throughout all stages of its lifecycle. In particular, costs are incurred in the development stage prior to production commencing, and the decline stage when the product is withdrawn from the market.

Lifecycle costing (LCC) recognises that costs are incurred prior and post production, and aims to cost a product, service, customer or project over its entire lifecycle. It therefore ensures that all costs are covered by sales revenue to ensure the product is profitable over its entire lifecycle.

Examples of costs that lifecycle costing aims to include are:

- Design costs
- Prototyping
- Programming
- Process design
- Equipment acquisition

Activity 2: Co X

Co X is in a high tech industry and is often first to market with new technological advances. It has recently spent £500,000 designing and developing a new product. The new product is expected to have an 18-month life cycle. Advertising spend immediately after the product's launch was £1.1m.

The anticipated performance of this product is as follows:

	Introduction	Growth	Maturity	Decline
Sales volume (units)	4,000	15,000	30,000	10,000
Per unit (£)				
Selling price	600	550	450	350
Variable cost	250	250	200	150
Overhead	100	100	60	75

Required

Calculate the profitability of the new product.

	Development	Introduction	Growth	Maturity	Decline	Total
Sales volume (units)		4,000	15,000	30,000	10,000	
	£000	**£000**	**£000**	**£000**	**£000**	**£000**
Revenue						
Variable cost						
Overhead						
Development cost						
Advertising cost						
Profit						

In an LCC exercise, the costs consist of present and future costs. Therefore, in order to arrive at a better picture of lifecycle costs, these may be discounted to their present value, and a net present value calculated. Net present value is covered in Chapter 10.

2 Target costing

Traditionally an organisation establishes the cost of producing a product and the profit margin they want to achieve from the product. A mark-up is then applied to the cost to generate the selling price needed to achieve the required profit margin.

Therefore, total cost + required profit = selling price.

In a target costing situation, an organisation may have an idea of the maximum amount customers are willing to pay for a product, and how much profit it wishes to achieve from the product. In these situations, the selling price is set first, followed by the profit margin that the company wishes to achieve.

A **target cost** is then calculated as follows:

Formula to learn

Target cost is calculated as:

	£
Target selling price/market price	X
Less target profit	(X)
Target cost	X

The target cost required is compared to the expected cost of the product. Any difference between the expected cost and the target cost is known as a cost gap, and managers will seek incremental improvements to both product design and production processes to ensure that the target cost is met.

2.1 Fixed costs within the target cost

Some costs may already be fixed. For example, it may not be possible to change the time taken to produce a unit or the hourly rate of pay for employees. These are costs that the company is unlikely to be able to influence in terms of making savings, and therefore they are deducted from the target cost.

Illustration 1: Lata Ltd

Lata Ltd is looking to manufacture a new product, the Boom. The market is very competitive and the company has established that to sell 10,000 units a year it should set the selling price at £24. It wishes to achieve a profit margin of 20%.

Current total production costs are estimated to be £22,000.

Required

(a) Calculate the target cost per unit to achieve a profit margin of 20%.

To calculate this, the target profit to be achieved needs to be subtracted from the target selling price of £24.00 as follows:

	£
Selling price	24.00
Profit margin (20%)	(4.80)
Target cost	19.20

(b) Indicate whether the new product should be introduced.

To answer this question, total target costs need to be compared to total estimated cost. If there is a cost gap, the product should not be introduced at this current time:

	£
Total target cost (£19.20 × 10,000 units)	19,200
Total estimated cost	22,000
Cost gap	2,800

As there is a cost gap the product should not be launched at this time. Steps need to be taken in order to reduce this cost gap before the product is launched.

We now have some further information to consider:

Market research has estimated that 12,000 units of the Boom could be sold if the selling price was reduced by £2.00 per unit. Lata will consider this reduction if the 20% profit margin can be maintained. However, it is aware it cannot reduce the cost of labour or fixed overheads.

Each Boom requires 2 hours of labour, at a rate of £6 per hour. In addition, the total fixed production costs have been estimated as £30,000.

(c) Calculate the target cost of materials required to maintain a profit margin of 20%.

To work this out, we need to calculate the total target cost per unit bearing in mind the sales price reduction. We then need to calculate the cost per unit of each of the costs, and deduct these costs from the total target cost per unit, to calculate how much can be spent per unit on materials:

	£
Reduced selling price per unit (£24.00 – £2.00)	22.00
Target profit per unit (22.00 × 0.2)	(4.40)
Target total cost per unit	17.60
Expected labour cost (2 hrs × £6)	12.00
Expected fixed cost per unit (£30,000/12,000 units)	2.50
Target material cost per unit (17.60 – 12.00 – 2.50)	3.10

Activity 3: Target costing

A business is deciding whether to introduce a new product:

- It needs to make a net profit margin of 25%.

- Market research suggests that, in total, the business will be able to sell 25,000 units of the product at £10 per unit.

- The total costs that the business expects to incur over the life of the product are shown in the table below:

Research and development £000	Variable manufacturing costs £000	Fixed manufacturing costs £000	End of life costs £000
39	125	15	5

(a) **Complete the following table to determine the target cost per unit for the new product (to the nearest penny).**

	£
Total anticipated sales revenue	
Target total net profit	
Target total costs	
Target cost per unit	

(b) **Using the information in (a), calculate the life cycle costs per unit (to the nearest penny) and provide a recommendation as to whether or not the product should be introduced.**

	£
Total life cycle costs	
Life cycle cost per unit	

The new product [   ] be launched.

Picklist:

should
should not

The market research, mentioned at the start of the task, also indicated that customers would purchase more of the product if its selling price was reduced by £1 per unit. The company would consider making this price reduction if it could sell enough units to maintain a profit margin of 25%.

(c) **Complete the table below. Assume the life cycle costs are expected to be as in (a) and (b) above. Enter your answers in the table below to the nearest penny.**

	£
Reduced selling price per unit	
Target net profit per unit	
Target total cost per unit	
Expected variable manufacturing cost per unit	
Target fixed costs per unit	

2.2 Value analysis and value engineering

Value analysis and value engineering are key techniques that an organisation can use to close a cost gap.

Value analysis is where every aspect of a product or service is analysed to determine whether it provides value to the customer and whether the same value can be provided in another way at a lower cost. It aims to reduce the cost of a product or service without any reduction in the value to the customer. This analysis is done to products currently in production.

Value engineering is value analysis but applied to new products. When designing a product each element is assessed to determine whether it adds value to the product and, if it does, that the element is included at the lowest possible cost.

2.3 Value adding and non-value adding activities

Value analysis and value engineering ensures that only value-adding activities should take place – those activities which create, or enhance, the quality of saleable products. Any other activity is deemed as non-value adding and should be reduced or eliminated. Examples include:

- Reworking of defective products
- Storage of materials
- Costs associated with staff turnover
- Movement costs (if sub-assemblies between production stages)
- Complex mix of components in products

The aim of value analysis is cost reduction. However, care must be taken to ensure short-term cost reduction does not affect long-term profitability. For example, costs could be reduced by cutting back on staff training, but this could lead to inefficiencies, low morale or high labour turnover.

Care also needs to be taken to ensure that the organisation's sustainability and corporate social responsibility is also not negatively impacted.

2.4 Sustainability and corporate social responsibility considerations

Sustainability refers to the need of organisations having enough resource to meet their current needs, without compromising the ability of the both the organisation, and other parties, to meet their future needs.

Sustainability considerations can be split into two broad categories:

- **Environmental sustainability** – This considers the organisation's use of natural resources and the impact its operations has on the natural environment. Examples of environmentally sustainable practices include replenishing natural resources and reducing emissions.

- **Economic sustainability** – This considers the impact the organisation has on both the local and national economy that it operates within. Examples of economical sustainable practices include ensuring job security, paying a fair wage to employees, providing a suitable product to customers at a reasonable price, and providing sufficient returns to shareholders.

Corporate social responsibility (CSR) is the responsibility that the organisation has to groups and individuals that are external to it. Examples of CSR practices include:

- Supporting local community activities, for example local fetes and litter picks/graffiti cleaning

- Donating profits to local and national charities

- Supporting disadvantaged groups within the local community

- Paying compensation to groups that have been negatively impacted by the organisation's actions, eg injury caused by an unsafe product

Activity 4: SF Ltd

SF Ltd are a premium food manufacturer. They are currently developing a new range of ready-made lasagnes.

Currently there is a substantial cost gap on the new lasagnes. In order to reduce this cost gap, the management have decided on the following actions:

- Use a lower grade of packaging to reduce the materials cost. The packaging selected will be non-recyclable, in contrast to the recyclable packaging they use on their other products.

- Moving production from their factory in Aton to a factory in Beaton. A lower grade of labour, and cheaper machinery, will be used as a result. The Beaton factory has been criticised for its heavy emissions from its production line.

Required

Explain the sustainability implications of the decisions the management have taken.

Chapter summary

- Most products have a limited lifecycle which involves the stages of development and launch, growth, maturity and decline. The position of the product within its lifecycle will affect sales and profitability patterns and be an important factor in cost management.

- The aim of lifecycle costing is to ensure that all the costs of a product (including development costs) are accumulated over the whole of its lifecycle, with or without discounting, in order to ensure that all costs are covered by revenue from the product.

- Target costing involves setting a target for the cost of a product or service by deducting the desired profit margin from the market selling price. The target cost represents the maximum amount of cost that the organisation can incur and still make the desired level of profit.

- Value analysis is a method of analysing the constituent elements of a product or service in order to try to reduce the cost with no loss in value to the customer. This method of analysis applied to new product design is known as value engineering.

Keywords

- **Corporate social responsibility:** the responsibility that the organisation has to groups and individuals that are external to it

- **Lifecycle costing:** costing of a product throughout all stages of its lifecycle, including costs incurred in the development stage and market withdrawal costs

- **Product lifecycle:** model to show different sales and profitability patterns at different stages of a product's life

- **Sustainability:** the need of organisations having enough resource to meet their current needs, without compromising the ability of the both the organisation, and other parties, to meet their future needs

- **Target cost:** the desired cost of a product which the designers must achieve, based on deducting the desirable profit margin from the target selling price

- **Value analysis:** analysis of every aspect of existing products/services in order to reduce the cost with no reduction in value to the customer

- **Value engineering:** value analysis in the design stage of a product or planning stage of a service

Test your learning

1 **Identify types of cost that could be incurred in each stage of the product life cycle.**

2 A business is considering investment in new machinery at a cost of £340,000 on 1 April 20X4. This machinery will be used to produce a new product which will give rise to the following net cash inflows:

31 March 20X5	£80,000
31 March 20X6	£70,000
31 March 20X7	£90,000
31 March 20X8	£120,000
31 March 20X9	£60,000

The cost of capital is 7%.

Complete the table below to calculate the net present value of this project.

Year	Cash flows £	Discount factor at 7%	Present value £
0		1.000	
1		0.935	
2		0.873	
3		0.816	
4		0.763	
5		0.713	
Net present value			

3 A business is considering investment in new plant and machinery on 1 January 20X6 at a cost of £90,000. The company has a cost of capital of 11%. The cash cost savings are estimated to be:

	£
31 December 20X6	23,000
31 December 20X7	31,000
31 December 20X8	40,000
31 December 20X9	18,000

(a) Complete the table below to calculate the net present value of the plant and machinery.

Year	Cash flows £	Discount factor at 11%	Present value £
0		1.000	
1		0.901	
2		0.812	
3		0.731	
4		0.659	
Net present value			

(b) Complete the following sentence:

The organisation [＿＿＿＿＿] invest in the plant and machinery.

Picklist:

should

should not

4   Fox Ltd are about to start developing a new product. It is anticipated that it will have a 5 year lifecycle.

Development costs are expected to be £400,000. It is anticipated that the product will have a 5 year lifecycle, at the end of which the machinery used to develop the product will be decommissioned at a cost of £60,000.

The expected cash flows from the product are expected to be as follows:

	Introduction	Growth	Maturity	Decline
Sales volume (units)	5,000	13,000	25,000	10,000
Selling price per unit	250	250	200	150
Variable cost per unit	150	130	70	85
Fixed Overhead (£000)	800	650	450	460

Calculate the profitability of the new product.

	Development	Introduction	Growth	Maturity	Decline	Total
Sales volume (units)		5,000	13,000	25,000	10,000	
	£000	**£000**	**£000**	**£000**	**£000**	**£000**
Revenue						
Variable cost						
Fixed Overhead						
Development cost						
Scrap cost						
Profit						

5 Jess Co are developing a product, the Catflap. Jess wants to achieve a profit margin of 20%, and needs to set the selling price at £90 per unit.

Calculate the target cost per unit.

The target cost per unit is £ [   ] .

6 **Explain the terms value analysis and value engineering.**

Activity based costing (ABC)

9

Learning outcomes

5.3	**Calculate and interpret activity based costing (ABC) information**
	• Calculate product costs using ABC
	• Recognise that ABC is a refinement on absorption costing, where production costs are analysed into cost pools affected by cost drivers other than simple production volumes
	• Explain why products with short production runs may have a higher production overhead absorbed into each unit

Assessment context

Calculation of various absorption rates using activity based costing (ABC) may be required in one question in the assessment.

Business context

The concepts of ABC were developed in the manufacturing sector of the US during the 1970s and 1980s. Absorption costing has become outdated for many businesses due to the diversity of product ranges and high level of overheads. As such ABC is becoming a much more appropriate tool for businesses to use when costing their products.

An example of an organisation that has used ABC successfully is the Chinese electricity firm Xu Ji. ABC was adopted by them in 2001, and analysis of their direct and variable costs into their respective activities helped them to standardise their processes. This enabled them to set more competitive prices to their customers.

Chapter overview

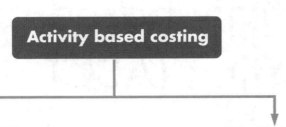

Calculation of cost/unit

- Overheads are grouped into activities **(cost pools)**
- Identify the item which causes cost to be incurred **(cost driver)**
- Calculate a cost per unit for **each** cost driver

$$\frac{\text{Cost pool}}{\text{Cost driver}} = \text{OAR}$$

- Absorb costs into production based on actual usage if cost drivers

Suitability of ABC

Better analysis of costs leads to better:

- Cost control
- Pricing decisions
- Profitability analysis

Criticisms:

- Time consuming
- Costly
- Some arbitrary apportionment may still exist
- Limited benefit if products have similar cost structures

Introduction

Traditional absorption costing uses a single basis for absorbing production overheads into cost units, usually using machine or labour hours, ignoring other reasons why overheads are incurred. Therefore, production overheads are absorbed using one overhead absorption rate (OAR):

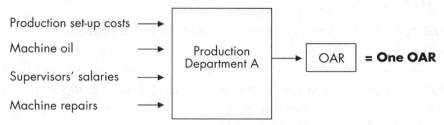

In modern manufacturing organisations, fixed overheads tend to form a large part of product costs over variable costs. Direct labour in particular is nowadays a much less significant part of production. **Activity based costing** (ABC) recognises this, and attempts to charge production costs in a more realistic way.

ABC identifies activities outside of production, and then charges overheads to cost units on the usage of these activities. The activities will vary from business to business, but some examples include:

- Material receipts into stores
- Material requisitions from stores to production
- Repairs and maintenance of production machinery
- Setting up machines for a production run
- Quality control checks

ABC matches overhead costs to individual activities. An OAR is calculated per activity, and these OARs are used to absorb production overheads into production units. As a result, ABC calculates multiple OARs depending on the amount of activities that take place in the organisation:

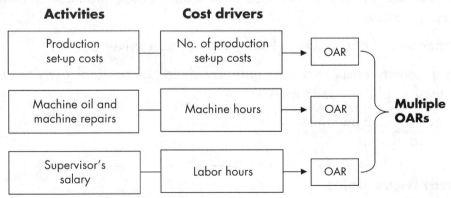

It's important to note that under ABC, a product that is made in small batches will incur more production overhead than a product made in larger batches. This is because it uses up more of certain activities, such as materials requisitions and production set-ups. If a single OAR was used, this additional activity usage would not be reflected, and the OAR is inaccurate as a result.

ABC is therefore beneficial when there are a number of different products being made by the organisation, with considerable differences in the use of activities between the products.

1 Calculation of costs per unit under ABC

1.1 ABC terminology

There is some specific terminology that you need to be comfortable with when using ABC:

Key terms

> **Cost pool** is a breakdown of total overheads into different categories depending on the activity that has generated the cost.
>
> **Cost driver** is a factor that drives a change in the usage of an activity.

An important step in ABC is to match the cost pool (ie the category of cost) to the cost driver (ie the factor that has caused the activity related to the cost pool to change).

1.2 Steps to take to calculate cost per unit under ABC

(1) Group total overheads into cost pools according to the nature of the activity that has caused the cost pool to be incurred.

(2) Identify what causes each cost pool to change, and match the cause to the cost driver ie identify a cost driver per cost pool.

(3) Calculate an OAR per unit of cost driver for each individual cost pool as follows:

$$\frac{\text{Total cost pool}}{\text{Total no of cost drivers}}$$

(4) Calculate total activity costs for each cost unit, based on the total usage of cost drivers, as follows:

OAR per unit of cost driver × Total usage of cost driver per unit

(5) Absorb activity costs into cost units by dividing the total activity cost by the total number of units as follows:

$$\frac{\text{Total activity cost per unit}}{\text{No of units}}$$

Assessment focus point

Step (2) requires you to match a cost pool to a cost driver. You will need to make a logical guess in the assessment as to the best cost driver to use for each cost pool, although the vast majority of the time it should be obvious.

Illustration 1: Copper Ltd

Copper Ltd produces two products, the C and P. The direct costs of the two products are given below:

	C	P
Direct materials	£3.50	£4.80
Direct labour	£2.00	£1.20

The budgeted production is for 120,000 units of C and 50,000 units of P.

The two main overhead activities identified for the production process are materials handling and production set-ups.

The budgeted overheads for Copper Ltd are £800,000 and they are made up as follows:

	£
Materials handling cost pool	300,000
Production set-up cost pool	500,000
	800,000

The use of these activities for each product is:

	C	P	Total
Number of materials requisitions	200	800	1,000
Number of production set-ups	100	400	500

Required

Calculate the total costs incurred and the unit cost of each product using ABC.

To calculate the cost per unit, we need to follow the ABC steps.

Step 1: Identify cost pools

Production overheads have already been split into separate cost pools, namely materials handling and production set-up.

Step 2: Identify cost drivers

Again, the cost drivers have already been identified as the number of materials requisitions, and the number of production set-ups.

Importantly, at this stage we need to match each cost pool to the cost driver. Looking at the cost pools and the cost drivers, it is logical to assume the following:

Cost pool	Cost driver
Materials handling	Number of materials requisitions
Production set-up	Number of production set-ups

Step 3: Calculate OAR per unit of cost driver.

The formula to do this is as follows:

$$\frac{\text{Total cost pool}}{\text{Total no of cost drivers}}$$

Therefore, the OAR per cost driver is:

Materials handling $\dfrac{£300,000}{1,000}$ = £300 per material requisition

Production set-ups $\dfrac{£500,000}{500}$ = £1,000 per production set-up

Step 4: Calculate total activity costs for each cost unit.

The formula to do this is as follows:

OAR per unit of cost driver × Total usage of cost driver per unit

Therefore, the total overhead incurred by each unit is calculated as follows:

	C £	P £
Materials handling overhead		
200 × £300	60,000	
800 × £300		240,000
Production set-up overhead		
100 × £1,000	100,000	
400 × £1,000	160,000	400,000
		640,000

Step 5: Absorb activity costs into cost units.

The formula to do this is as follows:

$$\frac{\text{Total activity cost per unit}}{\text{No of units}}$$

Therefore, the overhead cost per unit of C and P can be calculated as:

$$\text{Cost per unit} = \frac{£160,000}{120,000 \text{ units}} \qquad \frac{£640,000}{50,000 \text{ units}}$$

$$£1.33 \text{ per unit} \qquad £12.80 \text{ per unit}$$

Note that the overhead cost per unit of P is substantially more than the overhead cost per unit of C. This is due to P being much more activity-intensive, making more use of both materials requisitions and production set-ups.

The cost per unit for each of C and P can now be calculated as follows:

		C £	P £
Direct materials	(3.50 + 2.00)	5.50	
Direct labour	(4.80 + 1.20)		6.00
Production overhead		1.33	12.80
Unit cost		6.83	18.80

Activity 1: Dodo

Dodo Ltd manufactures three products, A, B and C. Data for the period just ended is as follows.

	A	B	C
Output (units)	20,000	25,000	2,000
	£/unit	£/unit	£/unit
Sales price	20	20	20
Direct material cost	5	10	10
Total production overheads	£190,000		
Labour hours/unit	2	1	1
Wages paid at £5/hr			

Required

(a) Calculate the overhead absorption rate if overheads are absorbed on the basis of labour hours.

The overhead absorption rate is £ _____ per labour hour.

(b) Calculate the total cost per unit for each of the products.

	A £/unit	B £/unit	C £/unit
Direct materials			
Direct labour			
Production overheads			
Total cost			

You have now been given the following breakdown of overheads and cost driver information for Dodo:

	£
Machining	55,000
Quality control and Set-up costs	90,000
Receiving	30,000
Packing	15,000
	190,000

Cost driver data	A	B	C
Labour hours/unit	2	1	1
Machine hours/unit	2	2	2
No. of production runs	10	13	2
No. of component receipts	10	10	2
No. of customer orders	20	20	20
Output (units)	20,000	25,000	2,000

(c) Calculate the following overhead absorption rates (cost driver rates):

    (i)   Machining
    (ii) Quality control and set-up costs
    (iii) Receiving
    (iv) Packing

(i)   [ ]   per [ ]

(ii)   [ ]   per [ ]

(iii) [ ]   per [ ]

(iv) [ ]   per [ ]

(d) Calculate the total overhead cost for each of the products.

	A £	B £	C £	Total £
Machining				
Quality control and set-up costs				
Receiving				
Packing				
Total				

(e) Calculate the overhead cost per unit for each of the products.

	A £	B £	C £
Total overhead costs			
Units produced			
Overhead cost per unit			

(f) Calculate the total cost per unit for each of the products.

	A £/unit	B £/unit	C £/unit
Direct materials	5.00	10.00	10.00
Direct labour	10.00	5.00	5.00
Production overheads			
Total cost			

Chapter summary

- Activity based costing (ABC) considers the activities that cause overheads to be incurred and the factors that give rise to these activity costs (cost drivers).

- It is a method of absorbing overheads into products on the basis of the amount of each activity that the particular product is expected to use in the period.

- ABC may be more suitable than traditional absorption costing in manufacturing businesses where overhead costs are much larger than direct production costs.

Keywords

- **Activity based costing (ABC):** a more complex approach to absorption of overheads, based upon an analysis of the detailed causes of the overheads

- **Cost driver:** a factor that drives a change in the usage of an activity

- **Cost pool:** a breakdown of total overheads into different categories depending on the activity that has generated the cost

1 **Explain how activity based costing differs from traditional absorption costing.**

2 A business produces two products, the LM and the NP. The direct costs of the two products are:

	LM	NP
Direct materials	£2.60	£3.90
Direct labour	£3.50	£2.70

The total overhead cost is made up as follows:

	£
Stores costs	140,000
Production set-up costs	280,000
Quality control inspection costs	180,000
	600,000

The budgeted production is for 50,000 units of LM and 20,000 units of NP.

Each product is expected to make the following use of the service activities:

	LM	NP	Total
Materials requisitions from stores	100	220	320
Production set-ups	80	200	280
Quality control inspections	30	60	90

Complete the following table to show the budgeted cost per unit for each product using activity based costing and how much total budgeted overhead is included in the unit cost for each product.

Product	Budgeted cost per unit £	Budgeted overhead per unit £
LM		
NP		

3 **Explain the benefits of activity based costing.**

4 **Explain the disadvantages of activity based costing.**

Decision-making techniques 10

Learning outcomes

1.3	Recognise and calculate measures of profitability and contribution
	• Explain the difference between contribution and profit
	• Identify when to use contribution analysis as a decision making tool
	• Calculate the contribution per unit and per £ of turnover
	• Calculate the breakeven point and margin of safety
	• Calculate the optimal production mix when labour, materials or machine hours are restricted, and the opportunity costs of limited resources
	• Explain the outcomes of the various decision-making tools to aid the decision-making process
4.3	Make recommendations using decision-making techniques
	• Recommend the optimal production mix when resources are limited and opportunity costs of limited resources
	• Recommend a course of action based on the breakeven point and margin of safety
	• Analyse decisions about make or buy, closure of a business segment and mechanisation
	• Use relevant and non-relevant costing information to aid decision making

Assessment context

The concepts contained in this chapter could be tested as either a numeric or written task in the assessment. You won't be tested on all of these concepts in the same assessment – it depends on the variant of the assessment you are allocated as to which one you get.

Business context

The tools demonstrated in this chapter are widely used by businesses. This is to ensure that risk has been adequately assessed, and that the most profitable option is adopted by the organisation.

Chapter overview

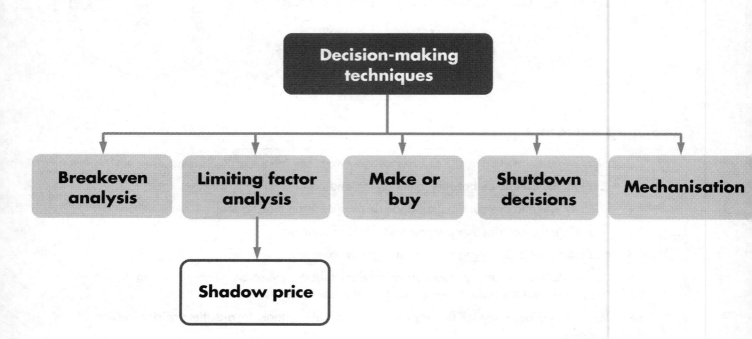

Introduction

When making short-term decisions profit should not be the basis of the decision made. Profit includes fixed overheads which are likely to still be incurred at the same rate regardless of the decision that is made. Instead **contribution** is the tool that should be used for decision making purposes.

Contribution is defined as selling price less all variable costs per unit.

When using contribution as a decision making tool the following assumptions are made:

(a)   Contribution per unit is a constant figure at each level of activity; but
(b)   Total contribution increases directly with increases in output and sales.

Fixed costs are different. As the volume of output and sales increases:

(a)   Total fixed costs are unchanged; but

(b)   The fixed costs per unit fall with increases in output and sales (because the fixed costs are spread over more units).

1 Cost-volume-profit analysis

Cost-volume-profit (CVP) analysis is the analysis of the relationship between activity levels, costs and profit. It is based on contribution analysis. A common application of CVP analysis is **breakeven analysis** to determine the breakeven point for business operations

Assessment focus point

Assessment tasks can take one of two formats:

- A numeric task requiring you to calculate each measure; or

- A written task where you are asked to compare two products, describing how each measure is calculated.

A good working knowledge of each formula is essential for you to be able to tackle both types of question.

1.1 Breakeven point

Key term

Breakeven point (BEP) is the level of activity where the sales revenue is equal to the total costs of the business.

The BEP helps managers to determine the point at which all costs are covered by sales revenue, but the company neither makes a profit or a loss:

	£
Sales	15,000
Less variable costs	(5,000)
Contribution	10,000
Fixed costs	(10,000)
Profit	0

Contribution 10,000 ⟶ = Must be **equal**
Fixed costs (10,000) ⟶

As you can see above, the BEP occurs when:

Total contribution = Fixed costs

Or

Contribution per unit × Sales units = Fixed costs

Sales units will therefore be the amount of units to sell to make neither a profit nor a loss, ie the BEP. Therefore:

Formula to learn

$$BEP = \frac{Fixed\,costs}{Cont'n/unit}$$

1.2 Breakeven revenue

An alternative to calculating the BEP in units is to calculate **breakeven revenue**.

Key term

Breakeven revenue is the amount of revenue required to cover total costs in order to make neither a profit or a loss.

The simplest way of calculating breakeven revenue is to take the breakeven point and multiply it by selling price per unit as follows:

Formula to learn

Breakeven revenue = BEP (units) × Selling price per unit

An alternative method of finding the breakeven revenue is to use the **contribution to sales (C/S) ratio** rather than the selling price per unit. The C/S ratio calculates the contribution per £ of sales revenue rather than contribution per sales unit, and is calculated as:

Formula to learn

$$C/S\ ratio = \frac{Contribution}{Sales}$$

Breakeven occurs when the total contribution generated by the C/S ratio equals the fixed costs of the business. This is calculated as:

Total sales revenue × C/S ratio = Fixed costs

This formula can then be re-arranged to find the breakeven revenue as follows:

Formula to learn

$$\text{Breakeven revenue (£)} = \frac{\text{Fixed costs}}{\text{C/S ratio}}$$

1.3 Margin of safety

Key term

Margin of safety is the amount by which sales units or revenue could fall before a loss is made.

Margin of safety (MOS) can either be calculated as an absolute figure, or as a percentage of budgeted sales.

To calculate MOS as an absolute amount of sales units, the following formula is used:

Formula to learn

MOS (absolute figure) = Budgeted sales units – breakeven sales units

To calculate the MOS as a percentage of budgeted sales, the following formula is used:

Formula to learn

$$\text{MOS (as \%)} = \frac{\text{Budgeted sales units} - \text{breakeven sales units}}{\text{Budgeted sales units}} \times 100$$

Assessment focus point

Make sure you express the margin of safety as a percentage of the budgeted sales units and not as a percentage of breakeven sales units.

1.4 Required profit level

The approach used to find the breakeven sales volumes can be extended to find the volume needed to attain a required profit level.

When an organisation wants to achieve a required profit level, the amount of contribution generated must be enough to cover both fixed costs and the required profit, thus:

Contribution per unit × sales units = Fixed costs + Required profit

Re-arranging this formula, we can calculate the sales units required to achieve a required profit, thus:

Formula to learn

$$\text{Sales volume to reach required profit level} = \frac{\text{Fixed costs} + \text{required profit}}{\text{Contribution per unit}}$$

Alternatively the C/S ratio can be used to find the sales revenue required to achieve a certain level of profit. To achieve required profit, we know that:

Required contribution = Fixed costs + Required profit

Therefore, the sales revenue can be isolated out from the required contribution as follows:

$$\text{Sales revenue required} = \frac{\text{Target contribution}}{\text{C/S ratio}}$$

Illustration 1: Reardon Enterprises 1

Reardon Enterprises manufactures a product called the PepperPot with a selling price of £10 per unit. The variable costs of producing the product are £6 per unit and the total annual fixed costs of the business are £200,000.

Budgeted sales for the PepperPot were 70,000 units.

Required

Calculate:

(a) The BEP in units
(b) The breakeven revenue
(c) The MOS in units
(d) The MOS %
(e) The sales units required for a target profit of £100,000

(a) To calculate the BEP in units, the following calculation needs to be made:

$$\text{BEP} = \frac{£200,000}{£10 - £6}$$

$$= 50,000 \text{ units}$$

(b) The breakeven revenue can then be calculated as follows:

50,000 units × £10 = £500,000

Alternatively the C/S ratio could be used to calculate the breakeven revenue:

$$\text{C/S ratio} = \frac{£10 - £6}{£10} = 0.4$$

This means that for every £1 of sales revenue generated, 40% translates into contribution.

This C/S ratio can then be used to calculate the breakeven revenue as follows:

$$\text{BEP (£)} = \frac{200,000}{0.40}$$

$$= £500,000$$

(c) We have calculated the breakeven sales units to be 50,000 units. The MOS in units can therefore be calculated as:

MOS = 70,000 units – 50,000 units

= 20,000 units

(d) Remember that the MOS is expressed as a percentage of budgeted sales. The MOS % is therefore calculated as:

$$\text{MOS} = \frac{20,000}{70,000} \times 100$$

$$= 28.6\%$$

This tells management that sales can drop below the budgeted figure by 28.6% before losses are made.

(e) Reardon will need enough sales units to generate contribution to not only cover the fixed costs of £200,000, but additional required profit of £100,000. These sales units can be calculated as:

$$\text{Activity level} = \frac{£200,000 + £100,000}{£10 - £6}$$

$$= 75,000 \text{ units}$$

Therefore, if the business sells 75,000 units, a profit of £100,000 will be made.

Activity 1: Widget A

Cooler Ltd produce one product called the Widget. Financial data for the Widget is as follows:

Per unit:	£
Materials	12
Labour	30
Variable production overhead	13
Variable distribution cost	5
Total variable cost	60
Selling price	100

	£
Factory cost	100,000
Administration costs	50,000
Total fixed costs	150,000

Sales units are budgeted at 5,000 units, and Cooler wish to make a profit of £30,000 for the Widget.

Required

Calculate:

(a) The BEP in units
(b) The breakeven revenue
(c) The MOS in units
(d) The MOS as a percentage of budgeted sales
(e) The sales volume required to make a target profit of £30,000

(a) The BEP is [   ] units.

(b) The breakeven revenue is £ [   ].

(c) The MOS in units is [   ] units.

(d) The MOS as a percentage of budgeted sales is [   ] %.

(e) The sales volume required to make a target profit of £30,000 is [   ] units.

1.5 Use of CVP analysis in risk analysis

CVP analysis can give useful information to managers to assess the risk associated with certain activities, or selling of particular products.

We have seen that the higher the BEP of a product, the lower the activity level can fall before a loss is made. If this high BEP is compared to budgeted sales, this would give a low MOS.

If the MOS is low, sales can't fall very far before a loss is made. This low MOS increases the risk associated with selling the product.

It is important to note that a low BEP does not necessarily increase the risk associated with the product. Instead, it is the amount that sales volumes need to drop by before a loss is made that increases the risk. This is why MOS is the more useful calculation when assessing risk.

1.6 Cost changes and impact on risk

When the costs of a business change this will impact the breakeven analysis. In general terms, an increase in costs will cause the BEP to rise whereas an increase in selling price will lower the BEP. However, we also need to be aware of the mix of variable and fixed costs within the activity of the business.

As fixed costs are unaffected by changing activity levels, they will be incurred at the same rate regardless of sales volumes generated. Variable costs on the other hand are only incurred when units are produced. Therefore, the greater the proportion of fixed costs in an activity, the greater the risk that they won't be covered if sales volumes drop. This increases the overall risk associated with that activity.

An organisation that has high fixed costs as a proportion of its total costs is known to have high **operational gearing**.

Illustration 2: Reardon Enterprises 2

Reardon Enterprises also sell another product called the SaltShaker. CVP analysis has been undertaken for the SaltShaker, and Reardon Enterprises would like to compare this with the PepperPot.

The analysis for each product is given below:

	PepperPot	SaltShaker
Contribution per unit (£)	4	6
Fixed costs (£)	200,000	210,000
Breakeven point (units)	50,000	35,000
Margin of safety (%)	28.6%	18%

Required

Comment on the risk associated with the PepperPot and the SaltShaker.

Looking at the BEP, it would appear that PepperPot is a more risky product than SaltShaker. This is because PepperPot would need to sell in greater volumes to start making a profit, and there is a risk that these high sales volumes may not be achieved.

However, the BEP does not take into account the budgeted sales volumes. If sales volumes of PepperPot are budgeted to be much higher than those of SaltShaker, the risk perspective changes. This is where the MOS becomes the more useful risk indicator.

According to the MOS, PepperPot's sales volumes could fall by 28.6% before a loss is made, compared to an 18% reduction in sales volumes for SaltShaker. This makes PepperPot a lower risk product as it is less sensitive to a reduction in sales volumes than SaltShaker.

Looking at the cost base of both products, we can establish the reason for this.

Whilst SaltShaker generates more contribution per unit than PepperPot, each unit sold needs to cover a greater amount of fixed costs. This has reduced SaltShaker's BEP and MOS. SaltShaker is, therefore, more operationally geared – the level of fixed costs will need to be covered regardless of the sales volumes achieved, thus increasing the risk associated with SaltShaker.

Assessment focus point

MOS is the more useful indicator to assess risk. Whilst an assessment task may require you to also discuss the BEP, always use MOS to conclude which product has greater risk attached.

Activity 2: Widget 2

It is now expected that the fixed costs will rise by 10%, variable costs by 5% and the selling price by 6%.

Required

(a) Using the information from Activity 1: Widget A, calculate the revised BEP.

The revised BEP is ⬚ units.

(b) Explain how this impacts on the risk associated with selling the Widget.

The following activity is an example of an assessment standard written task.

Activity 3: Chuck

Chuck Limited has two departments, Lob and Throw. Each department manufactures separate products.

It has supplied the following information for last month:

	Lob	Throw
Sales volume (units)	35,000	30,000
Selling price (£ per unit)	6	6
Variable production costs (£ per unit)	3.50	1.00
Fixed overheads (£)	43,750	120,000
Contribution per unit (£)	2.50	5.00
BEP (units)	17,500	24,000
MOS (%)	50	20

Required

Draft a report in which you provide analysis of these figures under the given section headings:

Implications of the differences in BEP between the two departments.

Which department has the better MOS and why?

Comment on the results from a risk perspective and suggest any potential ways of reducing it.

2 Limiting factor analysis

Normally, a business would want to maximise sales volumes in order to maximise profits. However, the amount of units that can be sold is limited by the amount of sales units that customers demand. Sales demand therefore limits the amount of sales volumes generated.

However, in practice, other production factors could limit the amount of units that can be produced and ultimately sold. These factors could be:

- Limited materials available to purchase
- Limited labour or machine hours available

If one of these factors is limiting activity, the plans of the business must be built around this factor rather than around sales demand. The challenge for management is how to maximise profit when one of these other factors is limited.

As fixed costs will need to be incurred regardless of the amount of units produced, profit is maximised by looking at the contribution each product earns per unit of the scarce production resource – in other words we maximise the contribution per unit of limiting factor.

2.1 Optimal production plan

If a business makes more than one product, we need to find the combination of products that makes the most profitable use of the scarce resource. This is known as the optimal production plan.

The approach establishing the optimal production plan is to determine the contribution per unit of limiting factor and concentrate on making the product with the highest contribution per unit of limiting factor.

The following steps are used to calculate the optimal production plan:

(1) Identify the limiting factor.

(2) Calculate contribution per unit.

(3) Calculate contribution per unit of limiting factor by making the following calculation:

Contribution per unit
Limiting factor per unit

(4) Rank products by contribution per unit of limiting factor.

(5) Prepare the optimal production plan.

Illustration 3: Farnham Engineering 1

Farnham Engineering makes three products, A, B and C. The costs and selling prices of the three products are:

	A	B	C
	£	£	£
Direct materials @ £4 per kg	8	16	12
Direct labour @ £7 per hour	7	21	14
Variable overheads	3	9	6
Marginal cost	18	46	32
Selling price	22	54	39

BPP
LEARNING MEDIA

Sales demand for the coming period is expected to be as follows:

Product A	3,000 units
Product B	7,000 units
Product C	5,000 units

The supply of materials is limited to 50,000 kg during the period and the labour hours available are 28,000.

Required

Calculate the optimal production plan for Farnham Engineering.

This can be done be following the above steps:

Step 1: Identify the limiting factor.

The following calculations can be done to identify the limiting factor:

	A	B	C	Total required
Materials				
(2/4/3 kg)	6,000 kg	28,000 kg	15,000 kg	49,000 kg
Labour				
(1/3/2 hrs)	3,000 hours	21,000 hours	10,000 hours	34,000 hours

From the above table we can see that labour hours are the limiting factor (28,000 labour hours are available whereas 34,000 hours are required to meet total sales demand).

Step 2: Calculate contribution per unit.

Using the above table, the contribution per unit of each of products A, B & C is as follows (remember that contribution per unit = selling price – marginal cost):

A: £22 – £18 = £4 per unit

B: £54 – £46 = £8 per unit

C: £39 – £32 = £7 per unit

Step 3: Calculate contribution per unit of limiting factor.

As labour hours is the limiting factor, the contribution earned per labour hour needs to be calculated. This will ensure that we are maximising contribution for every labour hour that is worked.

The calculations needed are as follows:

	A	B	C
Contribution	£4	£8	£7
Labour hours per unit	1 hour	3 hours	2 hours
Contribution per labour hour:			
£4/1	£4.00		
£8/3		£2.67	
£7/2			£3.50

Step 4: Rank products by contribution per unit of limiting factor.

Once the above calculation has been complete, the products are ranked in order of contribution per labour hour. This ensures that production priority is given to the most profitable product.

Product A makes the most contribution per unit of limiting factor (labour hours) and therefore, in order to maximise contribution, we must concentrate first on production of A up to its maximum sales demand. Then we can concentrate on producing C, and finally, if there are any remaining hours available, on B.

Step 5: Calculate the optimal production plan.

The optimal production plan can now be calculated as per the below table:

	Units produced	Labour hours required
A	3,000	3,000
C	5,000	10,000
		13,000
B (balance)	5,000 (15,000 hrs/3 hrs per unit)	15,000 (balancing figure)
		28,000

Activity 4: LF

LF is trying to work out its optimal production plan.

Machine time available is 300 hours.

Labour time available is 200 hours.

	A £/unit	B £/unit	C £/unit
Selling price	150	120	100
Variable costs	100	80	70
Fixed costs	20	20	20
Profit	30	20	10
Machine time	5 hrs	2 hrs	1 hr
Labour time	2 hrs	1 hr	0.5 hrs
Demand	50	50	50

Required

(a) Identify the limiting factor.

The limiting factor is [   ] .

Picklist:

labour hours
machine hours

(b) Calculate the contribution per unit of limiting factor for each product.

The contribution per limiting factor for:

A is [   ]

B is [   ]

C is [   ]

(c) Calculate the optimal production plan.

The optimum number of units to be produced of:

A is [   ] units

B is [   ] units

C is [   ] units

2.2 Opportunity cost and shadow price

We have seen above that when a resource is limited, an organisation will not be able to meet maximum production requirements, and therefore will not be able to meet maximum sales demand. This gives rise to an **opportunity cost** to the organisation.

Opportunity cost is the benefit which would have been earned, but which has been given up, by choosing one option instead of another.

Key term

Since the organisation needs to limit production of one of its products due to limited resources, it won't benefit from the contribution generated if those units were produced and subsequently sold. Therefore the opportunity cost in this situation would be the contribution lost as a result of lost sales of those units.

To overcome this opportunity cost, the business may choose to obtain additional units of the limited resource. However, the business needs to ensure that obtaining these resources is cost beneficial. Care needs to therefore be taken as to the **shadow price** of the limited resource.

Shadow price is the additional amount that an organisation is willing to pay to obtain an additional unit of limiting factor.

Key term

The contribution per unit of limiting factor will help the organisation decide how much extra should be paid for additional units of a scarce resource. Ideally the organisation would not want to pay more than the contribution generated by each unit of limiting factor as it would find itself in a loss making situation.

The resources obtained will be used to produce any units that remain outstanding. Therefore, the shadow price is calculated as the contribution per unit of limiting factor of the product whose production has not been maximised.

The shadow price can then be used alongside the standard cost of the limited resource to calculate the maximum amount that a business should pay to acquire additional units of the scarce resource.

Illustration 4: Farnham Engineering 2

Farnham Engineering is now considering obtaining additional production resource, and is considering how much extra they would need to pay.

Required

Calculate the maximum price Farnham Engineering should pay for 6,000 additional hours of labour.

The optimal production plan is:

	Units produced	Labour hours required
A	3,000	3,000
C	5,000	10,000
		13,000
B (balance)	5,000 (15,000 hrs/3 hrs per unit)	15,000 (balancing figure)
		28,000

We are not maximising production of product B, as sales demand is 7,000 units. This means that Farnham has generated an opportunity cost of £8 per unit, or £16,000 in total (£8 per unit × 2,000 units).

To overcome this opportunity cost, the additional 6,000 labour hours will be used to make an additional 2,000 units of B.

The contribution per labour hour of B was calculated as:

£8 contribution per unit/3 hours per unit = £2.67

This £2.67 represents the additional amount that Farnham should pay to obtain an additional labour hour, ie the shadow price for one hour of labour.

The standard cost per labour hour is £7, so the maximum amount to be paid per hour for an additional hour of labour is:

	£
Standard labour cost per hour	7.00
Contribution per labour hour (shadow price)	2.67
Maximum cost per hour	9.67

The total maximum amount to be paid for an additional 6,000 hours is now calculated as:

£9.67 per hour × 6,000 hours = £58,020

Paying more than £2.67 per hour would not be cost beneficial to Farnham, as the additional cost would offset the contribution generated by each additional unit of B, as demonstrated below:

	£
Contribution per unit	8.00
Additional cost of labour (£2.67 × 3 hrs)	8.00
Revised contribution per unit	5.33

Activity 5: LF Shadow Price

LF is deciding how much extra it should pay for additional resources.

Required

Using the information from Activity 4, calculate the maximum additional price that LF should pay for each of the following:

(a) 100 hours of additional labour: £ [_____] .

(b) 100 hours of additional machine time: £ [_____] .

3 Make or buy decisions

A company may want to consider whether it is best to manufacture a unit itself or whether it would be better to outsource the production to a sub-contractor. Some examples include:

(a) Whether a company should manufacture its own components or buy the components from an outside supplier

(b) Whether a construction company should do some work with its own employees or whether it should sub-contract the work to another company

(c) Whether a service should be carried out by an internal department or whether an external organisation should be employed

3.1 Relevant costs in make or buy decisions

To numerically analyse the make or buy decision, the **relevant costs** need to be considered. These are costs that will be incurred or saved purely as a result of making the decision.

In make or buy decisions, the following costs would be deemed relevant:

(a) All variable costs

(b) Fixed costs that would be avoided if the product was not being made, meaning that the fixed cost is directly attributable to the product. For example, by choosing to buy a component, the rental cost of a machine used to make that component would be saved. This wouldn't be the case for factory rent – as other components will still need to be made, the factory would still need to be kept on.

Any cost that would need to be incurred regardless of the decision being made (ie a committed cost), or any cost that has been made historically before the decision is taken (ie a sunk cost), is not relevant and is not included in the financial analysis of the make or buy decision.

Illustration 5: Shellfish Co

Shellfish Co makes three components W, X and Y. Costs of these components in the forthcoming year are as follows:

	W	X	Y
Production (units)	1,000	2,000	4,000
Unit marginal costs	£	£	£
Direct materials	4	5	2
Direct labour	8	9	4
Variable production overheads	2	3	1
	14	17	7

The fixed costs for the period are:

	£
W directly attributable fixed costs	1,000
X directly attributable fixed costs	5,000
Y directly attributable fixed costs	6,000
Other fixed costs (committed)	30,000
	42,000

A sub-contractor has offered to supply units of W, X and Y for £12, £21 and £10 respectively.

Required

Should Shellfish make or buy the components?

Firstly, we need to establish the relevant costs of this decision. The relevant costs are all the variable costs, plus the directly attributable fixed costs for all the products. We can ignore the committed fixed costs as these will need to be incurred regardless of whether the components are made in-house, or bought from the sub-contractor.

The total cost of making the components is:

	W £	X £	Y £
Total variable cost			
£14 × 1,000 units	14,000		
£17 × 2,000 units		34,000	
£7 × 4,000 units			28,000
Directly attributable fixed costs	1,000	5,000	6,000
Total cost of manufacture	15,000	39,000	34,000

Now, compare the total cost of manufacture to the total cost of buying in each product from the sub-contractor:

	W £	X £	Y £
Total sub-contractor cost			
£12 × 1,000 units	12,000		
£21 × 2,000 units		42,000	
£10 × 4,000 units			40,000
Total cost of manufacture	(15,000)	(39,000)	34,000
Additional cost of buying in	(3,000)	3,000	6,000

Shellfish would save £3,000 each year by sub-contracting component W, but would be incurring additional costs by sub-contracting components X and Y. Therefore, Shellfish should buy-in component W but keep producing components X and Y in-house.

Activity 6: Dolphin

Dolphin makes three components. Details for the following year are as follows:

	A	J	H
Production (units)	5,000	4,000	3,000
	£	£	£
Direct material/unit	15	6	18
Direct labour/unit	15	20	22
Variable production overheads/unit	5	4	4
Directly attributable fixed costs	2,000	3,000	6,000
Other general fixed costs are £20,000			
A subcontractor has quoted a price per unit of	30	39	50

Required

Indicate whether the components should be made or bought in.

Dolphin should buy in [▼] .

Picklist:

all of the components
none of the components
some of the components

3.2 Non-financial considerations in make or buy decisions

Assessment focus point

In the assessment you may have to explain other factors that need to be considered before making an outsourcing decision. Some ideas are given in the below table.

BPP
LEARNING MEDIA

Advantages of outsourcing	Disadvantages of outsourcing
Cost savings due to the flexibility provided by the outsource partner	Control of the operations is lost
Expertise that the organisation may have difficulty accessing themselves	Quality of the product could be impacted as the organisation is reliant on the processes of the outsourced partner
Capital can be released from the department or product to maximise opportunities	The outsourced partner will have other customers to service, so reliability could drop
Resources can be diverted to more value adding activities	Confidential information will need to be provided to the outsource partner, and there is potential that this could be misappropriated
	Skills are lost in-house, making it difficult to bring operations back in-house if required
	Employees are likely to be made redundant, negatively impacting morale and motivation

4 Shutdown decisions

Shutdown decisions will include the following:

(a) Whether or not to close down a product line, department or other activity, either because it is making losses or because it is too expensive to run

(b) If the decision is to shut down, whether the closure should be permanent or temporary

4.1 Relevant costs in shutdown decisions

The same relevant costing principles need to be applied as per make or buy decisions when numerically evaluating a shutdown position.

Illustration 6: Shutdown decisions

A company manufactures three products – Pawns, Rooks and Bishops. The net profit from these is shown below:

	Pawns £	Rooks £	Bishops £	Total £
Sales	50,000	40,000	60,000	150,000
Variable costs	30,000	25,000	35,000	90,000
Contribution	20,000	15,000	25,000	60,000
Fixed costs	17,000	18,000	20,000	55,000
Profit/loss	3,000	(3,000)	5,000	5,000

The company is concerned about the performance of Rooks and is deciding whether it should cease production of them in order to produce a new product, Crowners.

The fixed costs associated with the production of Rooks are £5,000.

The forecasted profit generated by Crowners is shown below:

	Crowners £
Sales	45,000
Variable costs	33,000
Contribution	12,000
Fixed costs	8,000
Profit/loss	4,000

Directly attributable fixed costs of Crowners are £6,000.

Required

Identify whether the company should cease the production of Rooks and start selling Crowners.

If Rooks were to stop being produced, the company would lose the benefit of the contribution generated by Rooks, but would save on the fixed costs:

	£
Loss of contribution	(15,000)
Savings in fixed costs	5,000
Incremental loss	(10,000)

If production stopped on Rooks, the company would see a fall of £10,000 in their profits.

The profit generated by Crowners would be as follows:

	£
Contribution	12,000
Directly attributable fixed costs	(6,000)
Incremental profit	6,000

If production was switched to Crowners, the company would only make £6,000 profit, so the company would suffer an overall drop in profits of £4,000. They should, therefore, keep making Rooks in preference to Crowners.

Activity 7: Duo

Duo Ltd owns two factories, A and B. The forecasts for both factories for the year ending 31 December 20X5 are below:

	A £000		B £000	
Revenue	2,200		2,850	
Direct materials	660		784	
Direct labour	440		448	
Fixed production overheads	220		420	
Cost of sales	1,320		1,652	
Gross profit	880	40%	1,198	42%
Sales and distribution costs	520		640	
Administration costs	210		250	
Profit from operations	150	6.8%	308	10.8%

Other information:

Inventories are of raw materials and will remain unchanged throughout the year.

Sales and distribution costs are variable with turnover from each factory.

Administration costs are fixed.

The Managing Director has proposed closing factory A. The impact to Factory B's results will be as follows:

- Revenue would increase by 40%

- Materials, labour and sales and distribution costs are all variable with sales revenue

- Fixed production overheads will increase by £100,000

- Administration costs will increase by £60,000

- It is forecast that purchasing costs will decrease by 5% as a result of the closure

Required

(a) Prepare a revised statement of profit or loss for factory B, assuming factory A is closed.

	Factory B £	
Revenue		
Materials		
Direct labour		
Fixed production overheads		
Cost of sales		
Gross profit		%
Sales and distribution costs		
Administration costs		
Profit from operations		%

(b) Indicate whether factory A should be closed.

Factory A [   ] be closed.

Picklist:

should
should not

4.2 Non-financial considerations of shutdown decisions

Shutdown decisions should not be judged purely on financial analysis. Some other factors to consider are:

- **Staff morale** – Staff will either need to be redeployed or made redundant, which negatively impacts morale and motivation.

- **Customers** – Market share could be lost if customers choose to source the discontinued product from a competitor.

- **Suppliers** – Some suppliers may be reliant on the organisation to stay in business. If the organisation chooses to stop making the product this could have severe consequences on these suppliers.

5 Mechanisation decisions

Management may face a decision about changing the technology that is used in production. For example, as technology plays a greater part in manufacturing, a business may be considering changing from a labour-intensive production process to a machine-intensive one.

5.1 Relevant costs in mechanisation decisions

Relevant costs can also be used to assess the impact on profit of a mechanisation decision. These costs include:

- Labour cost savings

- The capital cost of acquiring the machine

- Increased fixed overheads due to increased machine maintenance, depreciation and power. Many of these overheads are likely to be fixed.

- Increased revenue due to increased sales volumes

5.2 Mechanisation and impact on risk

As the majority of fixed overheads incurred is likely to increase as a result of mechanisation, the risk within the business is likely to increase. This is because the cost base will be the same regardless of the sales volumes achieved, so the business has a higher level of operational gearing. The profits of the business will therefore become more sensitive to changes in sales volumes.

Illustration 7: Mechanisation decision

A business is considering the rental of machines which would cost £47,500 per year to rent. The machine will allow the business to reduce the labour required to manufacture its product by 1.5 hours per unit. Currently the business makes and sells 4,000 units per annum at £125 each and total annual fixed costs are £180,000.

The product's standard cost card shows the following variable costs:

		£
Direct material	3 kg @ £5	15
Direct labour	6 hrs @ £10	60
		75

Required

Calculate the current profit and the profit that would be generated if the machine is purchased. Indicate whether the machine should be rented.

The current profit generated by the business is:

	£
Sales revenue (£125 × 4,000 units)	500,000
Total variable cost (£75 × 4,000 units)	(300,000)
Fixed costs	(180,000)
Profit	20,000

If the new machine is purchased there will be savings in labour cost, but additional fixed cost will be incurred.

The labour hours will change to 4.5 hrs (6hrs – 1.5hrs). The labour cost will now change to:

4.5hrs × £10 × 4,000 units = £180,000

This represents a cost saving of £60,000.

The fixed overheads will increase to £227,500 (£180,000 + £47,500).

The total profit generated with the new machine will be as follows:

	£
Sales revenue (£125 × 4,000 units)	500,000
Total variable cost (£300,000 – £60,000)	(240,000)
Fixed costs	(227,500)
Profit	32,500

As there will be an overall increase in profit, the machine should be rented.

However, the business becomes more risky as there are now higher fixed costs in the business. If sales volumes of 4,000 units are not achieved, the fixed costs of £227,500 still need to be covered. The achievement of £32,500 profit now becomes more dependent on achieving sales volumes of 4,000 units.

Activity 8: Hill Ltd

Hill Ltd is considering replacing one of its current machines with a new machine.

The table below shows how having the new equipment compares with the current situation:

	Current situation	**Proposed situation with new equipment**
Direct material	3 kg @ £5	Usage down by 10%
Direct labour	6 hrs @ £10	Time down by 25%
Sales	4,000 units at £125 each	No change
Fixed costs	£180,000	Up by £47,500

Required

Calculate the profit figures for the current and proposed situations, and indicate whether the machine should be acquired.

	Current situation	**Proposed situation**
Profit		

It ☐ be better to acquire the new equipment.

Picklist:

would
would not

Assessment focus point

Instead of being asked to calculate the difference in profit in a mechanisation decision, you could instead be asked to calculate the net present value of the decision. The net present value is covered later in this chapter.

5.3 Other considerations in mechanisation decisions

Other factors to consider in mechanisation decisions include:

- **Employee morale** – Due to mechanisation of a process, it is likely that fewer employees will be needed on the process. Employees will either need to be re-deployed or made redundant. This will have a detrimental impact on employee morale.

- **Environmental considerations** – Running more machines will require additional power usage. This will increase emissions from the business, negatively impacting its carbon footprint.

6 Long-term decision making

So far in this chapter we have looked at short-term decision making, where the financial benefits or costs of a decision are assessed by looking at annual costs or one-off changes in costs.

However, many decisions will incur costs and produce benefits over a longer period of time. For example, the purchase of a machine may generate an outflow today, but the costs and benefits associated with the machine will be produced over its useful life.

To analyse long-term decisions, the **time value of money** needs to be taken into account. This is the assumption that cash flows received in the future are worth less than if we received them today due to inflation and interest rates.

A common method of assessing long-term decisions taking into account the time value of money is the **net present value (NPV)** method.

6.1 Net present value

Key term

Net present value is the sum of discounted cash flows, showing the cash increase or decrease generated by a decision in today's monetary value.

The present value of a cash flow is a future cash flow discounted to today's value. It is calculated by discounting the future cash flow by the interest that could be earned between today and the time that the cash flow would occur. In essence, the present value is the value that would be incurred or received if the cash flow occurred today.

The NPV is the sum of discounted cash inflows less discounted cash outflows. It therefore shows the increase or decrease in cash as a result of the decision if the cash flows occurred today.

Note that only cash flows are included in the analysis. Accounting adjustments such as depreciation are ignored as there is no cash flow associated with them.

It is also assumed that cash flows occur at the end of the year, even if they occur at various points throughout the year.

6.2 Steps to calculate NPV

(1) Calculate/list the expected cash flows (per year) arising from the investment or decision.

(2) Calculate the net cash flow arising per year.

(3) Discount each net cash flow using a discount factor (DCF) for each year as follows:

Net cash flow × DCF

This discount factor is linked to either the interest rate or the company's cost of capital.

(4) Total up the cash flows, adding discounted cash inflows and subtracting discounted cash outflows, to arrive at the NPV.

Assessment focus point

Discount factors are given to you in the assessment. There is no need for you to calculate them.

6.3 Decision rules using NPV

If the NPV is positive, then the decision should be accepted because the value of the cash inflows received as a result of the decision exceed the value of the cash outflows incurred. This will increase cash in the business and increase value to shareholders.

However, if the NPV is negative the opposite is true as the future benefits do not justify the current capital spending. The decision should be rejected.

Illustration 8: JLK

A company is to invest in a project with an immediate cash outflow of £20,000. The receipts from this project are £10,000 in one year's time, £14,000 in two years' time and £6,000 in three years' time.

The interest rate applicable to the company is 8% and the discount factors at this rate are given below:

Period	Discount factor 8%
1	0.926
2	0.857
3	0.794

Required

What is the NPV of this project and should the company invest in it?

Here is the NPV analysis:

Time	Cash flow £	Discount factor	Present value £
0	(20,000)	1.000	(20,000)
1	10,000	0.926	9,260
2	14,000	0.857	11,998
3	6,000	0.794	4,764
NPV			6,022

The project has a positive NPV; therefore, the company should invest in it.

Activity 9: Caston Foods

Caston Foods Ltd is considering introducing a new type of oven-ready meal, and has produced the following estimates of capital expenditure, revenue and costs. This new product is expected to have a three-year lifecycle.

Year 0 development costs will be £600,000.

Other cash flows (£000):

	Year 1	Year 2	Year 3
Revenue	760	920	1,060
Operating costs	456	542	612

The company's cost of capital is 14%.

Present value (PV) factors for a 14% discount rate are:

	Year 0	Year 1	Year 2	Year 3
PV factor	1.000	0.877	0.769	0.675

Required

(a) Calculate the NPV:

	Year 0	Year 1	Year 2	Year 3
Revenue				
Operating costs				

	Year 0	Year 1	Year 2	Year 3
Capital expenditure				
Net cash flows				
PV factor				
Discounted cash flows				
NPV				

(b) Complete the following sentence:

The new type of meal [   ] be launched.

Picklist:

should
should not

6.4 Net present cost

Sometimes a project will not generate any cash inflows. The net present value method can still be used, but the outcome will be known as **net present cost**.

Activity 10: JLK

JLK is looking to purchase a new machine which would cost £600,000 incurring annual running costs of £90,000. The machine would be scrapped for £100,000 at the end of 5 years.

Required

Calculate the net present cost of the machine using the following 10% discount factors:

Time	0	1	2	3	4	5
Cash flow						
Discount factor	1.000	0.909	0.826	0.751	0.683	0.621
NPV						
Net present cost						

Chapter summary

- For short-term decision making we concentrate on marginal costing and contribution – total fixed costs are assumed to be constant for the period.

- The BEP in units is found by dividing the fixed costs by the contribution per unit.

- The unit sales to achieve a target profit can be found by dividing the fixed costs plus target profit by the contribution per unit.

- The difference between budgeted or actual sales and the breakeven point is the margin of safety. This is often expressed as a percentage of budgeted sales or actual sales.

- The contribution to sales ratio can be used to find the breakeven point in terms of sales revenue:

  BEP (sales revenue £) = Fixed costs ÷ C/S ratio

- Normally output in any period is limited by sales demand. However, occasionally a factor of production such as the availability of material, labour hours or machine hours may be a limiting factor on output and profitability.

- Where there is more than one product and a limiting factor, overall profit is maximised by concentrating production on the products with the highest contribution per limiting factor unit.

- In a make or buy decisions, the relevant costs are any variable costs incurred/saved as a result of the decision and any savings in attributable fixed costs.

- Qualitative aspects of make or buy, shutdown and mechanisation need to be considered alongside the financial analysis.

- Whether or not to move from a labour-intensive production process to a machine-intensive production process will also have many short- and some long-term effects.

Keywords

- **Breakeven analysis:** calculations to determine the breakeven point

- **Breakeven point (BEP):** level of sales where sales revenue and total costs are equal, so that there is no profit and no loss

- **Breakeven revenue:** amount of revenue required to cover total costs in order to make neither a profit or a loss

- **Contribution:** sales revenue less variable costs

- **Contribution to sales (C/S) ratio:** ratio of contribution to sales revenue

- **Cost-volume-profit analysis:** analysis of the relationships between activity levels, costs and profits using marginal costing

- **Limiting factor:** a factor that limits the amount of a product that can be produced or sold: it is often sales demand but may be a production factor in limited supply

- **Margin of safety (MOS):** excess of budgeted sales or actual sales over the breakeven point sales, which may be measured as a percentage of budgeted or actual sales

- **Net present cost:** the sum of discounted cash outflows, used where a project is not expected to generate cash inflows

- **Net present value (NPV):** the sum of discounted cash inflows less cash outflows

- **Operational gearing:** the ratio of fixed costs to variable costs within an organisation's activities

- **Opportunity cost:** the benefit which would have been earned, but has been given up, by choosing one option instead of another

- **Relevant cost:** costs that will be incurred or saved as a result of making a decision

- **Shadow price:** the additional amount that an organisation is willing to pay to obtain an additional unit of limiting factor

- **Time value of money:** the assumption that cash flows received in the future are worth less than if they were received today

1 A business making a single product has budgeted sales of 38,000 units. The selling price per unit is £57 and the variable costs per unit of production are £45. The fixed costs of the business are £360,000.

Required

Calculate:

(a) The breakeven point in units
(b) The margin of safety as a percentage

The breakeven point is ⬚ units.

The margin of safety is ⬚ %.

2 A business has fixed costs of £910,000. It sells a single product at a selling price of £24 and the variable costs of production and sales are £17 per unit.

Required

Calculate the amount of units that need to be sold to make a profit of £500,000.

The amount of units that need to be sold is ⬚ units.

3 A business sells its single product for £40. The variable costs of this product total £32 per unit. The fixed costs of the business are £100,000.

Required

Calculate the sales revenue required to make a profit of £200,000.

The sales revenue required in order to make a profit of £200,000 is

£ ⬚

4 A business produces three products, the production and sales details of which are given below:

	Product		
	R	S	T
Direct materials @ £2 per kg	£16	£12	£10
Direct labour @ £9 per hour	£18	£36	£9
Selling price	£40	£60	£25
Machine hours per unit	6	4	3
Maximum sales demand	10,000 units	20,000 units	5,000 units

During the next period the supply of materials is limited to 250,000 kg, the labour hours available are 120,000 and the machine hours available are also 120,000. Fixed costs are £50,000 per period.

Required

(a) Identify the limiting factor.
(b) Calculate the optimal production plan.
(c) Calculate the profit earned under the optimal production plan.

(a)   The limiting factor is ⬚ .

Picklist:

labour hours
machine hours
materials

(b)

Product	Units produced

(c)   The profit that will be earned under this production plan is **£** ⬚ .

5   A business has two products, X and Y, with the following costs per unit:

	X Cost per unit £	Y Cost per unit £
Direct materials	2.50	3.00
Direct labour	8.00	6.00
Fixed overheads	3.00	1.50

The business could buy in X from an external supplier at a cost of £11 per unit, and it could buy in Y at £10 per unit.

Fixed overheads are not directly attributable and will be incurred regardless of whether the products will be bought in or not.

Required

Which product(s) should be bought in?

The business should buy in ⬚ .

Picklist:

both products
neither product

X
Y

6 Timmy Co is short on labour hours meaning that it can't meet maximum sales demand.

Labour hours available to Timmy Co are 20,000 hours.

It has produced the following optimal production plan for its products Badger and Pelican:

	Badger	Pelican
Sales demand (units)	5,000	10,000
Labour hours per unit (Hrs)	1	2
Contribution per unit (£)	5.00	7.00
Contribution per unit of limiting factor (£)	5.00	3.50
Optimal production plan	5,000	7,500

How much should Timmy Co pay for 5,000 additional labour hours?

£ _____ .

Activity answers

CHAPTER 1 Costing techniques

Activity 1 – Cost behaviour

| Cost | Quarterly production | | Cost classification |
	2,000 units £	9,000 units £	
Direct materials (W1)	13,500	60,750	Variable
Rent (W2)	6,500	6,500	Fixed
Supervisors (W3)	2,000	8,000	Stepped
Electricity (W4)	3,850	12,950	Semi variable

W1 As the cost per kg will vary with production, it is a variable cost
@ 2,000 units: 1.5kg × £4.50 × 2,000 = £13,500
@ 9,000 units: 1.5kg × £4.50 × 9,000 = £60,750

W2 The rent cost will be unaffected by the volume of units produced, so is a fixed cost.

W3 As the cost will increase at a certain production volume, this is a stepped cost.
@ 2,000 units: 2,000 units / 2,500 = 0.8 = 1 supervisor required
∴ Cost = £2,000
@ 9,000 units: 9,000 / 2,500 = 3.6 = 4 supervisors required
∴ Cost = 2,000 × 4 = £8,000

W4 Electricity has a part fixed and part variable element, so is a semi-variable cost.
@ 2,000 units: £1,250 + (£1.30 × 2,000) = £3,850
@ 9,000 units: £1,250 + (£1.30 × 9,000) = £12,950

Activity 2 – High Low Method

Units	Fixed £	Variable £
17,000	10,000	170,000
25,000	15,000	212,500

	Units	£
High	19,000	290,000
Low	15,000	250,000
	4,000	40,000

Variable cost per unit = £40,000 / 4,000 = £10 per unit

@ 19,000 units:

	£
Total cost	290,000
Total variable cost (£10 × 19,000)	(190,000)
Fixed cost	100,000

@ 17,000 units

	£
Fixed cost	100,000
Variable cost (£10 × 17,000)	170,000
Total cost	270,000

@ 25,000 units

	£
Fixed cost (£100,000 + £5,000)	105,000
Variable cost ((£10 – £1.50) × 25,000)	212,500
Total cost	317,500

Activity 3: Classifying factory cost centres

Cost Centre	Type
Canteen	Service cost centre
Stores	Service cost centre
Stitching	Production cost centre
Maintenance	Service cost centre
Packing	Production cost centre
Finishing	Production cost centre

Activity 4: Classifying centres

Canteen in a factory – Cost centre
Car dealer – Revenue centre
Shop in chain – Profit centre
An independent restaurant – Investment centre

Activity 5: Galaxy

The overhead recovery rate will be **£7.60** per **machine hour**.

(£38,000/5,000 machine hours)

Overheads were under-absorbed by £9,600:

	£
Actual overheads	40,000
Absorbed overheads (£7.60 × 4,000 hours)	30,400
Under-absorption	9,600

Activity 6: Absorption vs. marginal costing

Cost per unit – absorption costing

		£
Direct materials		12,000
Direct labour		15,000
Variable overheads		23,000
Fixed overheads		25,000
Total cost		75,000
Cost per unit =		£75,000/5,000
=		£15 per unit

Cost per unit – marginal costing

		£
Direct materials		12,000
Direct labour		15,000
Variable overheads		23,000
Total cost		50,000
Cost per unit =		£50,000/5,000
=		£10 per unit

Activity 7: Marginal vs. absorption costing profit

| | Absorption Costing | | Marginal costing | |
	Month 1	Month 2	Month 1	Month 2
	£	£	£	£
Sales	1,100,000	1,320,000	1,100,000	1,320,000
Opening inventory	0	200,000	0	120,000
Production costs	750,000	750,000	450,000	450,000
Closing inventory	200,000	350,000	120,000	210,000
Cost of sales	550,000	600,000	330,000	360,000
Fixed overheads	0	0	300,000	300,000
Profit/Loss	550,000	720,000	470,000	660,000

Workings

Sales:

Month 1: £100 × 11,000 = £1,100,000

Month 2: £110 × 12,000 = £1,320,000

Production costs:

	£
Direct material	10
Direct labour	8
Variable production overhead (£180,000/15,000 units)	12
Marginal cost per unit	30
Fixed production overhead (£300,000/15,000 units)	20
Absorption cost per unit	50

Absorption production cost: £50 × 15,000 = £750,000

Marginal production cost: £30 × 15,000 = £450,000

Closing inventory:

	Month 1	Month 2
	Units	
Opening inventory	0	4,000
Production	15,000	15,000
Sales	11,000	12,000
Closing inventory	4,000	7,000

Month 1

Absorption costing: £50 × 4000 = £200,000

Marginal costing: £30 × 4,000 = £120,000

Month 2

Absorption costing: £50 × 7,000 = £350,000

Marginal costing: £30 × 7,000 = £210,000

(b)

	Month 1 £	Month 2 £
Absorption costing profit	550,000	720,000
Change in inventory	(80,000)	(60,000)
Marginal costing profit	470,000	660,000

Workings

Month 1: 4,000 units × £20 per unit = £80,000

Month 2: 3,000 units × £20 per unit = £60,000

CHAPTER 2 Statistical techniques

Activity 1: Moving averages

Month	Actual £	Three-month moving average £
March	226,504	
April	251,600	238,768
May	238,200	245,800
June	247,600	242,100
July	240,500	250,300
August	262,800	

Activity 2: JB Ltd

(a)

2X16 Cost per kg	Jan	Feb	Mar
Underlying cost per kg (£)	180	(222 – 12) 210	240
Seasonal variation (£)	(220 – 180) 40	12	–18
Seasonally adjusted cost (£)	220	222	(240 – 18) 222

(b)

2X17 Cost per kg	Jan	Feb	Mar
Underlying cost per kg (£)	540	570	600
Seasonal variation (£)	40	12	–18
Seasonally adjusted cost (£)	580	582	582

Trend is increasing by £30 per month. There are 10 additional periods between January 2X16 and January 2X17

∴ Jan 2X17 trend = 240 × (30 × 10) = 540

Activity 3: Linear regression – costs

The total production costs will be **£203,800**.

63,000 + 3.2 × 44,000

Activity 4: Linear regression – sales

y = 4.8 + 1.2x

The first two years account for x = 1 to x = 24

Therefore the x values in which we are interested are x = 25, 26, 27

Month 1   x = 25:   y = 4.8 + 1.2(25)   = 34.8   ie £34,800

Month 2   x = 26:   y = 4.8 + 1.2(26)   = 36.0   ie £36,000

Month 3   x = 27:   y = 4.8 + 1.2(27)   = 37.2   ie £37,200

Activity 5: Index numbers

Month	Cost per kg (£)	Index number
January	26.20	£26.20/£26.20 × 100 100
February	26.80	£26.80/26.20 × 100 102.29
March	26.90	£26.90/26.20 × 100 102.67
April	25.80	£25.80/26.20 × 100 98.47

Activity 6: Tees R Us

(a)

Month (20X7)	Actual cost per kg (£)	Index number	Costs at January prices
January	4.95	100	4.95 × 100/100 4.95
February	4.97	101	4.97 × 100/101 4.92
March	4.99	103	4.99 × 100/103 4.84
April	5.05	105	5.05 × 100/105 4.81
May	5.08	106	5.08 × 100/106 4.79
June	5.10	107	5.10 × 100/107 4.77

(b)

Month (20X8)	Index	Actual cost (£)
July	115	4.95 × 115/100 5.69
August	116	4.95 × 116/100 5.74
September	119	4.95 × 119/100 5.89
October	120	4.95 × 120/100 5.94
November	122	4.95 × 122/100 6.04
December	123	4.95 × 123/100 6.09

Activity 7: YSP Games

(a) The trend refers to the general direction in which a time series changes over time. For YSP games, this is the steady increase in sales volumes by 5,000 units per month, showing an upward sales growth trend.

The seasonal variation is a predicted increase or decrease away from the trend for segments of the time series, due to regular, repetitive events. In YSP games, there is a positive seasonal variation between September – December, reflecting gamers spending more time on games as winter approaches, or more games being sold in the run up to Christmas.

(b) The limitations of using time series analysis for YSP Games are:

Whilst the trend has shown a steady increase of 5,000 units per month historically, YSP may see this trend changing into the future. For example, the taste for the types of games YSP produce may change, impacting on the general upward sales growth previously experienced by YSP.

Seasonal variations are calculated on previous trading history, but the pattern of these variations may change. For example, an advancement in technology may adversely affect seasonal variations if YSP don't respond quickly enough, as their customers by a competitor game. This may mean that the positive seasonal variations experienced between September–December may be lower than previously, or become negative.

Random variations are ignored in time series analysis as they are hard to predict. For example, if YSP games have the rights to produce a game for a film franchise which subsequently flops, this could cause an unexpected decrease in demand for that game, causing a decline in sales volumes.

CHAPTER 3 Standard costing

Activity 1 – Latt

Unit	Quantity	Cost per unit	Total unit cost
Material	3 kg	5.00	15.00
Labour	2 hours	7.00	14.00
Fixed overheads	2 hours	5.00	10.00
Total			39.00

Activity 2: GreenGrass Ltd

Target standards are **more realistic** as they reflect current operating conditions within GreenGrass Ltd. This is because allowances are made for idle time, wastage and other inefficiencies in the production process. This will improve motivation as managers are appraised against realistic conditions.

Although target standards include some improvements to the current standard, they do not encourage excessive improvement such as an ideal standard does. This makes the target standard **more achievable** than ideal standards. Managers are therefore more motivated as the target set is within their reach.

Managers are likely to be **less tightly controlled** using an target standard. This is because the budget set will be more accurate as it reflects realistic operating conditions. Whilst there will still be an element of control it will be less strict than under ideal standards, which motivates managers in turn.

Activity 3: Press Co

(a) The standard quantity of labour per unit is 12 minutes.

(2,400hrs/12,000 units) × 60

(b) The budgeted quantity of materials needed to produce 15,000 units of C06 is 26,250 kg.

21,000kg/12,000 units × 15,000 units

(c) The budgeted labour hours to produce 15,000 units of C06 is 3,000 hours.

(12 mins × 15,000 units)/60

(d) The budgeted labour cost to produce 15,000 units of C06 is £ 45,000.

£36,000/12,000 units × 15,000 units

(e) The budgeted overhead absorption rate per unit is £ 4.50 .
£54,000 / 12,000 units

(f) The fixed production overheads were over by 7,500 .

	£
Over-head absorbed (£4.50 × 15,000 units)	67,500
Actual overheads	(60,000)
Over-absorption	7,500

CHAPTER 4 Variance analysis

Activity 1: News Co

(a) **Total material variance**

	£
Actual units should cost (27,000 × 2 kg × £2.50)	135,000
Actual material used did cost (53,000 kg × £2.38)	(126,140)
	8,860 (F)

(b) **Material price variance**

	£
Actual purchases should cost (53,000 × £2.50)	132,500
Actual purchases did cost (53,000 kg × £2.38)	(126,140)
	6,360 (F)

(c) **Material usage variance**

	Kg
Actual production should use (27,000 × 2 kg)	54,000
Actual production did use	(53,000)
	1,000 F
@ std cost £2.50	£2,500 F

Activity 2: Yard

(a) Total labour variance

	£
Actual units should cost (2,195 × 4 hrs × £12.50)	109,750
Actual labour used did cost	(110,750)
	(1,000) A

(b) Labour rate variance

	£
Actual hours paid should cost (9,200 × £12.50)	115,500
Actual hours paid did cost	(110,750)
	4,250 F

(c) Labour efficiency variance

	Hrs
Actual production should use (2,195 × 4 hrs)	8,780
Actual production did use	(9,200)
	(420) A
@ std cost £12.50	£5,250 A

Activity 3: Flight Co

The idle time variance is £700 A

	Hrs
Hours worked	2,200
Hours paid	(2,300)
	(100) A
X £7 per hour	£(700) A

Activity 4: Bee Co

(a) Total variable overhead variance

	£
Actual units should cost (1,000 units × £30)	30,000
Actual units did cost	(30,750)
	750 (A)

(b) Variable overhead expenditure

	£
Actual hours worked should cost (1,960 hrs × £15)	29,400
Actual hours worked did cost	(30,750)
	1,350 (A)

(c) Variable overhead efficiency

	Hrs
Actual units should take (1,000 units × 2 hrs)	2,000
Actual units did take	(1,960)
	40 F
@ std cost £15	£600 F

Activity 5: Armour

The standard fixed overhead cost of a Soul is 3 hours at £10 per hour = £30 per unit.

(a) The fixed overhead total variance

	£
Amount of overhead absorbed (1,000 units × £30 per unit)	30,000
Fixed overhead incurred	(33,980)
Fixed overhead total variance (under absorbed)	(3,980) (A)

(b) The fixed overhead expenditure variance

	£
Budgeted fixed overhead expenditure	33,000
Actual fixed overhead expenditure	33,980
Fixed overhead expenditure variance	980 (A)

(c) The fixed overhead volume variance

Budgeted production	1,100 units
Actual production	1,000 units
	(100) units (A)
× standard absorption rate per unit	× £30
Fixed overhead volume variance	(£3,000) (A)
Or	
Budgeted labour hours (3 hrs × 1,100 units)	3,300 hrs
Standard hours produced (3 hrs × 1,000 units)	3,000 hrs
	300 hrs (A)
× standard OAR per hour	× £10
Fixed overhead volume variance	£3,000 A

(d) The fixed overhead efficiency variance

1,000 units of Soul should take (× 3 hrs)	3,000 hours
But did take	3,500 hours
	500 hours (A)
× standard absorption rate per hour (× £10)	× £10
Fixed overhead volume efficiency variance	£5,000 (A)

(e) The fixed overhead capacity variance

Budgeted hours of work (3 hrs × 1,100 units)	3,300 hours
Actual hours of work	3,500 hours
	200 hours (F)
× standard absorption rate per hours (× £10)	× £10
Fixed overhead volume capacity variance	£2,000 (F)

Activity 6: Grace

(a) The fixed overhead volume variance is £ $\boxed{66,000 \ (A)}$.

	Units
Budgeted production	66,000
Actual production	60,000
Difference	6,000

Valued at standard OAR per unit = $\dfrac{£726,000}{66,000}$ = £11.00   £66,000(A)

(b) The actual fixed production overheads incurred were £ $\boxed{656,000}$.

Actual fixed production overhead incurred.

	£
Budget	726,000
Actual (balancing figure)	656,000
Fixed overhead expenditure variance	70,000(F)

CHAPTER 5 Operating statements

Activity 1: Tivell

(a) (i) Actual cost of £156,907 for 36,490 kg

∴ Actual cost per kg = $\dfrac{£156,907}{36,490}$ = £4.30

(ii) Actual cost of £252,938 for 51,620 hrs

∴ Actual cost per hour = $\dfrac{£252,938}{51,620}$ = £4.90

(iii) 8,900 bottles took 51,620 hours

∴ hours per bottle = $\dfrac{51,620}{8,900}$ = 5.80

(iv) Budgeted fixed overheads = £1,566,000 per year

Standard fixed overhead absorption rate per bottle = £15.00

$\dfrac{£1,566,000}{15.00}$ = 104,400 bottles = budget production level

(v) There are 48 operating weeks in the year and so budgeted production in a 4-week period represents 4/48 of the year's budgeted output.

$$\therefore \text{ 4 weeks' production} = 104,400 \times \frac{4}{48} = 8,700 \text{ bottles}$$

(vi) Standard fixed OAR = £15.00

Budgeted fixed overheads (4 weeks) = 8,700 × £15.00 = £130,500

$$\left(\text{or, } \frac{4}{48} \times £1,566,000 = £130,500\right)$$

(b) (i)

	£
36,490 kg should cost (× £4.50)	164,205
Did cost	156,907
Material price variance	7,298 (F)

(ii)

	Kg
8,900 units should use (× 4 kg)	35,600
Did use	36,490
	890 A
× std £/kg	4.50
Material usage variance	£4,005 (A)

(iii)

	£
51,620 hours should cost (× £5.00)	258,100
Did cost	252,938
Labour rate variance	5,162 (F)

(iv)

	Hrs
8,900 units should take (× 5 hrs)	44,500
Did take	51,620
	7,120 (A)
× std £/hr	5.00
Labour efficiency variance	35,600 (A)

(v)

	£
Budgeted fixed overheads	130,500
Actual fixed overheads	134,074
Fixed overhead expenditure variance	3,574 (A)

(vi)

	Bottles
Budget	8,700
Actual	8,900
	200 (F)
× std jar/bottle	15
Fixed overhead volume variance	£3,000 (F)

(vii)

	Hrs
Budged hours of work	43,500
(8,700 units × 5 hrs)	
Actual hours of work	51,620
Capacity variance in hrs	8,120 (F)
× std OAR/hr	3.00
Fixed overhead capacity, variance	£24,360 (F)

(viii)

	Hrs
Standard hours	44,500
(8,900 × 5 hrs)	
Actual hours	51,620
	7,120 (A)
× std OAR/hr	3
Fixed overhead efficiency variance	£21,360 (A)

(c) Statement of reconciliation

			£
Standard cost of production			
(8,900 units × £58.00)			516,200
	£(F)	£(A)	
Materials price	7,298		
Material usage		4,005	
Labour rate	5,162		
Labour efficiency		35,600	
Fixed overhead expenditure		3,574	
Fixed overhead capacity	24,360		
Fixed overhead efficiency		21,360	
	36,820	64,539	27,719 (A)
Actual cost of actual production			543,919

Activity 2: Blast Co

Variance	Fav	Ad	£
Standard cost of actual production (W1)			2,196,000
A1 material price (W2)		–106,000	
A1 material usage (W3)	2,500		
A2 material price (W4)	336,000		
A2 material usage (W5)		–1,750	
Direct labour rate (W6)		–190,000	
Direct labour efficiency (W7)		–48,750	
Fixed overhead expenditure (W8)	40,000		
Total variance	378,500	–346,500	32,000
Actual cost of actual production			2,164,000

BPP
LEARNING MEDIA

Workings

1   ((£500,000 + 490,000 + 450,000)/20,000 × 20,500) + 720,000 = £2,196,000

2

	£
51,000 kg should cost (× £10)	510,000
Did cost	616,000
Material price variance	106,000 (A)

3

	Kg
20,500 units should use (× 2.5 kg)	51,250
Did use	51,000
	250 F
× std £/kg	10
Material usage variance	£2,500 (F)

4

	£
72,000 kg should cost (× £7)	504,000
Did cost	168,000
Material price variance	336,000 (F)

5

	Kg
20,500 units should use (× 3.5 kg)	71,750
Did use	72,000
	250 A
× std £/kg	7
Material usage variance	£1,750 (A)

6

	£
51,000 hours should cost (× £10.00)	510,000
Did cost	700,000
Labour rate variance	190,000 (A)

7

	Hrs
20,500 units should take (× 2.25 hrs)	46,125
Did take	51,000
	4,875 (A)
× std £/hr	10.00
Labour efficiency variance	48,750 (A)

8

	£
Budgeted fixed overheads	720,000
Actual fixed overheads	680,000
Fixed overhead expenditure variance	40,000 (F)

Activity 3: Colin's Cakes

(a)

Variance	Variance amount £	Adverse/favourable/ no variance
Flour price (W1)	2,800	Favourable
Direct labour rate (W2)	9,000	Favourable

Workings

1   Flour price variance

	£
33,000 kg should cost (33,000 kg × £18,000/30,000 kg)	19,800
33,000 kg did cost	(17,000)
	2,800 F

2   Direct labour rate variance

	£
23,000 hrs should cost (23,000 hrs × £160,000/20,000 hrs)	184,000
23,000 hrs did cost	175,000
	9,000 F

(b)

	£
Standard direct cost of actual production (W1)	213,600
Flour price variance	–2,800
Flour usage variance (W2)	–1,800
Direct labour rate variance	–9,000
Direct labour efficiency variance (W3)	–8,000
Actual direct cost of production	192,000

Workings

1   (£18,000 + £160,000)/10,000 units × 12,000 units = £228,000

2

	kg
12,000 units should use (12,000 units × 30,000 kg/10,000 units)	36,000
12,000 units did use	33,000
	3,000 F
@ standard cost – 3,000 kg × £18,000/30,000 kg	£1,800 F

3

	Hrs
12,000 units should take (12,000 units × 20,000 hrs/10,000 units)	24,000
12,000 units did take	23,000
	1,000 F
@ standard cost – 1,000 hrs × £160,000/20,000 hrs	£8,000 F

CHAPTER 6 Interpreting variances

Activity 1: Causes of variances

- Lower grade of labour used
- More experienced staff used

Activity 2: Shoebox Ltd

To: Colleague	Subject: Variance explanations
From: Accounting Technician	Date: xx/xx/20xx

Supplier

The new supplier being more expensive has meant that more was paid for materials per kg than was originally planned. This has led to more being spent overall on materials and an adverse materials price variance.

The materials from the new supplier was of better quality. This has led to less wastage of material when the trainers were produced, and consequently less material being used overall in production. This has helped to generate a favourable material usage variance.

Machinery

The installation of the new machine caused production to be stopped in the month. Overtime then had to be worked to recover the lost time. This has led to more time being taken in production that was originally planned, and staff being less efficient as a result. This has led to adverse labour and fixed overhead efficiency variances.

As production had to be halted, production operatives could not produce trainers for four days. This has led to increased idle time and an adverse fixed overhead capacity variance.

As overtime had to be worked to recover the lost time staff were paid overtime premiums. This has led to a higher labour cost per hour than was planned and an adverse labour rate variance.

Warehouse

The renegotiation of the warehouse rent downwards has meant that less was spent on rent than was budgeted. This has led to reduced fixed overhead expenditure and a favourable fixed overhead expenditure variance. The reduced rent needs to be reflected in future budgets to stop this variance occurring again.

Activity 3: Tivvel

(a)

	£
36,490 kg at standard price (× £4.50)	164,205
36,490 kg at revised standard price (× £5.00)	182,450
Non-controllable price variance	18,245 (A)

(b)

	£
36,490 kg at revised standard price	182,450
But did cost	156,907
Controllable price variance	£25,543 (F)

Activity 4: Patch

(a)

	£
Actual purchases should cost	340,000
Actual purchases did cost	355,000
Material price variance	(15,000) (A)

(b)

	£
Actual purchases should cost	340,000
Actual purchases at revised standard cost 34,000 × (£10 × 115%)	391,000
Price variance due to difference in index value	(51,000) (A)

	£
Actual purchases at revised standard cost	391,000
Actual purchases did cost	355,000
Price variance due to other reasons	36,000 (F)

Activity 5: Blossom

(a)

	£
20,800 kg at standard price (× £90,000/22,500kg)	83,200
20,800 kg at revised standard price (× £90,000/22,500kg × 123.2/110)	93,184
Price variance due to difference in index value	9,984 (A)

(b)

	£
20,800 kg at revised standard price	93,184
20,800 kg at actual price	91,520
Price variance due to other factors	1,664 (F)

(c) **Response to the purchasing manager**

The incorrect standard for materials price makes up £9,984 of the total adverse materials price variance of £8,320. As this element is uncontrollable by the purchasing manager, it isn't fair to judge their performance on this part of the variance. Indeed the controllable variance is £1,664 favourable, implying that the purchasing manager has made good operational decisions to limit the total adverse variance suffered.

Response to personnel manager

The overtime working has had the effect of increasing the hourly rate paid to production staff. This would have had a negative effect on the labour rate variance and would be a key driver of the adverse variance reported. This can be substantiated as the actual hourly rate was £6.20; 20 pence more than the standard rate of £6.00.

CHAPTER 7 Performance indicators

Activity 1: LNG Ltd

(a)

Gross profit margin	23.6%
Operating profit margin	5.0%
Administration costs as a percentage of sales	5.7%
ROCE	5.5%

Average advertising revenue per newspaper produced	£0.56
Advertising revenue per employee	£60,000
Average advertising revenue per advertising transaction	£105
Current ratio	1.89
Average age of receivables in months	3 months
Average age of payables in months	2.2 months
Interest cover	3.5 times

Workings

(i) Gross profit margin $\dfrac{990}{4,200} \times 100$ = 23.6%

(ii) Operating profit margin $\dfrac{210}{4,200} \times 100$ = 5.0%

(iii) Administration costs as a % of sales $\dfrac{240}{4,200} \times 100$ = 5.7%

(iv) Return on capital employed (ROCE) $\dfrac{210}{3,800} \times 100$ = 5.5%

(v) Average advertising revenue per newspaper produced $\dfrac{4,200}{7,500}$ = £0.56

(vi) Advertising revenue per employee $\dfrac{4,200,000}{70}$ = £60,000.00

(vii) Average advertising revenue per advertising transaction $\dfrac{4,200}{40}$ = £105

(viii) Current ratio $\dfrac{1,135}{600}$ = 1.89

(ix) Average age of receivables in months $\dfrac{1,050}{4,200} \times 12$ = 3 months

(x) Average age of payables in months $\dfrac{600}{3,210} \times 12$ = 2.2 months

(xi) Interest cover $\dfrac{210}{60}$ = 3.5 times

(b)

Memo

To: Managing Director   From: Accounting Technician

Subject: Performance Indicators   Date: xx/xx/xxxx

Gross profit margin

LNG's gross margin is nearly 10% below that of its competitor. This is because of advertising selling prices being lower, as the advertising price per advertising transaction is £15 lower than Ads.

LNG are also not generating revenue as efficiently as Ads, as the average advertising revenue per newspaper produced is 19p lower than Ads, and revenue per employee is £28,500 lower.

The combined effect of lower prices and lower efficiency has reduced the gross profit margin for LNG in comparison to Ads.

Operating profit margin

LNG's operating profit margin is half that of Ads. This is due to a reduced gross profit margin and administration costs as a percentage of sales being 1.7% higher than Ads. This indicates reduced efficiency, which has reduced LNG's operating profit margin compared to Ads.

ROCE

LNG's ROCE is 10% below that of its competitor. This is due to the lower operating profit margin, indicating that LNG is not using capital employed as efficiently as Ads to generate profit. More information is needed on each company's capital employed figure to provide a fuller assessment.

Current ratio

LNG's ratio is below that of Ads. This means that Ads has a slightly better liquidity position than LNG. Although LNG take almost a month longer to pay their suppliers, it also takes them an extra month to collect its income from customers. The combined effect is a lower current ratio and a lower liquidity position.

Interest cover

The interest cover of the two companies is the same. This indicates that LNG and Ads have the same ability to service its debt. A similar level of financial risk is therefore apparent within both companies.

BPP
LEARNING MEDIA

Activity 2: Seat Co

(a)

	Actual	Budget
Gross profit margin	16.7%	20.0%
Operating profit margin	4.2%	8.0%
Return on capital employed	10.7%	20.0%
Inventory turnover (in months)	1.3	1.0

(b)

Memo

To: Finance Director   Date: xx/xx/xxxx

From: Accounting Technician   Subject: Performance Indicators

Gross profit margin

An increase in the selling price of a chair will result in an increase in the gross margin. However it may be deemed that increasing the selling price of a chair would result in an uncompetitive price, resulting in reduced sales volumes. If this is the case, efforts should be made to reduce the cost of production.

Operating profit margin

The net operating margin will increase if the company is able to reduce its distribution and administration costs. It would appear from the actual results that a reduction has already taken place since distribution and administration costs are £15,000 below budget.

ROCE

The ROCE will improve if operating profits improve with no increase in capital employed. The measures detailed above will, therefore, have the effect of improving the return. An alternative, however, would be to examine whether all the assets employed are required for use in the business. If not, an asset disposal programme could be implemented and the proceeds distributed to shareholders. This would have the effect of reducing capital employed and improving the return on capital employed.

Inventory turnover

The current inventory represents 1.3 months' production. An increase in sales volumes may lead to a reduction in the number of chairs held in inventory and will consequently improve this indicator.

Activity 3: Grippit

Email	
To: Finance Director	From: Accounting Technician
Subject: Analysis of scenarios	Date: xx/xx/20xx

(i) **Gross profit margin**

The gross profit margin for scenario 1 is 36% and scenario 2 is 28.57%. This is mainly driven by sales price per unit rather than the costs under each scenario.

Sales price per unit

Sales price per unit is higher under scenario 1 than scenario 2. This will increase contribution generated per unit within scenario 1, which has driven the gross profit margin to be higher than that of scenario 2.

Materials and labour cost

The materials and labour costs are exactly the same within both scenarios. However because the sales price in scenario 2 has not been set to recover these direct costs at the same rate as in scenario 1, contribution per unit is therefore lower. This has driven a lower gross profit margin in scenario 2.

Fixed costs per unit

Fixed costs per unit are higher in scenario 1 than scenario 2. The reason for this is because of the increased volumes within scenario 2, meaning that total fixed costs are spread over more units. Indeed, the total fixed costs are the same in both scenarios. This has had no impact on the gross profit margins in either scenario.

(ii) **Gearing and interest cover**

The level of gearing for both scenarios is at a similar level. This implies that a similar level of debt will be incurred in each scenario, and therefore the same level of financial risk is evident.

The level of interest cover in scenario 1 the profit is higher than that in scenario 2. This can be attributed to the fall in profits rather than increased debt, as the gearing ratio is broadly similar between both scenarios, meaning that a similar level of interest will be incurred.

(iii) **Recommendation**

It is recommended that scenario 1 is chosen. This is because it has a higher gross profit margin, driving greater profits throughout Grippit, and there is slightly less risk of default on long term debt as gearing is lower and interest cover is higher.

Activity 4: Blossom

The bonus system at Blossom makes it tempting for managers to manipulate the profit figures for their department. This represents a **threat of self-interest** for each manager.

If a manager chooses to manipulate their department's profit figures, then their results will not be showing a true picture of what is actually happening within their department. This will **undermine the manager's integrity**.

Managers may also **choose to not invest in new machinery.** This is because new machinery will likely drag down the department's ROCE as capital employed increases, and due to a higher depreciation charge which will suppress the profit. This is also not goal-congruent, as new machines can improve the efficiency of Blossom in the long term.

Managers may also choose to **keep other costs low** in order to keep their operating profit high. For example, managers may choose to use a lower quality supplier in order to reduce materials cost. This is also non-goal congruent as it is likely that the garden statues produced will be of lower quality, impacting on Blossom's reputation.

Activity 5: Baker's Biscuits

Effectiveness indicators:

- Number of customer complaints
- Number of customer recommendations
- Reworked biscuits as a percentage of total production
- Market share
- Industry awards won

Productivity indicators:

- Average batches of biscuits per employee
- Average number of batches produced per labour hour
- Average number of batches per machine hour
- Percentage of labour time spent in production

Activity 6: Barnes

(i) Efficiency ratio $= \dfrac{(14,000 \times 3)\text{ hours}}{40,000\text{ hours}} \times 100\% = 105\%$

(ii) Capacity ratio $= \dfrac{40,000\text{ hours}}{36,000\text{ hours}} \times 100\% = 111\%$

(iii) Activity ratio $= \dfrac{(14,000 \times 3)\text{ hours}}{36,000\text{ hours}} \times 100\% = 117\%$

$E \times C = A$ ie $105\% \times 111\% = 117\%$

The activity ratio of 117% (more output than budgeted and more standard hours produced than budgeted) is explained by the 111% capacity working, and by good efficiency of 105%.

Activity 7: The Balanced Scorecard

Financial Perspective

- Gross profit margin
- Operating profit margin
- Return on Capital Employed
- Asset turnover
- Working capital cycle

Customer perspective

- Number of customer complaints
- Customer satisfaction scores
- Market share
- Number of repeat purchases

Internal

- Labour hours per unit
- Machine hours per unit
- Order processing time
- Average time per customer
- Average queue lengths
- Value added per employee

Innovation and Learning

- Percentage of sales from new products
- Average training cost per employee
- Percentage of employee time spent in training

CHAPTER 8 Cost management

Activity 1: Product lifecycle costs

Development – Research and development costs will be mostly fixed. Few direct variable overheads are incurred.

Introduction – Advertising and promotion costs, alongside continuing recovery of research and development costs will mean that fixed costs are still the highest proportion of overall cost

Growth – Direct material and labour costs become the biggest proportion of overall cost, so costs switch from fixed to variable.

Maturity – Economies of scale reduce the level of variable cost. Mechanisation will mean that more fixed overheads are incurred. Costs switch from variable to fixed.

Decline – Increased obsolescence costs increase the proportion of variable cost incurred.

Activity 2: Co X

	Development	Introduction	Growth	Maturity	Decline	Total
Sales volume (units)		4,000	15,000	30,000	10,000	
	£000	**£000**	**£000**	**£000**	**£000**	**£000**
Revenue		2,400	8,250	13,500	3,500	27,650
Variable cost		(1,000)	(3,750)	(6,000)	(1,500)	(12,250)
Overhead		(400)	(1,500)	(1,800)	(750)	(4,450)
Development cost	(500)	–	–	–	–	(500)
Advertising cost	–	(1,100)	–	–	–	(1,100)
Profit	(500)	(100)	3,000	5,700	1,250	9,350

Activity 3: Target costing

(a)

	£
Total anticipated sales revenue (£10 × 25,000 units)	250,000
Target total net profit (£250,000 × 0.25)	(62,500)
Target total costs	187,500
Target cost per unit (£187,500/25,000 units)	7.50

(b)

	£
Total life cycle costs (39,000 + 125,000 + 15,000 + 5,000)	184,000
Life cycle cost per unit (£184,000/25,000 units)	7.36

The new product [should] be launched.

This is because the expected life cycle cost per unit is below the total target cost, so the product will achieve the desired profit margin when it is launched.

(c)

	£
Reduced selling price per unit (£10 – £1)	9.00
Target net profit per unit (£9 × 0.25)	(2.25)
Target total cost per unit	6.75
Expected variable manufacturing cost per unit (£125,000 /25,000 units)	(5.00)
Target fixed costs per unit	1.75

Activity 4: SF Ltd

Using non-recyclable packaging will mean that more of SF's packaging will end up in landfills. This will have a damaging effect on the environment as it contributes to the destruction of wildlife habitats as well as generating excess methane which is unpleasant to local populations.

The lower grade of packaging also detracts from the quality perception that SF wants to portray on its premium lasagne range. This could have a damaging effect on profit and shareholder returns as a result.

The move towards using a lower grade of labour in Beaton will have a damaging effect on staff in the factory in Aton. It is likely that the staff in the Aton factory will have reduced working hours or be made redundant. This will have a negative impact on the Aton local economy as the local population will have less disposable income and skills levels will reduce.

The machinery used in the Beaton factory has been criticised for heavy emissions. Moving production will see these emissions increasing as more production units are produced, damaging the Beaton local natural environment. SF also may contravene emissions regulation, incurring fines that will impact profits and returns to shareholders.

CHAPTER 9 Activity based costing (ABC)

Activity 1: Dodo

(a) Under traditional absorption costing

OAR = £190,000/67,000(W) = £2.836/hr

Working: Total hours

	A	B	C	Total
Units	20,000	25,000	2,000	
Hrs/unit	2	1	1	
Total hours required	40,000	25,000	2,000	67,000

(b)

	A £/unit	B £/unit	C £/unit
Direct materials	5.00	10.00	10.00
Direct labour	10.00	5.00	5.00
Production overheads	5.67	2.84	2.84
Total cost	20.67	17.84	17.84

(c) (i) Machine costs $\dfrac{£55,000}{40,000+50,000+4,000}$ = £0.585 per machine hour

(ii) QC and set-up $\dfrac{90,000}{10+13+2}$ = £3,600 per production run

(iii) Receiving $\dfrac{£30,000}{10+10+2}$ = £1,363.64 per component receipt

(iv) Packing $\dfrac{£15,000}{20+20+20}$ = £250 per customer order

(d)

	A £	B £	C £	Total £
Machining costs (40:50:4)	23,404	29,255	2,341	55,000
Quality control and set-up (10:13:2)	36,000	46,800	7,200	90,000
Receiving (10:10:2)	13,636	13,636	2,728	30,000
Packing (20:20:20)	5,000	5,000	5,000	15,000
Total overhead costs	78,040	94,691	17,269	190,000

(e)

	A £	B £	C £
Total overhead costs	78,040	94,691	17,269
Units produced	20,000	25,000	2,000
Overhead cost/unit	£3.90	£3.79	£8.63

(f)

	A £/unit	B £/unit	C £/unit
Direct materials	5.00	10.00	10.00
Direct labour	10.00	5.00	5.00
Production overheads	3.90	3.79	8.63
Total cost	18.90	18.79	23.63

CHAPTER 10 Decision-making techniques

Activity 1: Widget

(a) Contribution per unit = £100 – £60 = £40

∴ £150,000/£40 = 3,750.

(b) 3,750 units x £100 = £375,000

(c) 5,000 units – 3,750 units = 1,250 units

(d) (5,000 – 3,750)/5,000 × 100 = 25%.

(e) (150,000 + 30,000)/£40 = £180,000/£40 = 4,500 units.

Activity 2: Widget 2

(a) Fixed costs rise by 10% = 165,000

Variable costs rise by 5% = £63 per unit

Selling price rises by 6% = £106 per unit

Therefore contribution per unit = £43

$$BEP = \frac{165,000}{43} = 3,838 \text{ units}$$

(b) The BEP rises by 88 units.

This reduces the MOS to: 23.24%.

The BEP should still be achieved; the MOS falls but only marginally. There is a greater risk that the fixed costs will not be covered but this risk has only been impacted slightly by the change.

Activity 3: Chuck

Implications of the differences in BEP between the two departments:

The BEP of Lob is lower than that of Throw, despite having a lower contribution per unit. This is because Lob has a lower fixed cost base, so the contribution generated per unit has less fixed cost to cover.

As a consequence Lob needs to sell much fewer units to cover its fixed cost base than Throw does in order to recover its fixed costs.

Which department has the better margin of safety and why?

Lob has a much higher MOS than Throw. This is because the proportion of budgeted sales to BEP is much lower than that of Throw. Indeed Lob can drop 17,500 units before it starts making a loss compared to Throw's 6,000 units.

The main reason for this is not only because of the lower fixed costs generating a low BEP, but because there is more demand for Lob's product, generating higher sales volumes.

Comment on the results from a risk perspective and suggest any potential ways of reducing it.

Throw is the more risky department as, although its BEP is higher than that of Lob, its MOS is substantially lower. This means that sales volumes within Throw cannot fall as far as within Lob before a loss is made, increasing the risk of Throw.

Throw is also much more operationally geared as it has a much higher proportion of fixed costs than Lob. Since these fixed costs need to be incurred regardless of the sales volume Throw achieves, it is therefore more sensitive to a change in sales demand. This further increases the risk of Throw.

To reduce the risk within Throw the following improvements could be made:

Sales volumes could be increased. This will generate more contribution towards fixed costs. However, there will be an impact on fixed costs as advertising spend may increase which, if the sales volume increase didn't materialise, would further increase breakeven point and reduce margin of safety.

Alternatively sales prices could increase. This would increase contribution without any impact on fixed costs. Care must be taken here as a substantial increase in price could impact on sales volumes, which may cancel out the price increase.

Automation of the production process in Throw may improve efficiency. This will reduce variable production costs, especially labour, and will improve contribution per unit. The BEP will reduce in turn.

Throw could also analyse their fixed costs and work towards reducing these. This will improve Throw's BEP as contribution generated will be covering fewer fixed costs.

Activity 4: LF

(a)   The limiting factor is | machine hours |.

Labour time required = (50 × 2 hr) + (50 × 1 hr) + (50 × 0.5 hr) = 175 hrs

Labour time available = 200 hrs

Machine time required = (50 × 5 hr) + (50 × 2 hr) + (50 × 1 hr) = 400 hrs

Machine time available = 300 hrs

(b)   A is | £10 |

B is | £20 |

C is | £30 |

(c)   A is | 30 units |

B is | 50 units |

C is | 50 units |

Workings

	A	B	C
Contribution/unit	£50	£40	£30
Contribution/machine hour	£10	£20	£30
Rank	3rd	2nd	1st

Production schedule	Hrs used
(1) Produce maximum 50 of C	50
(2) Produce maximum 50 of B	100
(3) Produce A with remaining hours	
$\dfrac{150}{5}$ = 30 units	150
	300

Activity 5: LF Shadow Price

(a)   100 hours of additional labour: £0

There are enough labour hours available to make all require units so no additional labour hours need to be obtained.

(b)   100 hours of additional machine time: £1000 (£10 per hour × 100 hours)

The additional hours will be used to make the maximum amount of A.

The shadow price is therefore the contribution per machine hour on production of A.

Activity 6: Dolphin

Dolphin should buy in some of the components .

The company would save £27,000 by buying in A, but would lose a total of £45,000 if they bought in J & H. This is demonstrated in the below table:

	A	J	H
Cost of making			
Direct material/unit	15	6	18
Direct labour/unit	15	20	22
Variable production overheads/unit	5	4	4
Variable cost of making/unit	35	30	44
Production (units)	5,000	4,000	3,000
Total variable production cost	175,000	120,000	132,000
Incremental fixed costs	2,000	3,000	6,000
Total cost of making	177,000	123,000	138,000

	A	J	H
Cost of buying			
Cost per unit	30	39	50
Production (units)	5,000	4,000	3,000
Total cost of buying	150,000	156,000	150,000
Total cost of making	(177,000)	(123,000)	(138,000)
Additional cost of buying the units	(27,000)	33,000	12,000
Production (units)	0	4,000	3,000

Activity 7: Duo

(a)

	Factory B £000	
Revenue (2,850 × 1.4)	3,990.0	
Materials (784 x 1.4 × 0.95)	1,042.7	
Direct labour (448 × 1.4)	627.2	
Fixed production overheads (420 + 100)	520.0	
Cost of sales	2,189.9	
Gross profit	1,800.1	45.1%
Sales and distribution costs (640 × 1.4)	896.0	
Administration costs (250 + 60)	310.0	
Profit from operations	594.1	14.8%

(b)   Factory A ⬚ should ⬚ be closed down.

This is because the company will be more profitable:

Current profit = 150 + 308 = £458

New profit = £594.1

Activity 8: Hill Ltd

	Current situation £	Proposed situation £
Sales	4,000 units × £125 = 500,000	500,000
Direct materials	3 kg × £5 × 4,000 units = (60,000)	3 kg × £5 × 4,000 units × 90% = (54,000)
Direct labour	6 hrs × £10 × 4,000 units = (240,000)	6 hrs × £10 × 4,000 units × 75% = (180,000)
Fixed costs	(180,000)	180,000 + 47,500 = (227,500)
Profit	**20,000**	**38,500**

It | would | be better to acquire the new equipment.

This is because there will be an increase in profit of £18,500 if the new machine was purchased.

Activity 9: Caston Foods

(a)

	Year 0	Year 1	Year 2	Year 3
Revenue		760,000	920,000	1,060,000
Operating costs		(456,000)	(542,000)	(612,000)
Capital expenditure	(600,000)			
Net cash flows	**(600,000)**	**304,000**	**378,000**	**448,000**
PV factors	1.000	0.877	0.769	0.675
Discounted cash flows	**(600,000)**	**266,608**	**290,682**	**302,400**
Net present value 259,690				

(b) The new type of meal | should | be launched.

This is because it produces a positive NPV, therefore generating additional wealth to the owners of the business.

Activity 10: JLK

Time	0	1	2	3	4	5
Cash flow	(600,000)	(90,000)	(90,000)	(90,000)	(90,000)	10,000
Discount factor	1.000	0.909	0.826	0.751	0.683	0.621
Present value	(600,000) × 1.000 = (600,000)	(90,000) × 0.909 = (81,810)	(90,000) × 0.826 = (74,340)	(90,000) × 0.751 = (67,590)	(90,000) × 0.683 = (61,470)	(10,000) × 0.621 = 6,210
Net present cost	(600,000) + (81,810) + (74,340) + (67,590) + (61,470) + 6,210 = (879,000)					

Test your learning: answers

Chapter 1 Costing Techniques

1

True ☑

| 10,000 units | Cost per unit £43,600/10,000 = | £4.36 |
| 12,000 units | Cost per unit £52,320/12,000 = | £4.36 |

As the cost per unit is the same at each level of production this would appear to be a purely variable cost.

2

Activity level	Total fixed cost £	Fixed cost per unit £
3,000 units	64,000	21.33
10,000 units	64,000	6.40
16,000 units	64,000	4.00

Working

3,000 units	£64,000/3,000 = £21.33
10,000 units	£64,000/10,000 = £6.40
16,000 units	£64,000/16,000 = £4.00

3   The marginal cost per month is

£52,500 .

The full production cost per month is

£70,000 .

Workings

	Production cost £
Direct material costs (£5 × 3,500)	17,500
Direct labour costs (£10 × 3,500)	35,000
Marginal cost	52,500
Rent	10,000
Supervisor cost	7,500
Full production cost	70,000

4   (a)   The variable element of the production cost is

| £3 per unit |
.

The fixed element of the production cost is

| £169,000 |
.

(b)

Level of production	Production cost £
120,000 units	529,000
150,000 units	619,000

Workings

(a)

		£
Highest level	126,000	547,000
Lowest level	101,000	472,000
Increase	25,000	75,000

$$\text{Variable rate} = \frac{£75,000}{25,000} = £3 \text{ per unit}$$

Using highest level:

	£
Variable cost 126,000 × £3	378,000
Fixed costs (balancing figure)	169,000
Total cost	547,000

(b)   (i)

120,000 units	£
Variable cost 120,000 × £3	360,000
Fixed cost	169,000
Total forecast cost	529,000

(ii)

150,000 units	£
Variable cost 150,000 × £3	450,000
Fixed cost	169,000
Total forecast cost	619,000

5 (a)

	✓
£62.50	
£20.00	✓
£15.00	
£100.00	

(b)

	✓
£62.50	
£20.00	
£15.00	✓
£100.00	

Workings

$$\text{Department P1} = \frac{£50,000}{2,500\,h}$$
$$= £20 \text{ per direct labour hour}$$

$$\text{Department P2} = \frac{£60,000}{4,000\,h}$$
$$= £15 \text{ per machine hour}$$

6

	Amount of under-/over-absorption £	Under- or over-absorption	Add or subtract in statement of profit or loss (income statement)
An overhead absorption rate of £3 per unit, based on expected production levels of 500 units. Actual overheads turn out to be £1,600, and actual production is 650 units.	350.00	Over-absorption	Add
The budget is set at 1,000 units, with £9,000 overheads recovered on the basis of 600 direct labour hours. At the end of the period, overheads amounted to £8,600, production achieved was only 950 units and 590 direct labour hours had been worked.	250.00	Over-absorption	Add

Workings

1

	£
Actual overheads	1,600
Absorbed overheads (650 units @ £3 per unit)	1,950
Over-absorption	350

The over-absorption of £350 would be added to profit in the statement of profit or loss (income statement).

2

	£
Actual overheads	8,600
Absorbed overheads (590 hrs × £15* per hr)	8,850
Over-absorption	250

$$\text{* Overhead absorption rate} = \frac{£9,000}{600 \text{ direct labour hours}}$$

= £15 per direct labour hour

The over-absorption of £250 would be added to profit in the statement or profit or loss (income statement).

7   (a)

Department	Overhead absorption rate
X	£2.60 per machine hour
Y	£3.17 per direct labour hour

Workings

$$X = \frac{£260,000}{100,000}$$

= £2.60 per machine hour

As X is a highly mechanised department, most of the overhead will relate to the machinery therefore machine hours have been used to absorb the overhead.

$$Y = \frac{£380,000}{120,000}$$

= £3.17 per direct labour hour

As Y is a highly labour-intensive department, most of the overhead will relate to the hours that are worked by the labour force therefore labour hours are used to absorb the overhead.

(b) The overhead to be included in the cost of product A is £25.68.

Workings

Product A – department X overhead	£2.60 × 5	=	£13.00
Product A – department Y overhead	£3.17 × 4	=	£12.68
			£25.68

8 In an absorption costing system all fixed production overheads are absorbed into the cost of the products and are included in unit cost. In a marginal costing system the fixed production overheads are written off in the statement or profit or loss (income statement) as a period cost.

9

Method of costing	Budgeted cost £
Absorption costing	59.70
Marginal costing	57.11

Workings

1 Absorption costing – unit cost

	£
Direct materials	12.50
Direct labour assembly (4 × £8.40)	33.60
Finishing (1 × £6.60)	6.60
Assembly overheads (£336,000/60,000)	5.60
Finishing overheads (£84,000/60,000)	1.40
	59.70

2 Marginal costing – unit cost

		£
Direct materials		12.50
Direct labour assembly	(4 × £8.40)	33.60
Finishing	(1 × £6.60)	6.60
Assembly overheads	$\dfrac{£336,000 \times 60\%}{60,000}$	3.36
Finishing overheads	$\dfrac{£84,000 \times 75\%}{60,000}$	1.05
		57.11

10 Unit cost

	£
Direct materials	12.00
Direct labour	8.00
Variable overhead (£237,000/15,000)	15.80
Marginal costing unit cost	35.80
Fixed overhead (£390,000/15,000)	26.00
Absorption costing unit cost	61.80

(a) (i) **Absorption costing – statement of profit or loss (income statement)**

	November		December	
	£	£	£	£
Sales				
(12,500/18,000 × £75)		937,500		1,350,000
Less cost of sales				
Opening inventory				
(2,000 × £61.80)	123,600			
(4,500 × £61.80)			278,100	
Production costs				
(15,000 × £61.80)	927,000		927,000	
	1,050,600		1,205,100	
Less closing inventory				
(4,500 × £61.80)	278,100			
(1,500 × £61.80)			92,700	
		772,500		1,112,400
Profit		165,000		237,600

(ii) Marginal costing – statement of profit or loss (income statement)

	November £	November £	December £	December £
Sales				
(12,500/18,000 × £75)		937,500		1,350,000
Less cost of sales				
Opening inventory				
(2,000 × £35.80)	71,600			
(4,500 × £35.80)			161,100	
Production costs				
(15,000 × £35.80)	537,000		537,000	
	608,600		698,100	
Less closing inventory				
(4,500 × £35.80)	161,100			
(1,500 × £35.80)			53,700	
		447,500		644,400
Contribution		490,000		705,600
Less fixed overheads		390,000		390,000
Profit		100,000		315,600

(b)

	November £	December £
Absorption costing profit	165,000	237,600
Inventory changes	(65,000)	78,000
Marginal costing profit	100,000	315,600

Workings

	November £	December £
Increase in inventory × fixed cost per unit		
((4,500 – 2,000) × £26)	(65,000)	
Decrease in inventory × fixed cost per unit		
((4,500 – 1,500) × £26)		78,000

Chapter 2 Statistical techniques

1

	Actual £	Three-month moving average £
July	397,500	
August	403,800	400,300
September	399,600	402,900
October	405,300	403,667
November	406,100	406,633
December	408,500	407,500
January	407,900	408,933
February	410,400	411,433
March	416,000	413,167
April	413,100	415,533
May	417,500	417,467
June	421,800	

2

		Actual £	Four-quarter moving average £	Centred moving average = TREND £	Seasonal variations £
20X5	Quarter 1	383,600			
	Quarter 2	387,600			
			365,400		
	Quarter 3	361,800		365,688	−3,888
			365,975		
	Quarter 4	328,600		366,575	−37,975
			367,175		
20X6	Quarter 1	385,900		366,013	+19,887
			364,850		
	Quarter 2	392,400		366,125	+26,275
			367,400		
	Quarter 3	352,500		368,225	−15,725
			369,050		
	Quarter 4	338,800		371,288	−32,488
			373,525		
20X7	Quarter 1	392,500		375,575	+16,925
			377,625		
	Quarter 2	410,300		378,325	+31,975
			379,025		
	Quarter 3	368,900		379,750	−10,850
			380,475		
	Quarter 4	344,400		382,388	−37,988
			384,300		
20X8	Quarter 1	398,300			
	Quarter 2	425,600			

3

	Cost £	Index
January	59,700	100.0
February	62,300	104.4
March	56,900	95.3
April	60,400	101.2
May	62,400	104.5
June	66,700	111.7

Workings

January	59,700/59,700	= 100.0
February	62,300/59,700	= 104.4
March	56,900/59,700	= 95.3
April	60,400/59,700	= 101.2
May	62,400/59,700	= 104.5
June	66,700/59,700	= 111.7

4 (a)

	Wages cost £	RPI	Adjusted cost £
January	126,700	171.1	126,848
February	129,700	172.0	129,172
March	130,400	172.2	129,718
April	131,600	173.0	130,307
May	130,500	172.1	129,893
June	131,600	171.3	131,600

Workings

	Wages cost £	Adjusted cost £
January	126,700 × 171.3/171.1	126,848
February	129,700 × 171.3/172.0	129,172
March	130,400 × 171.3/172.2	129,718
April	131,600 × 171.3/173.0	130,307
May	130,500 × 171.3/172.1	129,893
June	131,600 × 171.3/171.3	131,600

(b)

	Adjusted cost £	Working	Index
January	126,848	126,848/126,848	100.0
February	129,172	129,172/126,848	101.8
March	129,718	129,718/126,848	102.3
April	130,307	130,307/126,848	102.7
May	129,893	129,893/126,848	102.4
June	131,600	131,600/126,848	103.7

5     $y = 5,000 + 10x$

Production cost of 1,400 units = £19,000

Workings

£15,000 = a + (1,000 × b)

£25,000 = a + (2,000 × b)

£(25,000 − 15,000) = (a + (2,000 × b)) − (a + (1,000 × b))

£10,000 = a + 2,000b − a − 1,000b

£10,000 = 1,000 × b

b = £10,000/1,000 = £10

£15,000 = a + (1,000 × 10)

a = £15,000 − £10,000

a = £5,000

so the regression line is y = 5,000 + 10 b

Production cost of 1,400 units = 5,000 + (10 × 1,400) = £19,000

6

	Production Units	Costs £
January	5,400	17,320
February	5,600	17,480
March	5,700	17,560
April	6,000	17,800
May	5,500	17,400
June	6,100	17,880

Workings

Stores costs:		
January	13,000 + (0.8 × 5,400)	17,320
February	13,000 + (0.8 × 5,600)	17,480
March	13,000 + (0.8 × 5,700)	17,560
April	13,000 + (0.8 × 6,000)	17,800
May	13,000 + (0.8 × 5,500)	17,400
June	13,000 + (0.8 × 6,100)	17,880

7

	Value of x	Trend	Seasonal variation	Forecast sales
Quarter 1 20X9	13	2,785	–200	2,585
Quarter 2 20X9	14	2,830	+500	3,330
Quarter 3 20X9	15	2,875	+350	3,225
Quarter 4 20X9	16	2,920	–650	2,270

Workings

Value of x for Quarter 1, 20X9

Quarter 1 20X6   =   1

Add 3 years of 4 quarters   12

            =   13

Trend for Quarter 1, 20X9: 2,200 + (45 × 13) = 2,785
Trend for Quarter 2, 20X9: 2,200 + (45 × 14) = 2,830
Trend for Quarter 3, 20X9: 2,200 + (45 × 15) = 2,875
Trend for Quarter 4, 20X9: 2,200 + (45 × 16) = 2,920

Chapter 3   Standard costing

1   The information for the amount of labour time for each cost unit would come from payroll records such as time sheets or from physical observations such as time and motion studies. Factors that should be taken into account include:

- The level of skill or training of the labour grade to be used on the product
- Any anticipated changes on the grade of labour used on the product
- Any anticipated changes in work methods or productivity levels
- The effect of any bonus scheme on productivity

The hourly rate for the direct labour can be found from payroll records but the following factors should be considered:

- Anticipated pay rises
- Anticipated changes in grade of labour
- Effect of any bonus scheme on the labour rate
- Whether any anticipated overtime is built into the hourly rate

2   The information for the amount of material required for each unit of a product can be found from the original product specification – the amount originally considered necessary for each unit. Factors that should be taken into account include:

- The level of skill of the labour to be used on the product

- Any anticipated changes to the quality of material sourced

- Any anticipated changes in work methods/equipment used to work the material

However, this figure may be amended over time as the actual amount used in production is monitored.

The basic price of the material can be found from suppliers' quotations or invoices. However, when setting the standard, the following should also be taken into account:

- General inflation rates

- Any foreseen increases in the price of this particular material

- Any seasonality in the price

- Any discounts available for bulk purchases

- Any anticipated scarcity of the material which may mean paying a higher price

3   Ideal standards are set on the basis of perfect working conditions. No allowance is made for normal wastage or inefficiencies.

Target standards are standards that are set on the basis of normal working conditions by building in some element to reflect normal wastage or inefficiencies. Target standards are capable of being met by efficient operations.

Basic standards are the original historical standards based upon the original expectations of cost for the product.

4   Ideal standards assume perfect operating conditions exist at all times, making them very difficult to achieve. As a result, staff performance is controlled on very tight targets, putting them under extreme pressure. This can therefore result in demotivated staff.

Chapter 4 Variance Analysis

1   (a)   Total materials cost variance

	£
Standard cost of actual production	
1,800 units should have cost (× 7 kg × £6.00)	75,600
But did cost	70,800
	4,800 (F)

(b)   Materials price variance

	£
12,000 kg should have cost (× £6.00)	72,000
But did cost	70,800
	1,200 (F)

(c)   Materials usage variance

1,800 units should have used (× 7 kg)	12,600
But did use	12,000
Variance in kg	600 (F)
× standard price per kg	× £6
Material usage variance in £	3,600 (F)

2   (a)   Total labour cost variance

	£
Standard cost of actual production	
1,800 units should have cost (× £17)	30,600
But did cost	25,000
	5,600 (F)

(b)   Labour rate variance

Actual hours at standard rate	
5,000 hrs should cost (× £6.80)	34,000
But did cost	25,000
	9,000 (F)

(c)   Labour efficiency variance

Standard hours for actual production at standard rate	
1,800 units should have taken (× 2.5 hrs)	4,500
But did take	5,000
	500 (A)
× standard rate per hour	× £6.80
	3,400 (A)

3   (a)   Standard materials for 6,400 units:

6,400 units × 5,500 kg/7,000 units = 5,029 kg

(b)   Standard labour hours for 6,400 units:

6,400 units × 10,000 hrs/7,000 units = 9,143 hrs

(c)   Standard machine hours for 6,400 units:

6,400 units × 21,000 hrs/7,000 units = 19,200 hrs

4 (a) Fixed overhead expenditure variance

	£
Budgeted fixed overhead	52,500
Actual fixed overhead expenditure	56,000
Fixed overhead expenditure variance	3,500 (A)

(b) Fixed overhead volume variance

	Units
Budgeted output	7,000
Actual output	6,400
Volume variance in units	600 (A)
Standard fixed overhead cost per unit	£7.50
Fixed overhead volume variance in £	4,500 Adv

(c) Fixed overhead efficiency variance

6,400 units should take (× 3 hrs)	19,200 hrs
But did take	20,000 hrs
Efficiency variance in hours	800 hrs (A)
× Standard absorption rate per hour	× £2.50
Fixed overhead efficiency variance	£2,000 Adv

(d) Fixed overhead capacity variance

Budgeted hours of work (7,000 × 3 hrs)	21,000 hrs
Actual hours of work	20,000 hrs
Capacity variance in hours	1,000 hrs (A)
× Standard absorption rate per hour	× £2.50
Capacity variance in £	2,500 (A)

Chapter 5 Operating Statements

1 (a) Materials price variance

	£
7,500 kg should have cost (× £3.60)	27,000
But did cost	25,900
	1,100 (F)

Materials usage variance

	£
1,750 units should have used (× 4.2 kg)	7,350 kg
But did use	7,500 kg
Materials usage variance in kg	150 kg (A)
× Standard price per kg	× £3.60
Materials usage variance in £	540 (A)

(b) Labour rate variance

	£
2,580 hrs should have cost (× £7.80)	20,124
But did cost	20,600
	476 (A)

Labour efficiency variance

1,750 units should have taken (× 1.5 hrs)	2,625 hrs
But did take	2,580 hrs
Efficiency variance in hrs	45 hrs (F)
× Standard rate per hour	× £7.80
Labour efficiency variance in £	351 (F)

(c) Fixed overhead expenditure variance

Budgeted fixed overhead 1,800 × £4.20	7,560
Actual fixed overhead	8,100
Fixed overhead expenditure variance	540 (A)

Fixed overhead efficiency variance

Efficiency variance in hours (same as labour efficiency)	45 hrs (F)
× Standard fixed overhead absorption rate per hour	£2.80
Fixed overhead efficiency variance in £	126 (F)

Fixed overhead capacity variance

Budgeted hours of work (1,800 × 1.5)	2,700 hrs
Actual hours of work	2,580 hrs
Capacity variance in hours	120 hrs (A)
× Standard fixed overhead absorption rate per hour	× £2.80
Capacity variance in £	336 (A)

(d) Standard cost of actual production

Direct materials 1,750 × 4.2 × £3.60	26,460
Direct labour 1,750 × 1.5 × £7.80	20,475
Fixed overhead 1,750 × £4.20	7,350
Total cost 1,750 × £31.02	54,285

Operating statement – Absorption costing

	Favourable variances	Adverse variances	£
Variances:			
Materials price	1,100		
Materials usage		540	
Labour rate		476	
Labour efficiency	351		
Fixed overhead expenditure		540	
Fixed overhead efficiency	126		
Fixed overhead capacity		336	
	1,577	1,892	315 (A)
Actual cost of production			54,600

2 (a) Total direct materials cost variance

	£
Standard cost of actual production	
2,400 × 12 × £4.80	138,240
Actual cost of actual production	145,000
	6,760 (A)

Materials price variance

	£
Actual quantity should have cost	
29,600 × £4.80	142,080
But did cost	145,000
	2,920 (A)

Materials usage variance

Actual production should have used (2,400 × 12)	28,800 kg
But did use	29,600 kg
Materials usage variance in kg	800 kg (A)
× Standard price per kg	£4.80
Materials usage variance in £	3,840 (A)

(b) Total direct labour variance

Standard labour cost of actual production	
2,400 × 3 × £8.00	57,600
Actual labour cost of actual production	56,200
	1,400 (F)

Labour rate variance

Actual hours should have cost	
6,900 × £8.00	55,200
But did cost	56,200
Labour rate variance	1,000 (A)

Labour efficiency variance

Actual production should have taken	
2,400 × 3	7,200
But did take	6,900
Labour efficiency variance in hours	300 hrs (F)
× Standard rate per hour	£8
Labour efficiency variance in £	2,400 (F)

(c) Fixed overhead expenditure variance

Actual fixed overhead	92,000
Budgeted fixed overhead	95,000
	3,000 (F)

(d) Standard cost of production

	£
Direct materials 2,400 × 12 × £4.80	138,240
Direct labour 2,400 × 3 × £8.00	57,600
Standard variable cost (2,400 × 81.60)	195,840

			£
Standard variable cost of actual production			195,840
Budgeted fixed overhead			95,000
Variances	**Favourable variances**	**Adverse variances**	
Materials price		2,920	
Materials usage		3,840	
Labour rate		1,000	
Labour efficiency	2,400		
Fixed overhead expenditure	3,000		
	5,400	7,760	2,360 (A)
Total actual cost			293,200

Chapter 6 Standard costing – further aspects

1   REPORT

To: Managing Director
From: Accountant
Date: xx.xx.xx
Subject: November production cost variances

The November production cost is 5% more than the standard cost for the actual production, due to a number of fairly significant adverse variances.

The main cause appears to have been the labour that was used in production for the month which was a more junior grade than normal due to staff shortages. Although this has given a favourable labour rate variance, it has also caused adverse labour efficiency and materials usage variances due to inefficiencies and wastage from the staff. This inefficiency in labour hours has also led to the fixed overhead efficiency adverse variance.

For future months we should either ensure that we have enough of the normal grade of labour for production of this product or train the junior staff in the production process.

There is also an adverse materials price variance which has been due to an increase in the price of our materials. As it is believed that this is a permanent price increase by all suppliers, we should consider altering the direct materials standard cost to reflect this, otherwise each month we will have adverse materials price variances.

The factory now has an additional rent cost which has presumably caused the adverse fixed overhead expenditure variance. If the additional inventory requirement and hence the additional rent is a permanent change then this should be built into the budgeted fixed overhead figure.

Due to the labour inefficiency, more hours have been worked than were budgeted for, leading to the favourable capacity variance. This indicates that the factory has more capacity than we have been making use of which, if the inefficiencies are sorted out, could be used to increase monthly production if required.

2

Scenario	Possible effects
A business replaces machinery with new equipment	• Favourable materials usage variance, if new machinery leads to less waste • Alternatively, adverse materials usage variance, if workers have to adapt to using new machinery • Adverse fixed overheads expenditure variance (higher depreciation charged, although overheads may decrease leading to favourable variance if more power-efficient) • Favourable labour efficiency if workers can work faster (and so favourable overhead efficiency variance)
A company has supply issues with a raw material	• Adverse materials price variance • Possible adverse materials usage variance, if can only source inferior material • Adverse labour efficiency variance (idle time) if no material for production • Possible adverse labour rate efficiency, if must use overtime to catch up, when material does become available

3   Materials price variance

	£
Actual kg should cost (1000 + 268)	1,268
Actual kg did cost	1,000
	268 F

The actual quantity of materials purchased = £1,268/£22 = $\boxed{58}$ kg

Labour rate variance

	£
768 hours should cost (22,560 – 636)	21,924
768 hours did cost	22,560
	636 A

The standard labour rate = £21,924/768 hrs = £ $\boxed{28.55}$

4 Fixed overhead expenditure variance

	£
Budgeted overheads	78,000
Actual overheads (78,000 – 8,500)	69,500
	8,500 F

Fixed overhead total variance

	£
Overheads absorbed (69,500 – 4,400)	65,100
Actual overheads	69,500
Under-absorbed overhead (8,500 – 12,900)	4,400

The standard labour hours for the period = $\dfrac{65,100}{4.2}$ = $\boxed{15,500}$ hours

5 Uncontrollable variance

	£
800 hours should cost (800 × £5.00)	4,000
800 hours should now cost (800 × £6.50)	5,200
	1,200 A

Controllable variance

	£
800 hours should now cost	5,200
800 hours did cost	4,900
	300 F

1

	April	May	June	Total
Productivity per labour hour	10.9 units	10.7 units	11.1 units	10.9 units
Efficiency ratio	98.8%	97.6%	101.2%	99.2%
Capacity ratio	102.7%	101.2%	101.2%	101.7%
Activity ratio	101.4%	98.8%	102.4%	100.9%
Value added per employee	£2,552	£2,524	£2,717	£2,598

Workings

	April	May	June	Total

(a) Productivity per labour hour

$$\frac{121,700}{11,200} \qquad \frac{123,500}{11,500} \qquad \frac{128,000}{11,500} \qquad \frac{373,200}{34,200}$$

$$= 10.9 \text{ units} \quad = 10.7 \text{ units} \quad = 11.1 \text{ units} \quad = 10.9 \text{ units}$$

(b) Standard hours for actual production

$$\frac{121,700}{11} \qquad \frac{123,500}{11} \qquad \frac{128,000}{11} \qquad \frac{373,200}{11}$$

$$= 11,064 \qquad = 11,227 \qquad = 11,636 \qquad = 33,927$$

Efficiency ratio

$$\frac{11,064}{11,200} \times 100 \quad \frac{11,227}{11,500} \times 100 \quad \frac{11,636}{11,500} \times 100 \quad \frac{33,927}{34,200} \times 100$$

$$= 98.8\% \qquad = 97.6\% \qquad = 101.2\% \qquad = 99.2\%$$

(c) Budgeted hours

$$\frac{120,000}{11} \qquad \frac{125,000}{11} \qquad \frac{125,000}{11} \qquad \frac{370,000}{11}$$

$$= 10,909 \qquad = 11,364 \qquad = 11,363 \qquad = 33,636$$

Capacity ratio

$$\frac{11,200}{10,909} \times 100 \quad \frac{11,500}{11,364} \times 100 \quad \frac{11,500}{11,363} \times 100 \quad \frac{34,200}{33,636} \times 100$$

$$= 102.7\% \qquad = 101.2\% \qquad = 101.2\% \qquad = 101.7\%$$

(d) Activity ratio

$$\frac{11,064}{10,909} \times 100 \quad \frac{11,227}{11,364} \times 100 \quad \frac{11,636}{11,363} \times 100 \quad \frac{33,927}{33,636} \times 100$$

$$= 101.4\% \qquad = 98.8\% \qquad = 102.4\% \qquad = 100.9\%$$

(e) Value added

£625,000 – £418,300	£206,700			
£634,000 – £424,500		£209,500		
£656,000 – £430,500			£225,500	£641,700
Value added per employee	$\dfrac{206,700}{81}$	$\dfrac{209,500}{83}$	$\dfrac{225,500}{83}$	$\dfrac{641,700}{247}$
	= £2,552	= £2,524	= £2,717	= £2,598

2

	Mar	Apr	May
Gross profit margin	42.2%	37.3%	39.3%
Net profit margin	10.9%	10.6%	11.3%
% expenses to revenue	31.3%	26.7%	28.0%
Return on capital employed	15.0%	16.5%	17.1%
Asset turnover	1.38	1.55	1.52

Workings

(a)

		Mar	Apr	May
(i)	Gross profit margin	$\dfrac{190}{450}$	$\dfrac{190}{510}$	$\dfrac{220}{560}$
		42.2%	37.3%	39.3%
(ii)	Operating profit margin	$\dfrac{49}{450}$	$\dfrac{54}{510}$	$\dfrac{63}{560}$
		10.9%	10.6%	11.3%
(iii)	Expenses to revenue	$\dfrac{141}{450}$	$\dfrac{136}{510}$	$\dfrac{157}{560}$
		31.3%	26.7%	28.0%
(iv)	Return on capital employed	$\dfrac{49}{(396-69)}$	$\dfrac{54}{(413-85)}$	$\dfrac{63}{(467-99)}$
		15.0%	16.5%	17.1%
(v)	Asset turnover	$\dfrac{450}{(396-69)}$	$\dfrac{510}{(413-85)}$	$\dfrac{560}{(467-99)}$
		1.38	1.55	1.52

(b) Gross profit margin

The decrease in the gross profit margin in April has mainly been driven by increasing cost of sales. Although revenue has increased between the two months, cost in sales did not increase in line with it. This has worsened the gross profit margin between March and April.

The increase in May is predominantly due to good cost control within cost of sales. Once again cost of sales have not increased in line with revenue – they have increased only marginally. This has led to an improved gross profit margin.

Return on capital employed

The increase of return on capital employed between March and April can be attributed to improving asset turnover and operating profit margin. Assets are being used more efficiently to generate revenue whereas the expense as a percentage of revenue has dropped. This has enabled more profit to be made, hence a greater return being generated.

Between April and May asset turnover has dropped, meaning the business is using assets less efficiently to generate revenue. However even better cost control has been managed, helping to improve the operating profit margin. The increase in ROCE can therefore be attributed more to good cost control rather than good revenue performance.

3

	20X6	20X7	20X8
Gross profit margin	46.3%	47.6%	44.4%
Operating profit margin	11.0%	11.8%	9.4%
Return on capital employed	18.0%	16.4%	12.7%
Asset turnover	1.64	1.39	1.34
Non-current asset turnover	2.13	1.88	1.81
Current ratio	4.8:1	5.6:1	5.2:1
Quick ratio	3.2:1	4.0:1	3.6:1
Receivables' collection period	38 days	48 days	52 days
Inventory days	41 days	45 days	49 days
Payables' payment period	25 days	28 days	30 days
Interest cover	N/A	33.3	28.3
Gearing ratio	N/A	8.9%	8.1%

Workings

		20X6	**20X7**	**20X8**
(a)	Gross profit margin	$\frac{380}{820} \times 100$	$\frac{405}{850} \times 100$	$\frac{400}{900} \times 100$
		46.3%	47.6%	44.4%
(b)	Operating profit margin	$\frac{90}{820} \times 100$	$\frac{100}{850} \times 100$	$\frac{85}{900} \times 100$
		11.0%	11.8%	9.4%
(c)	Return on capital employed	$\frac{90}{500} \times 100$	$\frac{100}{610} \times 100$	$\frac{85}{670} \times 100$
		18.0%	16.4%	12.7%
(d)	Asset turnover	$\frac{820}{500}$	$\frac{850}{610}$	$\frac{900}{670}$
		1.64	1.39	1.34
(e)	Non-current asset turnover	$\frac{820}{385}$	$\frac{850}{453}$	$\frac{900}{498}$
		2.13	1.88	1.81
(f)	Current ratio	$\frac{145}{30}$	$\frac{191}{34}$	$\frac{213}{41}$
		4.8	5.6	5.2
(g)	Quick ratio	$\frac{95}{30}$	$\frac{136}{34}$	$\frac{146}{41}$
		3.2	4.0	3.6
(h)	Receivables' collection period	$\frac{85}{820} \times 365$	$\frac{112}{850} \times 365$	$\frac{128}{900} \times 365$
		38 days	48 days	52 days
(i)	Inventory days	$\frac{50}{440} \times 365$	$\frac{55}{445} \times 365$	$\frac{67}{500} \times 365$
		41 days	45 days	49 days
(j)	Payables' payment period	$\frac{30}{440} \times 365$	$\frac{34}{445} \times 365$	$\frac{41}{500} \times 365$
		25 days	28 days	30 days
(k)	Interest cover	N/A	100/3	85/3
			= 33.3	= 28.3
(l)	Gearing ratio	N/A	50/560 × 100	50/620 × 100
			= 8.9%	= 8.1%

4

		Firmwell	**Hartfield**
	Cost of sales	$51 + 210 - 56$	$45 + 165 - 50$
		$= £205,000$	$= £160,000$
(i)	Gross profit margin	$\dfrac{335,000}{540,000} \times 100$	$\dfrac{210,000}{370,000} \times 100$
		62.0%	56.8%
(ii)	Operating profit margin	$\dfrac{65,000}{540,000} \times 100$	$\dfrac{35,000}{370,000} \times 100$
		12.0%	9.5%
(iii)	Return on net assets	$\dfrac{65,000}{550,000} \times 100$	$\dfrac{35,000}{410,000} \times 100$
		11.8%	8.5%
(iv)	Net asset turnover	$\dfrac{540,000}{550,000}$	$\dfrac{370,000}{410,000}$
		0.98	0.90
(v)	Average inventory	$\dfrac{51+56}{2}$	$\dfrac{45+50}{2}$
		£53,500	£47,500
	Inventory days	$\dfrac{53,500}{205,000} \times 365$	$\dfrac{47,500}{160,000} \times 365$
		95 days	108 days
(vi)	Payables' payment period	$\dfrac{25,800}{205,000} \times 365$	$\dfrac{27,500}{160,000} \times 365$
		46 days	63 days
(vii)	Sales per sq m	$\dfrac{540,000}{2,400}$	$\dfrac{370,000}{1,700}$
		£225	£218
(viii)	Sales per employee	$\dfrac{540,000}{28}$	$\dfrac{370,000}{13}$
		£19,286	£28,462
(ix)	Sales per hour worked	$\dfrac{540,000}{30,500}$	$\dfrac{370,000}{14,100}$
		£17.70	£26.24

(b)   REPORT

To: Sales Director

From: Accounts Assistant

Date: xx.xx.xx

Subject: Performance of stores

I have considered the performance figures for our two stores in Firmwell and Hartfield for the first six months of the year. The key factors that have appeared from these figures are addressed below.

Firmwell has a higher gross profit margin than Hartfield. This could be because sales volumes are not as high in Hartfield, as its inventory days are higher than that of Firmwell. This implies that revenue is not being generated as efficiently in Hartfield, having a negative impact on their gross profit margin. Hartfield could try and emulate Firmwell's revenue per square metre by looking at their store layout. This should help to drive up the gross profit margin in the future.

Hartfield, however, does have the highest productivity as sales per employee and sales per hour worked are higher than Firmwell. This implies that the lower gross profit margin is not due to inefficient use of staff – indeed its direct costs are much lower than that of Firmwell.

Firmwell has a higher operating profit margin and return on net assets. Firmwell therefore has better control of its expenses than Hartfield. If the Firmwell practices can be emulated in Hartfield, this could improve Hartfield's profitability.

Hartfield does have a better liquidity position as, despite having longer inventory days, it has a longer payables period, meaning its working capital cycle is lower. Both stores can learn from each other to improve their liquidity – Firmwell can emulate Hartfield's payables control, and Hartfield can emulate Firmwell's inventory control.

5   Financial performance indicators are **not useful on their own.** They need to be assessed to a comparator, either a previous financial indicator or a financial indicator of a competitor

Financial performance indicators are an **historic measurement.** They therefore give little reassurance to the future performance of an organisation.

Financial performance indictors **do not convey the full picture** of what is happening within an organisation. A range of non-financial indicators is therefore useful to the organisation to put their financial performance into context.

As financial indicators are mostly based around profit they encourage managers to **focus on the short-term**. Managers may therefore be discouraged to take decisions for the long-term benefit of the organisation.

6

(a) Gross profit margin $= \dfrac{\text{Gross profit}}{\text{Revenue}}$

44% $= \dfrac{\text{Gross profit}}{£106,500}$

44% × £106,500 = Gross profit

Gross profit = £46,860

(b) Gross profit margin $= \dfrac{\text{Gross profit}}{\text{Revenue}}$

37.5% $= \dfrac{£105,000}{\text{Revenue}}$

Revenue $= \dfrac{£105,000}{0.375}$

Revenue = £280,000

(c) Gross profit = £256,000 × 41%

= £104,960

Operating profit = £256,000 × 13.5%

= £34,560

Expenses = £104,960 − 34,560

= £70,400

(d) ROCE $= \dfrac{\text{Operating profit}}{\text{Capital employed}}$

12.8% $= \dfrac{£50,000}{\text{Capital employed}}$

Capital employed $= \dfrac{£50,000}{0.128}$

= £390,625

(e) ROCE = Operating profit margin × Asset turnover

15% = 10% × Asset turnover

$\dfrac{15\%}{10\%}$ = Asset turnover

Asset turnover = 1.5

(f) Average inventory $= \dfrac{118,000+104,000}{2}$

= £111,000

Inventory turnover $= \dfrac{\text{Cost of sales}}{\text{Average inventory}}$

$= \dfrac{£118,000+465,000-104,000}{£111,000}$

= 4.3 times

(g) Receivables' collection $=\dfrac{\text{Receivables}}{\text{Revenue}}\times 365$
     period

     64 days $=\dfrac{64{,}000}{\text{Revenue}}\times 365$

     Revenue $=\dfrac{64{,}000}{64\,\text{days}}\times 365$

              $=\ \pounds 365{,}000$

7   Financial
     Customer
     Innovation and learning
     Internal

Chapter 8 Cost management

1   **Development** – Fixed research and development costs

     Introductory – Continuing research and development costs, fixed advertising expenditure, low level direct materials and labour costs

     Growth – Continuing advertising and promotion expenditure, high level of direct materials and labour costs, high fixed and variable production overheads

     Maturity – Lower level of direct materials and labour costs due to economies of scale, higher level of production overheads due to mechanisation

     Decline – Low level of direct materials and labour, production overheads low, decommissioning and opportunity costs high due to wastage of obsolete stock

2

Year	Cash flows £	Discount factor at 7%	Present value £
0	(340,000)	1.000	(340,000)
1	80,000	0.935	74,800
2	70,000	0.873	61,110
3	90,000	0.816	73,440
4	120,000	0.763	91,560
5	60,000	0.713	42,780
NPV			3,690

Remember that depreciation is not a cash flow and is therefore excluded from the net present value calculations.

3　(a)

Year	Cash flows £	Discount factor at 11%	Present value £
0	(90,000)	1.000	(90,000)
1	23,000	0.901	20,723
2	31,000	0.812	25,172
3	40,000	0.731	29,240
4	18,000	0.659	11,862
NPV			(3,003)

(b)　The organisation ⟨should not⟩ invest in the plant and machinery

4

	Development	Introduction	Growth	Maturity	Decline	Total
Sales volume (units)		5,000	13,000	25,000	10,000	
	£000	£000	£000	£000	£000	£000
Revenue		£250 × 5 1,250	£250 × 13 3,250	£200 × 25 5,000	£150 × 10 1,500	11,000
Variable cost		£150 × 5 (750)	£130 × 13 (1,690)	£70 × 25 (1,750)	£85 × 10 (850)	(5,040)
Fixed Overhead		(800)	(650)	(450)	(460)	(2,360)
Development cost	(400)					(400)
Scrap cost					(60)	(60)
Profit	(400)	(300)	910	2,800	130	3,140

5

	£
Target selling price	90
Target profit margin (90 × 20%)	(18)
Target cost	72

6　**Value analysis** assesses the composition of a product that is currently in production, and its associated production process. Improvements are then sought to both the product and the process. This reduces the cost of production, resulting in a lower cost per unit.

Value engineering assesses the composition of a product that is not currently in production and is currently in its design stage. It looks at elements of the proposed product and assess whether each element adds value to the overall product. Elements that don't add value are subsequently eliminated, reducing the production cost of the product once it goes into production.

Chapter 9 Activity Based Costing

1   Activity based costing absorbs costs using **multiple bases,** and therefore establishes different reasons why overheads are incurred. This differs to absorption costing which assumes that overheads are incurred for one reason and therefore uses one base, such as labour or machine hours.

Due to the fact the activity based costing recognises there are different reasons for overheads to be incurred it therefore absorbs overhead using **multiple overhead absorption rate.** This differs from absorption costing that absorbs overhead using a single overhead absorption rate.

Activity based costing assumes that overheads are **not volume related,** ie if more units are produced the overhead remains unaffected. This differs from absorption costing which assumes that as more units are produced more overheads are incurred as a result.

2

Product	Budgeted cost per unit £	Budgeted overhead per unit £
LM	9.78	3.68
NP	27.41	20.81

Workings

1   Stores cost
$$= \frac{£140,000}{320}$$
$$= £437.50 \text{ per materials requisition}$$

2   Production set-up costs
$$= \frac{£280,000}{280}$$
$$= £1,000 \text{ per set-up}$$

3   Quality control costs
$$= \frac{£180,000}{90}$$
$$= £2,000 \text{ per inspection}$$

Product costs		LM £	NP £
Direct materials	50,000 × £2.60	130,000	
	20,000 × £3.90		78,000
Direct labour	50,000 × £3.50	175,000	
	20,000 × £2.70		54,000

Product costs		LM £	NP £
Stores costs	100 × £437.50	43,750	
	220 × £437.50		96,250
Production set-up costs	80 × £1,000	80,000	
	200 × £1,000		200,000
Quality control costs	30 × £2,000	60,000	
	60 × £2,000		120,000
Total cost		488,750	548,250
Cost per unit		488,750	548,250
		50,000	20,000
		= £9.78	= £27.41

Analysis of total unit cost

Direct costs	(2.60 + 3.50)	6.10	
	(3.90 + 2.70)		6.60
Overheads	$\dfrac{(43,750+80,000+60,000)}{50,000}$	3.68	
	$\dfrac{(96,250+200,000+120,000)}{20,000}$		20.81
		9.78	27.41

3   Activity based costing gives a **more realistic estimate** of cost usage by products. This in turn gives a more accurate reflection of profits, meaning a more realistic price can be set to recover those costs.

Activity based costing aids better **cost control and reduction** as cost drivers are more visible. This helps managers to find methods to reduce usage of cost drivers that are generating high overheads.

Activity based costing aids better **profitability analysis** of products as a more realistic profit is calculated. This will enhance the organisation's performance reporting.

Activity based costing recognises the **complexity and diversity** of the production process. It therefore enables managers to establish the true reasons why costs are incurred rather than assuming that overheads are incurred simply because more units have been produced.

4   Activity based costing is **time consuming** and therefore expensive, as it relies on collection and interpretation of a vast array of data.

Activity based costing has **limited use if only one product is produced** as the production overheads incurred tend to be more complex if a diverse product range is produced.

Activity based costing will still need some **arbitrary apportionment** as it is sometimes not obvious which cost driver is related to which cost pool.

The **amount of overhead absorption rates** calculated can be vast. It therefore makes standard cost cards complicated and difficult to interpret.

Chapter 10   Decision-making techniques

1   The BEP is ⎡ 30,000 ⎤ units.

The MOS is ⎡ 21 ⎤ %.

Workings

BEP $= \dfrac{£360,000}{£57-£45}$

$=$ 30,000 units

MOS $= \dfrac{38,000-30,000}{38,000}$

$=$ 21%

2   The amount of units that needs to be sold is ⎡ 201,429 ⎤ units.

Target profit sales $= \dfrac{£910,000+£500,000}{£24-£17}$

$=$ 201,429 units

3   The sales revenue required in order to make a profit of £200,000 is £ ⎡ 1,500,000 ⎤ .

Workings

1   Profit volume ratio $= \dfrac{£(40-32)}{£40}\times100$

$=$ 20%

2   Target profit sales revenue $= \dfrac{£100,000+£200,000}{0.20}$

$=$ £1,500,000

4   (a)   The limiting factor of production resources is ⎡ machine hours ⎤ .

Working

Resource requirements for maximum demand

	R	S	T	Total
Materials	80,000 kg	120,000 kg	25,000 kg	225,000 kg
Labour hours	20,000 hours	80,000 hours	5,000 hours	105,000 hours
Machine hours	60,000 hours	80,000 hours	15,000 hours	155,000 hours

The limiting factor is machine hours.

(b)

Product	Units produced
S	20,000
T	5,000
R	4,166

Workings

Contribution per machine hour

	R	S	T
Contribution	£6	£12	£6
Machine hours	6	4	3
Contribution/machine hour	£1.00	£3.00	£2.00
Ranking	3	1	2

Production plan

Product	Units produced	Machine hours used
S	20,000	80,000
T	5,000	15,000
R (balance 25,000/6 = 4,166.67 = 4,166 complete units)	4,166	24,996
		119,996

(c) The profit that will be earned under this production plan is £ 244,996 .

Workings

Product contribution:	£
R (4,166 × £6)	24,996
S (20,000 × £12)	240,000
T (5,000 × £6)	30,000
Total contribution	294,996
Less fixed costs	(50,000)
Profit	244,996

5 The business should buy in neither product .

	X £	Y £
Direct materials	2.50	3.00
Direct labour	8.00	6.00
Variable cost of production	10.50	9.00
External price	11.00	10.00

On the basis of costs alone, neither product should be purchased externally as they are cheaper to make.

6 Timmy should pay £ 17,500 for additional labour hours (£3.50 × 5,000 hours).

Synoptic assessment preparation

The questions below are ones to consider once you have completed and passed your assessment. Thinking these questions through will enable you to consider the topics covered in the *Management Accounting: Decision and Control* syllabus in a 'real world' context. This is a vital skill to develop before you attempt the synoptic assessment.

The questions presented are short-form questions. In the real synoptic assessment they will be attached to a wider case study.

Questions

(1) You are asked to consider the pricing strategy for two new products of a business. You have been given the following information regarding the new products:

	£ per unit	
	P1	**P2**
Direct materials	3.00	7.00
Direct labour	5.00	11.00
Variable production overhead	2.50	5.30
Fixed production overhead	1.45	3.30
Competitor sales price	14.50	32.00

The sales manager has suggested that you should price the products at 20% mark-up over marginal cost.

(a) Calculate the marginal cost of each product.
(b) Calculate the sales price of each product.
(c) Explain the impact that this pricing policy will have on the business.

(2) In order to close a cost gap of a new product, the production manager of JamJar Ltd. has proposed mechanising part of the production process. Alongside reducing the cost of production, mechanisation will also bring the JamJar in line with developments in the wider industry – indeed most of JamJar's competitors have installed this machinery and are seeing improvements in sales volumes as a result.

The costs of mechanising the production line are given below:

	20X1	20X2	20X3	20X4	20X5
Purchase cost	100,000				
Labour cost saving		10,000	8,000	6,400	5,120
Annual running costs		7,500	7,500	7,500	7,500
Increase in sales revenue		25,000	27,500	30,000	33,000

The discount rates for 12% cost of capital are given below:

0	1.000
1	0.893
2	0.797
3	0.712
4	0.636

(a) Calculate the net present value of mechanising the production line.

	Yr 0	Yr 1	Yr 2	Yr 3	Yr 4
Purchase cost					
Labour cost saving					
Annual running costs					
Increase in sales revenue					
Net cash flow					
Discount factor					
Present value					
Net present value					

(b) What are the potential advantages of mechanising the production line?

(c) What are the potential drawbacks of mechanising the production line?

(3) You are analysing resource utilisation for the coming periods and have established that there isn't enough labour hours available to cover production.

(a) What actions can the business take to access more labour hours?

(b) What are the potential consequences of the above actions?

(4) HeetMe Ltd has been reviewing the quality of the solar panels and has engineered two new products, the SP2000 and the SP3000.

The SP2000 is a low quality product with an economic life of 5 years. The SP3000 is a high quality product with an economic life of 20 years.

The Sales Director has provided information about the expected demand and price for the SP2000 and SP3000 for the coming year.

- SP2000 will be priced at £200 per panel and demand is expected to be around 9,000 units per year.

- SP3000 will be priced at £300 per panel and demand is expected to be around 5,000 units per year.

Forecast statement of profit or loss

	SP2000	SP3000
Volume	9,000 units	5,000 units
	£	£
Turnover	1,800,000	1,500,000
Cost of production		
Direct materials (glass)	540,000	300,000
Direct labour	126,000	175,000
Fixed production overheads	120,000	120,000
Total cost of sales	786,000	595,000
Gross profit	1,014,000	905,000
Selling and distribution costs	400,000	400,000
Administration costs	200,000	200,000
Operating profit	414,000	305,000
Extracts from the forecast statement of financial position		
	£	£
Material inventory (glass)	60,000	60,000
Finished goods inventory	0	0
Turnover	2,014,000	1,905,000

(a) Calculate the following performance indicators for both products:

    (i)   **Gross profit margin**

    (ii)   **Operating profit margin**

    (iii) **Direct materials cost per unit**

    (iv) **Direct labour cost per unit**

    (v)   **Fixed production overheads cost per unit**

    (vi) **Return on net assets**

    (vii) **Raw materials inventory turnover in days**

(b) Compare the performance of each product, referring to the following:

    (i)   **Sales price per unit**

    (ii)   **Materials, labour and fixed cost per unit**

    (iii) **Return on net assets**

Potential answers

(1)

    (a)

	£ per unit	
	P1	**P2**
Direct materials	3.00	7.00
Direct labour	5.00	11.00
Variable production overhead	2.50	5.30
Total marginal cost	**10.50**	**23.30**

    (b)   P1: 10.50 × 1.2 = £12.60

          P2: 23.30 × 1.2 = £27.96

    (c)   The prices set for each product are lower than those of its competitor. It is likely that the business will be able to attract high sales volumes, which will increase sales revenue to the business.

          However, the price set is not adequate to cover the fixed overhead of the product. If this price is set over the long-term these products are likely to be unprofitable. They therefore will not be generating an adequate return to the owners of the business.

          The lack of profit being generated is likely to put more pressure on other profitable products that the business sells. This will mean that cost efficiencies will need to be made elsewhere to support the profitability of the whole business.

(2)   (a)

	Yr 0	Yr 1	Yr 2	Yr 3	Yr 4
Purchase cost	(100,000)				
Labour cost saving		10,000	8,000	6,400	5,120
Annual running costs		(7,500)	(7,500)	(7,500)	(7,500)
Increase in sales revenue		25,000	27,500	30,000	33,000
Net cash flow	(100,000)	27,500	28,000	28,900	30,620
Discount factor	1.000	0.893	0.797	0.712	0.636
Present value	(100,000)	24,558	22,316	20,577	19,474
Net present value	(13,075)				

(b) The potential advantages of mechanising the production line are as follows:

JamJar is able to realise cost savings per unit as both labour and material costs will decrease as a result of mechanisation. This will enable JamJar to close the cost gap currently experienced on the product.

JamJar will see potential sales volumes increases as the target price can be set lower. This increase in sales volume will increase sales revenue, boosting profits.

By mechanising the production line, JamJar will be brought in line with its competitors. This will mean that JamJar is able to compete more effectively in the market by using competitive pricing arrangements.

(c) The potential disadvantages of mechanising the production line include:

Mechanisation is likely to cause anxiety amongst the existing workforce due to the threat of redeployment or redundancy. This will cause demotivation within the workforce, meaning that the labour efficiency savings won't be realised.

If staff will be made redundant, the wider community will also be impacted. This is because disposable income levels will be lower, which will threaten other local business and therefore the local economy. The skill set of the local workforce may also decrease, making it difficult for those affected staff to gain other employment.

The machine produces a negative net present value. This indicates that the new machinery will not produce an adequate return to shareholders. They may resist the mechanisation as it is will deteriorate value within JamJar.

The existing machine may not fit the current production process entirely. Extensive re-design of the process may need to be implemented which is time consuming and expensive.

(3) (a) Suitable answers could include:

- Increase overtime working
- Outsource additional hours required
- Access temporary staff
- Reduce amount of production units

(b) Suitable answers could include:

- Overtime working – this will have a negative impact on labour rates being paid, pushing up labour cost and driving an adverse labour rate variance.

- Outsourcing – there is reliance on the supplier to deliver the additional units in time for them to be sold.

- Temporary staff – if these staff are less experienced this will mean more time spent in production and subsequent impacts on wastage levels, affecting the materials usage and labour efficiency variances.

- Reduce production units – will affect sales volumes and therefore will reduce short-term profits. This could also affect long-term profits if customers defect to the competitor.

(4) (a)

		SP2000	SP3000
(i)	Gross profit margin SP2000: 1,014,000/1,800,000 × 100 SP3000: 905,000/1,500,000 × 100	56.3%	60.3%
(ii)	Operating profit margin SP2000: 414,000/1,800,000 × 100 SP3000: 305,000/1,500,000 × 100	23%	20.3%
(iii)	Direct materials cost per unit SP2000: 540,000/9,000 SP3000: 300,000/5,000	£60 per unit	£60 per unit
(iv)	Direct labour cost per unit SP2000: 126,000/9,000 SP3000: 175,000/5,000	£14 per unit	£35 per unit
(v)	Fixed production overhead cost per unit SP2000: 120,000/9,000 SP3000: 120,000/5,000	£13.33 per unit	£24 per unit
(vi)	Return on net assets SP2000: 414,000/2,014,000 × 100 SP3000: 305,000/1,905,000	20.6%	16%
(vii)	Raw materials inventory turnover in days SP2000: 60,000/786,000 × 365 SP3000: 60,000/595,000 × 365	27.9 days	36.8 days

(b) **Sales price per unit**

The sales price per unit is £100 more expensive for SP3000 than SP2000. This is due to the fact that it's higher quality and can therefore command a higher selling price per unit. Although the increased sales revenue has suppressed sales volume for SP3000, the additional revenue

generated by selling SP3000 at a higher selling price has pushed SP3000's gross profit margin above that of SP2000, as more contribution is being generated per unit.

Materials cost per unit

The materials cost per unit is constant between SP2000 and SP3000 despite SP3000 being sold for a higher price. This has had no impact on the gross profit margin as there is no impact on contribution generated per product.

Labour cost per unit

The labour cost per unit is £19 higher for SP3000 than SP2000. This is because the SP3000 is of higher quality, meaning that more labour time needs to be spent producing each unit. However, combined with SP3000's higher selling price, contribution per unit is much higher than on SP2000 (£126 for SP2000 and £206 for SP3000 respectively). This additional contribution earned by SP3000 has had a positive impact on its gross profit generated, pushing its gross profit margin above SP3000.

Fixed overhead cost per unit

The fixed overhead cost per unit is £10.67 higher for SP3000 than SP2000. This is predominantly due to fewer units of SP3000 being produced, as the same level of fixed overhead is being spread over fewer units. Whereas this will have a negative impact on the profitability per unit, there is ultimately no impact on the gross profit margin as, in total, the fixed overheads are constant between each product.

Return on net assets

The return on net assets is lower for SP3000 than SP2000. This is ultimately due to the lower operating profit margin (20.3% for SP3000 compared to 23% for SP2000). The lower operating profit margin performance can be attributed to the selling and distribution costs. Even though fewer units of SP3000 are produced and sold, selling and distribution costs are projected to be incurred at the same rate as that of SP2000. This could be attributed to the quality of the products, and the need to transport them more carefully than SP2000.

Bibliography

Kaplan, R.S. and Norton, D.P. (1996) Using the Balanced Scorecard as a Strategic Management System. *Harvard Business Review*, 74(1), 75–85.

Index

M

Make or buy, 241
Margin of safety, **227**
Margin of safety (MOS), 257
Marginal costing, 16, 21, 23, 30, 34, 36
Material price variance, **82**, 103
Material usage variance, **83**, 103
Mechanisation, 249
Moving average, 39, 61
Multiplicative model, 47

N

Net present cost, 257
Net present value, **252**, 257
Non-current asset turnover, 185
Non-financial performance indicators, 177, 185
Non-value adding activities, 202
Normal standard, **71**, 77

O

Operating profit margin, 185
Operating statement, 122
Operational gearing, 231, 257
Opportunity cost, **239**, 257
Over-absorption, 19, 30
Overhead Absorption Rate (OAR), **17**, 30

P

Payables' payment period, 185
Performance indicators, 186
Prime cost, **14**, 30
Product life cycle, 206
Production cost centres, 15
Production volume ratio, 179
Productivity, 186
Profit centres, **15**, 30

Q

Quick ratio, 186

R

Random variation, 40, 61
Receivables' collection period, 186
Relevant costs, 241, 257
Required profit level, 227
Retail price index, 61
Return on capital employed, 186

Return on net assets, 186
Revenue centres, **15**, 30
Revenue expenditure, 30
Risk, 230

S

Seasonal variations, 39, 61
Semi-variable costs, **5**, 30
Service cost centres, 15
Shadow price, **239**, 257
Shutdown, 245
Standard cost, **69**
Standard cost card, 77
Standard costing system, 77
Stepped fixed cost, **5**, 30
Sustainability, 203, 206

T

Target cost, 206
Target standard, **71**, 77
Time series, **39**, 61
Time series analysis, 61
Time value of money, 252, 257
Total fixed overhead variance, 103
Total labour variance, **86**, 103
Total material variance, **82**, 103
Total variable overhead variance, **92**
Trend (T), 39, 61

U

Uncontrollable variance, 136, 143
Under-absorption, 19, 30

V

Value added, 186
Value analysis, 206
Value engineering, 206
Variable costs, **4**, 30
Variable overhead efficiency variance, **93**
Variable overhead expenditure variance, **92**
Variance analysis, 81
Variances, 103

W

Weightings, 51
Working capital, 186

REVIEW FORM

How have you used this Course Book?
(Tick one box only)

☐ Self study

☐ On a course_____

☐ Other _____

Why did you decide to purchase this Course Book? *(Tick one box only)*

☐ Have used BPP materials in the past

☐ Recommendation by friend/colleague

☐ Recommendation by a college lecturer

☐ Saw advertising

☐ Other _____

During the past six months do you recall seeing/receiving either of the following?
(Tick as many boxes as are relevant)

☐ Our advertisement in Accounting Technician

☐ Our Publishing Catalogue

Which (if any) aspects of our advertising do you think are useful?
(Tick as many boxes as are relevant)

☐ Prices and publication dates of new editions

☐ Information on Course Book content

☐ Details of our free online offering

☐ None of the above

Your ratings, comments and suggestions would be appreciated on the following areas of this Course Book.

	Very useful	Useful	Not useful
Chapter overviews	☐	☐	☐
Introductory section	☐	☐	☐
Quality of explanations	☐	☐	☐
Illustrations	☐	☐	☐
Chapter activities	☐	☐	☐
Test your learning	☐	☐	☐
Keywords	☐	☐	☐

	Excellent	Good	Adequate	Poor
Overall opinion of this Course Book	☐	☐	☐	☐

Do you intend to continue using BPP Products?   ☐ Yes ☐ No

Please note any further comments and suggestions/errors on the reverse of this page. The BPP author of this edition can be emailed at: lmfeedback@bpp.com.

Alternatively, the Head of Programme of this edition can be emailed at: nisarahmed@bpp.com.

REVIEW FORM (continued)

TELL US WHAT YOU THINK

Please note any further comments and suggestions/errors below